Third Edition

Teaching Personal and Social Responsibility
Through Physical Activity

Don Hellison

Human Kinetics

Library of Congress Cataloging-in-Publication Data

Hellison, Donald R., 1938-
   Teaching personal and social responsibility through physical activity / Don Hellison. -- 3rd ed.
       p. cm.
   Rev. ed. of: Teaching responsibility through physical activity, c2003.
   Includes bibliographical references and index.
   ISBN-13: 978-0-7360-9470-2 (soft cover)
   ISBN-10: 0-7360-9470-9 (soft cover)
   1. Physical education and training--Sociological aspects--Study and teaching. 2. Responsibility--Study
and teaching. I. Hellison, Donald R., 1938- Teaching responsibility through physical activity. II. Title.
   GV342.27.H45 2011
   796.071--dc22

                                                    2010030868
ISBN: 978-0-7360-9470-2

This book is a revised edition of *Teaching Responsibility Through Physical Activity, Second Edition,* published in 2003 by Human Kinetics, Inc.

The Web addresses cited in this text were current as of September 2010, unless otherwise noted.

Acquisitions Editor: Scott Wikgren; **Developmental Editor:** Ray Vallese; **Assistant Editors:** Derek Campbell and Rachel Brito; **Copyeditor:** Patsy Fortney; **Indexer:** Sharon Duffy; **Permission Manager:** Dalene Reeder; **Graphic Designer:** Fred Starbird; **Graphic Artist:** Denise Lowry; **Cover Designer:** Keith Blomberg; **Visual Production Assistant:** Joyce Brumfield; **Photo Production Manager:** Jason Allen; **Art Manager:** Kelly Hendren; **Illustrator:** © Human Kinetics; **Associate Art Manager:** Alan L. Wilborn; **Printer:** Total Printing Systems

Printed in the United States of America   20 19 18 17 16 15 14 13 12 11

The paper in this book is certified under a sustainable forestry program.

Human Kinetics
1607 N. Market Street
Champaign, IL 61820
USA

United States and International
Website: **US.HumanKinetics.com**
Email: info@hkusa.com
Phone: 1-800-747-4457

Canada
Website: **Canada.HumanKinetics.com**
Email: info@hkcanada.com

Tell us what you think!
Human Kinetics would love to hear what we can do to improve the customer experience. Use this QR code to take our brief survey.

                                                                                    E5167

Contents

Foreword   ix
Preface to the Third Edition   xi
Acknowledgments   xiii

P · A · R · T

I

IDEAS

CHAPTER **1**   **What's Worth Doing? 3**

What's Worth Doing in Our Professional Lives? 3

Birth of Teaching Personal and Social Responsibility. 5

Toward a Working Theory-in-Practice 6

After-School, Youth Development, and Alternative
      School Programs 8

Influence of Related Social and Educational Issues. 10

There Are No Silver Bullets. 14

Take-Aways. 15

CHAPTER **2**   **A Framework for Teaching Personal
                  and Social Responsibility 17**

Core Values 18

Assumptions. 19

Levels of Responsibility 20

Program Leader Responsibilities 22

Daily Program Format. 27

Other Aspects of the TPSR Framework 28

Take-Aways. 29

CHAPTER **3** Levels of Responsibility **31**

Progression of Levels 32

Cumulative Levels 33

Five Levels 35

Level Modifications 44

Levels and Empowerment 45

Take-Aways 45

P·A·R·T

II

STRATEGIES

CHAPTER **4** Daily Program Format **49**

Relational Time 50

Awareness Talk 53

Physical Activity Plan 55

Group Meeting 56

Reflection Time 58

Take-Aways 62

CHAPTER **5** Embedding Responsibility in
the Physical Activity Content **63**

Physical Activity Content 63

Strategy Progression 66

Level I Strategies 67

Level II Strategies 69

Level III Strategies 73

Level IV Strategies 78

Level V Strategies 85

Take-Aways 86

CHAPTER 6 **Strategies for Specific Problems and Situations. 87**

Self-Reflection 87
Reflection-in-Action. 88
Fattening Our Bag of Tricks. 90
Level I: Individual Discipline Problems 91
Level I: Conflict Resolution Strategies 96
Level II: Teaching by Invitation 98
Level III: Struggles With Empowerment 98
Level IV: Helping and Leadership Problems 100
Level V: Specific Problems Outside the Gym 101
Take-Aways. 101

CHAPTER 7 **Being Relational With Kids 103**

Four Relational Qualities 103
Having the Courage to Confront. 105
Relational Qualities and Relational Time 106
Program Leader Qualities and Skills. 106
Teaching Students With Different Cultural Backgrounds. 112
Take-Aways. 114

P·A·R·T

III

IMPLEMENTATION

CHAPTER 8 **TPSR in PE Teacher Education: One Teacher's Explorations 117**

Sarah Doolittle

Teaching TPSR in PE Teacher Education. 118
Apprenticeship 120
Site-Based Practicum or Internship .121

Conference Workshop or Short Course .122

One-Week Intensive Elective 123

Semester-Long Elective 124

Within a Required Activity Course 124

Within a Required On-Site Undergraduate Methods Course 125

Required Methods Course in an After-School Program 125

Framework for a Teacher Education Program. 126

Summary Thoughts 128

Take-Aways. 130

CHAPTER 9 Coaching Clubs and Other TPSR Program Structures 131

Coaching Clubs 132

Cross-Age Teaching and Leadership 138

TPSR in Organized Sport. 139

Responsibility-Based Fitness Centers 141

TPSR on the Playground and at Recess 142

TPSR in the Classroom 142

Schoolwide Adoptions of TPSR 146

Take-Aways. 147

CHAPTER 10 Getting Started 149

Context 149

Self-Assessment. 151

First Steps. 152

Advanced Steps 154

Teaching as a Subversive Activity. 158

Take-Aways. 159

CHAPTER **11 Assessment and Evaluation Strategies . . . 161**

with Paul M. Wright

Student Assessment. 162

Teacher Evaluation. 173

Program Evaluation 175

Take-Aways. 180

Epilogue   183

Appendix: Assessment Tools   185

References and Resources   196

Index   203

About the Author   209

Foreword

Don Hellison's career is unique in physical education teacher education. It is most unusual in any profession to find someone who

- has an idea (in this case, the need to develop positive character traits among youth);
- develops that idea into a beginning vision of key pedagogical strategies for developing character among youth by helping them to, as he describes it, take personal and social responsibility;
- searches for ways to put that vision into practice by implementing those strategies with differing youth populations;
- is committed to examining the outcomes related to those strategies so as to constantly modify the practices to better achieve the primary goals; and
- for 40 years has devoted all of his considerable talents to achieving that vision and to sharing it with other professional educators so that they may use some or all of his strategies in their own teaching.

Don has never wavered in his commitment to helping children and youth take responsibility for their own behavior. He started in the early 1970s with general goals and ideas shared in his book *Humanistic Physical Education* (1973); then provided more detail about strategies for practice in *Beyond Balls and Bats* (1978).

I first met Don at an AAHPERD convention in California in the mid-1970s. We had been asked to debate humanist and behaviorist approaches to physical education. He was a committed humanist, and I was a committed behaviorist. The primary outcome for each of us was the beginning of a strong and enduring friendship and the understanding that, although our approaches differed, we shared similar values and could learn from each other. We also discovered that we had actually played high school baseball against each other in the spring of 1955 in the West Suburban conference outside Chicago.

We have done several other "debate shows" at AAHPERD conventions, but they have typically focused on the similarities of what we do rather than the differences. Don discovered that when you attempt to effect change among students in the real world, you have to offer students methods for gaining control over their behavior before they can work toward developing and valuing self-control and responsibility. I found that when you develop behavioral programs for students, you have to understand that they all have hopes, dreams, and problems and that behavioral management programs have to take those into consideration to be successful.

Don's work is thoroughly grounded in the important and relevant literature on youth development, and his own work has served to substantially increase the literature base in that area. Among his many admirable qualities, what stands out most to me has been his perseverance, shown through his own field work with troubled youth, his work to train physical educators and youth workers to implement his model, and his unambiguous commitment to the world of practice. This edition adds specific information for professionals who work in the emerging physical activity domains. Don always took his ivory tower to gymnasiums, fitness centers, and playing fields as quickly as possible!

As usual, this new edition continues to show more fully developed techniques and strategies enabling teachers and youth workers to be more successful in their endeavors to help children and youth develop qualities of character that substantially increase their chances to grow up successfully.

It has been my privilege to have Don as a friend and colleague. His unique contributions to physical education have no parallel in my professional lifetime. We all owe him our thanks.

—Daryl Siedentop

Preface

TO THE THIRD EDITION

If you want to write about the truth
you must write about yourself.
I am the only truth I know.

—*Jean Rhys*

■ ■ ■ ■ ■

It has now been 40 years since the first glimmer of an idea about teaching life skills and values through physical activity was prematurely rushed into practice with unsuspecting low-income urban youth, an approach Daryl Siedentop aptly called "ready-fire-aim." Since that initial experience, the idea of teaching kids to take personal and social responsibility (known as TPSR or the TPSR model; the T refers to both *teaching* and *taking* personal and social responsibility) gradually and sometimes painfully jelled, first in my work with kids, and then in my professional preparation of university students, teachers, youth workers, and coaches in the United States and several other countries. TPSR is still jelling. This book is the latest version of a career-long effort to develop and share whatever ideas and insights have surfaced in this ongoing process.

This edition is updated in a number of ways. The second edition was written specifically for in-school PE teachers, because they had shown the most interest in the first edition. However, as I explain in chapter 1, my work in urban high schools led to more involvement in alternative settings, particularly alternative schools and after-school programs, and more recently the emerging youth development movement. These forces have contributed to the recent upswing of interest in, attention to, and available funding for helping kids in all communities meet the challenges they now face. I have tried to address these developments and the physical education (PE) and physical activity (PA) professionals engaged in this work.

This shift in orientation required a total overhaul of the first two chapters as well as modifications in all chapters. I asked two colleagues to fill some gaps in earlier editions. TPSR assessment guru Paul Wright substantially rewrote the assessment chapter (chapter 11), and Sarah Doolittle contributed a new chapter on combining responsibility-based youth development with PE teacher education (chapter 8). My thanks to them for strengthening some of the earlier weaknesses in my work.

In addition to the updated kid quotes and opening chapter quotes, this edition includes numerous vignettes called "TPSR in Action" sprinkled throughout the chapters that were written by a wide range of TPSR users working either with kids or in professional preparation. Each is a short story about applying TPSR in a specific setting. Their generous contributions add very important dimensions of reality, validity, and contextual variety to the study of TPSR.

In this edition, I frequently refer to the intended audience for this book as PE and PA professionals or program leaders, generic terms for teacher, youth worker, and coach. I stopped short of referring to the reader as "you" to be consistent with the spirit of TPSR, which is about empowerment and encouraging reflection with the goal of making smart personal and social choices. The "you" who reads this book needs to be free to say, for example, "That idea certainly isn't for me."

The following thought was expressed in the last edition, but it bears repeating here. Although teaching certainly involves specific skills and strategies, it also ought to have a spirit—a moral compass, a sense of purpose, a passion, a vision. Ian Culpan, who spearheaded PE curriculum reform in New Zealand, told me that he doesn't want just a competent teacher; he wants an inspirational teacher. So do I. I want (and kids need) imaginative, creative program leaders who, instead of connecting the dots, can create the dots (another of Culpan's ideas).

Other recent changes include a Web site (www.tpsr-alliance.org), thanks to colleague Gloria Balague, and a yearly conference, now in its third year, also thanks to Gloria. Our latest plan is to offer one-week TPSR academies in the summer to help interested professionals bring TPSR concepts to their work with kids. Stay tuned.

Acknowledgments

There is no such thing as an individual.
We have an illusion of self-sufficiency, but actually
other people support us throughout
the entire process of our development.

—Urie Bronfenbrenner

■ ■ ■ ■ ■

I agree with Urie Bronfenbrenner. Almost no one works alone. Support from others comes in many ways, and some, probably too many, go unacknowledged. In past editions I have thanked many of the key people who directly or indirectly made those books possible. This time around, I want to acknowledge those who have contributed many of the insights, ideas, and examples used in this edition. It's a long list, yet I'm sure I've omitted some deserving friends and colleagues.

The work and influence of several people deserve special mention. Sarah Doolittle and Paul Wright improved this edition immeasurably by adding (in Sarah's case) a new chapter or revising (in Paul's case) an existing chapter, both of which expand the potential use of TPSR. A big thank-you also goes to the vignette authors, whose specific examples of TPSR in practice are sprinkled throughout the book. Gloria Balague dragged me (kicking and screaming) to join her in developing a Web site (www.tpsr-alliance.org) and holding a yearly TPSR conference, which have, among other things, brought together many of my colleagues and close friends and introduced others, which has increased collaboration and communication. It was at these meetings that I found and twisted the arms of more than a few of the vignette authors. These recent developments also helped to fuel the motivation to do a third edition of this book.

Nick Cutforth, Nikos Georgiadis, Tom Martinek, Dave Walsh, and Bill White provided a number of ideas and examples in the book. Others whose work I've described include Hal Adams, Kit Cody, Terary Cooper, Nick Forsberg, Barrie Gordon, Karyn Hartinger, Pete Hockett, Aleita Holcombe, Steve Hoy, Vicki Jorgensen, Walt Kelly, Tim Kramer, Bobby Lifka, Jeff Walsh, Mike Reeder, Missy Parker, Darin Kennedy, Jimmy Jones, Don Andersen, Mike DeBusk, Cynthia Luebbe, and Kathy Woyner.

My thanks to all and to those I've inadvertently omitted.

IDEAS

TPSR

1

What's Worth Doing?

Never doubt that a small group of thoughtful, committed citizens can change the world. Indeed, it is the only thing that ever has.

—Margaret Mead

■ ■ ■ ■ ■

What's worth doing in school physical education (PE) and after-school physical activity (PA) programs is a question Tom Templin and I raised over a decade ago (Hellison and Templin, 1991). Another way of stating this question is this: What kind of professional contribution does each of us want to make? I now realize that this question has driven my work from the beginning, along with its follow-up questions: Is it working? and What's possible? *Is it working?* asks whether my answer to what's worth doing actually works for both the kids I work with and me. *What's possible?* (Lampert, 1987) asks whether my answer to what's worth doing explores what's possible to accomplish, whether I have fully explored the possibilities. These three questions are revisited throughout this book and, from my perspective, ought to be revisited throughout our careers.

WHAT'S WORTH DOING IN OUR PROFESSIONAL LIVES?

Some PE and PA professionals find it compelling to teach kids to enjoy an active lifestyle, others want to teach them how to be competitive in sports, and still others want to help them take care of their bodies. Some want kids to understand the role feedback plays in learning a skill or how the overload principle improves fitness, or even to learn life skills such as "a sense of personal worth . . . [and] attitudes of persistence, reflection, responsibility, and reliability" (McLaughlin, 2000, p. 4)—the list goes on.

In the in-school physical education (PE) world, many teachers and in-school curriculum planners both locally and nationally have a simple answer to what's worth doing: Everything! They want development in fitness, motor skills, and cognitive knowledge, and they want to achieve any number of affective and social goals. In an effort to standardize these professional preferences, PE teachers have been handed a bewildering and shifting array of purposes, goals, and standards both local and national.

This trend raises two related questions: First, can kids really be helped to develop in all of these recommended ways? As PE scholar and teacher educator

Daryl Siedentop (2001) argued, we often turn out kids who are overexposed to but underdeveloped in sport and fitness. The second question this trend raises is, How can PE professionals hang on to their own values and passions—those things that provided motivation in the first place? Pressure to align our beliefs and values with standards or the opinions of other physical educators can become another barrier to doing what's worth doing. Fortunately, in their analysis of the PE standards movement, Jackie Lund and Deborah Tannehill (2010) recognized these issues and offered sound and flexible advice to PE teachers and supervisors: "It will be up to each teacher, and each school district to interpret the standards based on values, beliefs, and philosophy, and what is ultimately deemed important for students to know and do as a result of their physical education programs . . . we need to continually remember that the activities we select are not the outcomes but the means to achieving an outcome" (p. 29).

Compared to in-school PE teachers, many after-school and summer PA program leaders have fewer standards and directives. In fact, youth development–based PA programs are intended to occupy the intermediate space between formal in-school instruction and free play (Noam, Biancarosa, and Dechausay, 2003). Because these programs are not as structured as PE or as loose as recess or "the open gym," those who implement them have the obligation to contribute to kids' development but are given more room to choose and may be able to follow their passions more easily than PE teachers can. As McLaughlin (2000) reported, "each of the [successful out-of-school] programs we studied build from an individual's passion" (p. 18). Her investigation offers a rationale for emphasizing what's worth doing. Passion is essential to answering this question.

TPSR *in Action*

As director of the San Mateo Police Activities League (PAL), I found myself suddenly in the middle of a gang war in the winter of 2006. I was tasked with intervening between two gangs at the high school. Fortunately, one half of the combatants, the Surenos, agreed to join PAL under the assumption that they would be learning soccer. My agenda was different. TPSR was my secret weapon of peace. We spent two days a week on a patch of dirt learning the games of soccer and life. Leroy, an ex-professional player, and I infused TPSR levels into every practice. Surprisingly, they accepted TPSR with open arms, and one later commented, "God, there's no other adults that treat us like you, that have taught us." Like many on the team, Jimmy came to the program with a 0.0 GPA and little hope for his future. Two years later, Jimmy was selected PAL Youth of the Year over 600 others. In his acceptance speech, Jimmy acknowledged the impact TPSR had on his life: "I learned five words . . . that I always have with me wherever I go, and they are respect, self-control, leadership, participation, and effort. . . . Those five words . . . have changed my life."

Mike Buckle, Sergeant, San Mateo Police Department, California, and graduate student, San Francisco State University

Some PE and PA professionals turn to research for answers to what's worth doing, but science cannot answer this question. Research can give us some idea of what works (see chapter 11) but not necessarily what's best for kids and certainly not what individual teachers and program leaders (e.g., PE teachers, youth workers, youth sport coaches) are passionate about. It might be argued that daily physical activity is best for kids, but is that more important than promoting human decency or teaching kids how to control emotional outbursts? Is competitive sport more important than aerobic exercise? These questions are more appropriately the province of philosophy, not science. When research is consulted, those things harder to measure are relegated to the end of the line. What's worth doing probes our beliefs and values about life, kids, and physical activity rather than what research says. Moreover, McLaughlin reported that no one type of program was consistently associated with youth development, that "there are no cookie cutter practices," (2000, p. 18) only some guiding principles. In other words, a program must be about something, not—as Ted Sizer (1992) reminded us—about everything.

This discussion highlights the second important question for PA and PE professionals: Is it working? Whether it is worth doing or not, if it doesn't work, what's the point? It is important to ask both, What's worth doing? and Is it working? in professional practice. A wide range of approaches are available to address whether something is working, from the insights of the program leader to quantitative assessments, as chapter 11 on assessment shows.

The third question central to professional practice is, What's possible? Because this question explores one's vision and long-range plan, it is usually best to put it on the back burner until relationships with kids and a microculture for the program have been established.

BIRTH OF TEACHING PERSONAL AND SOCIAL RESPONSIBILITY

I entered college a history major, with no purpose other than to graduate, and I graduated in the same state. The question What's worth doing? began to concern me, but work experience plus another degree (in sociology) didn't improve my sense of purpose, so I joined the U.S. Marine Corps as an officer candidate to at least provide a challenge and some excitement. It did that all right, about as much as I could handle, but it contributed something far more important to my life. My platoon included young men from low-income urban neighborhoods who were sometimes court-referred (i.e., go to jail or go to the Marine Corps). I loved working with them in this highly physical environment and, in the process, found my answer to my question of what's worth doing, my sense of purpose, a calling that has lasted 40 years (and counting). However, I had not yet confronted the questions, Is it working? and more remotely, What's possible?

When my active tour of duty ended, I went back to school and earned a PE teacher certification, thinking that this was the closest I could come to using physical activity to help low-income urban kids. That's when the "fun" started (translation: wake-up call). I had earned a doctorate in PE along with my teacher certification, so I took a position at a university and at the same time began teaching part-time in an urban high school, armed with my Marine Corps experiences and a flimsy belief in the value of building character (see Hellison, 1973). But without the military authority and not having earned "a PhD in the streets" (McLaughlin 2000, p. 20)—that is, without much experience negotiating the low-income urban environment—I found myself defenseless in the face of kids who were for the most part unmotivated and hostile. In short, nothing worked.

TOWARD A WORKING THEORY-IN-PRACTICE

In its earliest form, taking personal and social responsibility (TPSR) was a survival response to my first teaching situation and others like it in other urban high schools my first few years. Giving them a few choices and some small decisions to make reduced the adversarial climate in the gym. But I needed a much clearer purpose and set of goals as well as some intervention strategies. I came to realize that helping my students to take more responsibility for their own development and well-being and for supporting the well-being of others was perhaps the best contribution I could make, especially given the personal and social problems my students faced. Any external control I might be able to impose would be transient at best, and they would still have to figure out life for themselves, if they could, without much help from social institutions. Law enforcement would do the rest, a dubious proposition at best.

If TPSR was going to be the purpose of my program, I needed to embed it in everything we did in the gym so that while my students were doing fitness activities or learning a motor skill, they were also learning something about taking personal and social responsibility. But TPSR was too vague to help me plan specific lessons. I still needed a better grasp of what it meant to be responsible. I also needed some specific strategies for putting this purpose into practice. What do students need to take responsibility for? And how do they go about taking this responsibility?

I couldn't see how I could avoid teaching values, because values are central to human relationships, decision-making, and the development of life skills (e.g., which life skills to promote). The key, I reasoned, is to treat the values not as absolutes but as qualities to experience and reflect on. The kids need to be ultimately responsible for adopting, modifying, or rejecting these values in their lives. Later, I developed the TPSR core values (see chapter 2) with the caveat that they were values, not scientific facts, and therefore PE and PA professionals needed to decide whether these values lined up with their own perspectives. (This argument is further developed later in this chapter.)

In the early development of TPSR, I was just trying to identify key value-based responsibilities for the kids. I selected two values related to personal well-being (effort and self-direction) and two related to social well-being (respect for others' rights and feelings and caring about others). I wanted to give attention to being both personally and socially responsible, although this personal–social balance can be precarious, as illustrated by the split of John Dewey's followers into two sects after his death, one child-centered and one society-centered (Jones and Tanner, 1981).

Following Sizer's less-is-more principle, I had to exclude many other possible values. If I wanted students to remember the values, let alone become involved in trying them out, the values had to be simply stated, concise, and few in number. Level V, exploring the application of these values outside the gym, complicated matters but was just a vague idea at this point. Actually, everything became more complicated as I tried to put these ideas into practice. Gradually the concepts were clarified and expanded in an effort to capture the essence of taking responsibility (see table 2.1 in chapter 2).

To simplify my approach, I placed my chosen values in a loose progression (see figure 1.1), referring to them as awareness levels (Hellison, 1978) or developmental levels (Hellison, 1985). Students thus learned a vocabulary as well as a sequence, and I was able to sidestep the term *values.* As long as I was flexible in its application, this progression

- helped me plan my lessons,
- helped kids focus on issues of respect and motivation right away, and

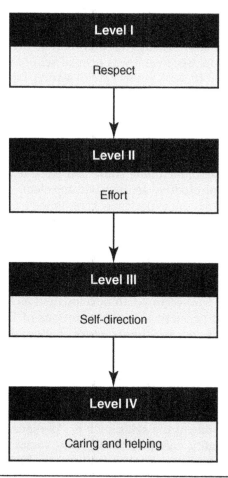

FIGURE 1.1   An early version of the TPSR values, at the time referred to as awareness levels or developmental levels.

- helped them to understand that self-direction and helping others were higher values.

Later, working with smaller groups of kids in alternative settings, I found the levels structure less important. Just calling the "levels" the kids' responsibilities seemed to work, as long as the issue of respect/self-control was addressed early and often in the program.

In short, I created my own emerging theory-in-practice, my answer to the question, What's worth doing? I call TPSR a theory-in-practice because it is a framework of values and ideas that are constantly being tested in practice, even now, 40 years after its inception.

AFTER-SCHOOL, YOUTH DEVELOPMENT, AND ALTERNATIVE SCHOOL PROGRAMS

My career was just beginning. But after a few years in urban public high schools, I had the opportunity to work for eight years in an alternative high school for court- and school-referred adolescents, both as a PE teacher (sometimes as a sex education and history teacher as well) and as the program leader of an after-school PA program. Because it was a small school with small classes and had faculty who wanted to work in this kind of setting, I quickly realized that my learning was just beginning. It was there that I became aware of what's possible. Despite having students with dismal records academically and behaviorally, I found that so much more was possible in a small school with small classes, and a small, caring faculty. I knew the kids better, saw them in a variety of settings, became a much more relational teacher, and had faculty support to try whatever new ideas I came up with, including some bad ones! It was also here that the potential strengths of alternative settings became clear.

After my alternative school experience, I continued to work in alternative settings, both in alternative school PE and after-school PA programs. I also began to teach younger kids as well as adolescents. This work became what was worth doing for me while opening up opportunities for exploring what was possible with youth. It also influenced my view of the field, not as just PE or PA, but both, an orientation reflected in the language and organization of this book. It wasn't until much later that I learned of youth development as both a philosophy and an emerging field. It fit perfectly with the intentions of TPSR, the development of after-school PA programs, and the structure of alternative schools. See figure 1.2 for a list of the key criteria of youth development programs.

The gradual coalescence of PA, youth development, and alternative schools was facilitated by the work of Richard Rothstein (2004), who argued for an expanded version of schooling during out-of-school hours as part of his plan to close the black–white achievement gap in urban communities. He promoted after-school programs that taught life skills such as "perseverance, self-confidence, self-discipline, punctuality, communication skills, social responsibility, and the ability to work with others and resolve conflicts" (p. 7). Raywid (2006) pointed out that alternative schools also teach life skills similar to those recommended by Rothstein.

Key Criteria for State-of-the-Art Youth Development Programs

1. Treat youth as resources to be developed. Build on the strengths they already possess, and emphasize their competence and mastery.
2. Focus on the whole person—the emotional, social, and cognitive as well as physical dimensions of the self.
3. Respect the individuality of youth, including cultural differences and developmental needs.
4. Empower youth.
5. Give youth clear, demanding (but not unreasonable) expectations based on a strong, explicit set of values.
6. Help youth envision possible futures for themselves.
7. Provide both a physically and psychologically safe environment.
8. Keep program numbers small and encourage participation over a long period of time; emphasize belonging and membership.
9. Maintain a local connection.
10. Provide courageous and persistent leadership in the face of systemic obstacles.
11. Provide significant contact with a caring adult.

FIGURE 1.2 The 11 key criteria of youth development programs.

From Hellison, D., & Cutforth, N. (1997). Extended day programs for children and youth: From theory to practice. In Walberg, H., Reyes, O., & Weissberg, R. (Eds), *Children and youth: Interdisciplinary perspectives* (pp. 223-249). Thousand Oaks, CA: Sage. Copyright 1997 by Sage Publications, Inc.

Youth development, which initially emerged in the 1990s as a response to the inadequacies of after-school programs in low-income urban communities (DeWitt-Wallace Reader's Digest Fund, 1995), has evolved to the point that life skills teaching such as that recommended by Rothstein and Raywid is now being embedded in PA programs. Examples include Project Coach (Intrator and Siegel, 2008), Harlem RBI (Berlin et al., 2007), and youth development programs based on the ideas in this book (Hellison et al., 2000; Martinek and Hellison, 2009). In particular, the exemplary work of Al Petitpas and his associates (Petitpas, Cornelius, and Van Raalte, 2008) has resulted in several popular programs that embed life skills teaching in PA programs, such as Project Rebound, First Tee, and Play It Smart.

The South Carolina state legislature, spearheaded by Judy Rink's concerns about childhood obesity and inactive kids, passed the Student Health and Fitness Act in 2005 requiring that each student receive at least 30 minutes of physical activity a day. The position of PA director was created to lead the development and implementation of PA programs to supplement the contribution of in-school PE. PA directors were trained to work with teachers and administrators in schools to take a comprehensive approach to school physical activity programs including before-school programs, after-school programs, lunch programs, recess, all-school events, and physical activity breaks in the classroom. Although motivated by different concerns, this legislation opens the door to supporting school PA programs that engage students in life skills similar to those described by Rothstein and Raywid.

INFLUENCE OF RELATED SOCIAL AND EDUCATIONAL ISSUES

The expansion of after-school PA in the United States, the recent emphasis on alternative and other small schools, and the emergence of youth development have been, at least in part, a response to the "surge of social pathology" among youth in recent years (Csikszentmihalyi and McCormack, 1986, p. 417), which is reflected in increases in school dropout rates, drug abuse and trafficking, delinquency, teen pregnancy, gangs, suicide, violence, and vandalism. Although there is some controversy over the interpretation of the data, it is quite clear that more children and youth are at risk.

These trends have been blamed on more families becoming dysfunctional (with increased incidences of child neglect and abuse, homelessness, and "kids raising kids"); on the increased availability of drugs and guns; on images from the Internet and other media; and on social, political, and economic conditions, including poverty, racism, and joblessness, which have made war zones of the areas in which many low-income families live.

Certainly, the growth of a disenfranchised underclass accounts for some of the problem. Few people question that inner-city kids are growing up in environments that put them at risk. As Kunjufu (1989) observed, "We have youth who are being killed because they stepped on someone's shoe or brushed up against someone in a crowded hallway between classes" (p. 48). Not all inner-city families are dysfunctional, however, and some kids who grow up in underserved neighborhoods become productive parents and citizens and distinguish themselves in their chosen line of work and as citizens. Moreover, not all kids who are at risk of being affected by social problems live in inner cities. A principal of one of the most affluent suburbs in the Chicago area has estimated that 50 percent of the families in his school district are rich but dysfunctional. Aggregated data for all youth reflect a substantial rise in crime, violence, sex, and drug use (Lickona, 1991). As Benson (1997) observed, "These concerns cannot be dismissed as urban issues alone. Part of the American dilemma is that these issues affect all sizes of communities" (p. 3).

Institutions that have traditionally provided support and guidance for children and youth often find it difficult to respond adequately to these trends. The Carnegie Council on Adolescent Development (1992) concluded that community programs designed to serve adolescents are not reaching most of the kids who are unsupervised after school and most likely to harm themselves and others. McLaughlin and Heath (1993) also found that most inner-city community programs and policies do not respond to the needs of kids; the programs are, for the most part, not developmental, not empowerment oriented, and not focused on the whole person. In public schools, teachers face the escalation of crime, violence, sex, and drug use as well as depression, attempted suicide, and school absenteeism (Benson, 1997).

KID QUOTES STUDENT QUOTES KID QUOTES STUDENT QUOTE
STUDENT QUOTES KID QUOTES KID QUOTES KID QUOTES
QUOTES STUDENT QUOTES KID QUOTES STUDENT QUOTES KI
QUOTES KID QUOTES STUDENT QUOTES KID QUOTES STUDEN

KID QUOTES

"This class helps you become a better person."—Eighth-grader

"I didn't change. I'm the same old person."—Sixth-grader

Overall, American kids are receiving less support and guidance in a society that bombards them with more choices than ever before and places many of them at a social, economic, and political disadvantage from the start. It is no wonder that many feel alienated and powerless and turn to withdrawal or rebellion. All of these forces have contributed to the emergence of the youth development movement, alternative schools, and PA programs, which have, in turn, begun to address these issues. However, the battle is nowhere near being won, especially in low-income communities.

Increasing Emphasis on Life Skills in PE and PA

Increasing social problems emphasized the need for teaching life skills in kids' programs. Schools are overburdened with subject matter and standards requirements, but, as described previously, alternative schools and after-school programs have stepped in. Although character development claims have been an integral part of PE and PA historically, the actual implementation of life skills teaching in PE and PA programs was slow to unfold.

PE and PA got a boost from well-known education scholar Nel Noddings (1992), who pointed out the potentially holistic nature of physical activity programs:

> [T]he physical self is only part of the self. We must be concerned also with the emotional, spiritual, and intellectual self, and clearly these are not discrete. We separate and label them for convenience in discussion, but it may be a mistake to separate them sharply in curriculum. (p. 49)

Think about it this way: In the academic world, we can separate the social, emotional, cognitive, and physical domains; offer courses on them; and prepare domain-specific specialists. But those of us who work in the world of practice have no such luxury. Kids bring all of these aspects of themselves into the gym. Program leaders have no choice (except in severe cases) other than to deal with the whole person.

Quincy Howe (1991), a former academic turned teacher of urban foster care kids ages 10 to 20, agreed, noting that specialists such as social workers and nurses can do part of the job, but only the teacher sees the whole person. This is arguably even more the case for PE and PA professionals, who deal with kids in highly active, interactive, and emotional environments. Helping kids develop life skills comes with the territory.

Social-emotional learning (SEL), a programmatic approach in alternative and some mainstream schools, is a recent response to the "surge of social pathology." Although definitions of SEL differ markedly, from caring and diversity to behavioral control strategies, the SEL literature is beginning to show life skills development, such as academic achievement and reduced discipline problems (Hoffman, 2009).

Some, but certainly not all, PE and PA professionals have responded to these developments. Examples include the sport-based youth development programs cited earlier, as well as the PE and PA work in adventure education (Hattie et al., 1997; Jim Stiehl's chapter in Hellison et al., 2000), character development (Beedy and Zierk, 2000), cooperation (Bressan, 1987; Orlick, 1978), moral development (Gibbons, Ebbeck, and Weiss, 1995; Romance, Weiss, and Bokoven, 1986; Shields and Bredemeier, 1995), good sporting behavior and fair play (Gibbons, Ebbeck, and Weiss, 1995; Giebink and McKenzie, 1985; Horrocks, 1977), empowerment (Ennis et al., 1999; Siedentop, 1994), and social responsibility (Horrocks, 1978; Trulson, 1986).

Conceptualization and implementation of these kinds of programs are difficult because personal and social development involves "soft skills," value orientations and intentions, and attitudes as well as specific behaviors. Personal and social behaviors, such as working independently, helping someone, or cooperating with a group, may be more easily identified; but attitudes, values, beliefs, feelings, and self-perceptions matter as well. How someone feels—an intangible mix of perceptions and intentions toward the self or someone else—may have greater personal and social implications than more visible behaviors. Wright (cited in Arnold, 1988) put it this way:

> [A person] cannot be defined through an inventory of actions performed [but rather] by a description of the principles that give coherence and meaning to an individual's behavior, and of the relatively enduring dispositions that underlie it. (p. 35)

It is as if both an inside self and an outside self are present in all of us, one very visible, the other existing mostly below the surface (Thomas, 1983).

The potential and demonstrated benefits of PE and PA can be further strengthened if they take place in a supportive setting, such as that created by recent developments in alternative schools and youth development programs, many of which embrace a "caring community." A particularly promising approach is the concept of wraparound programs, in which participants experience similar value-based ideas and strategies in all of their classes and programs, not just in PA and PE. One community-based example is Harlem RBI (Berlin et al., 2007), Another is the full-service schools that employ medical and dental practitioners, social workers to assist families, and enrichment programs after school. Yet another variation is the collaboration of a community resource coordinator, a social worker, and a mental health worker who are assigned to a school to work with teachers, kids, and parents (including making home visits and providing employment assistance for parents) (Quinn and Dryfoos, 2009).

Role of Values

Because values are embedded in teaching life skills (or more appropriately, life skills and values), teaching values cannot be avoided, despite some concerns by parents and others regarding the teaching of values in public schools. Much of what we do and say reflects our values. Values-based programs such as TPSR acknowledge this up front (i.e., the TPSR core values). In fact, many alternative schools and youth development–based PA programs openly acknowledge the importance of values (Hellison and Cutforth, 1997). Some of the debate focuses on interpretation. Concepts such as responsibility can be interpreted many ways—for example, "responsibility means do as I say" versus "responsibility means do whatever you please." In TPSR it has yet another meaning. It can be a slippery slope.

I was uncomfortable with the possibility of indoctrination from the outset. I struggled in my experiences and in my mind to find ways of teaching that could convey values without resorting to indoctrination, as I explained earlier. Fortunately, others have provided support. Tappan (1992) argued that proponents of universal conceptions of morality need to address the problem of employing "techniques of indoctrination to transmit certain values [rather than encouraging] students to discuss, examine, and reflect critically on values and ethical positions within a diverse, complex, and ever changing society" (p. 387).

DeCharms (1976) argued that we must help people to become origins in their lives. By this he meant teaching them how to set internal standards, including doing as one must rather than as one pleases and striving for goals in the face of opposing external forces, although this striving may not always pay off. DeCharms believed that being an origin has a moral dimension, because it requires us to take responsibility for the consequences of our goals and to treat others as origins rather than as pawns to be manipulated. He demonstrated the power of these ideas by implementing them in inner-city elementary schools and collecting data to demonstrate their effectiveness.

Cultivating the decision-making process involves giving young people the opportunity to share their beliefs and knowledge and to test these ideas in a controlled forum. Such experimentation is good not only because it follows a democratic perspective but also because it acknowledges that students know things that program leaders (i.e., PE and PA professionals) don't know. In an increasingly diverse society, in which teachers and program leaders are often of a different subculture than their students, giving students the power to apply the special knowledge of their world to make decisions can lead to better decisions and a better education. As an added benefit, the process of sharing decision-making power also raises the important question of who has the power to determine what is of value in a diverse society.

Giving kids responsibility yields psychological benefits. As Alfie Kohn (1993) put it: "All else being equal, emotional adjustment is better over time for people who experience a sense of self-determination" (p. 11). Instructors benefit as well because there is less occasion for the "I tell you what to do and you try to get out of doing it" game that teachers and students often play.

Teaching life skills addresses the emotional and social dimensions of being a whole person. For this reason and many others, teaching kids life skills, despite the difficulties, makes sense. And helping students take personal and social responsibility means sharing power with students and gradually shifting decision making to them. TPSR does not mean getting inside kids' heads but getting them inside their own heads.

THERE ARE NO SILVER BULLETS

No matter what values they promote, PE and PA programs are no panacea for the social problems we face today. Pete Mesa (1992), superintendent of schools in Oakland, California, outlined three levels of causes of social problems:

- Immediate causes, such as guns in schools
- Intermediate causes, including the need for skills in and a disposition toward social competence, problem solving, autonomy, and a sense of purpose and future
- Root causes, such as poverty, racism, inadequate health care, inadequate parent education, and lack of opportunity

In Mesa's conceptualization, PE and PA programs focus on intermediate causes. TPSR, to the extent that it works, is one small intermediate piece of the puzzle. Weiner (1993) persuasively argued that none of this intermediate work will make much of a difference "unless social and economic relations are utterly transformed, and that process will take a sustained, vigorous struggle by all who recognize the inequality and injustice of the status quo" (p. 2). Dryfoos (1991) agreed but argued for doing what we can:

> It is too little too late, too fragmented, too categorical, too inconsistent. . . . Child advocates are admittedly hanging on the incremental edge, chipping away at those situations that are amenable to change, with insufficient force to alter the social environment that generates many of these problems. *Even so, there is much incremental work that can and must be done.* (p. 634; italics added)

It is difficult but not out of reach to institute wraparound programs that address the whole person, such as full-service schools. These efforts represent a mini-version of systemic change. Extended-day programs are sometimes promoted as being more flexible and open to new ideas, and although this is true in some settings, Mesa's root causes remain resistant to change in all institutions.

Lawson (2005), by conceptualizing our field as SEPE (sport, exercise, and physical education), offered his vision of an empowerment-based community-wide change that would "contribute to sustainable economic and social development" (p. 135). It struck me as a brilliant, if idealistic, set of "grand conceptual frameworks" (p. 136). It is a "what's possible" idea that would shake up the way we do business.

TPSR stands for a set of ideas that have grown out of my attempt to help underserved and high-needs kids take more responsibility for their personal and social development in physical activity settings, rather than succumbing to external forces that are not in their best interests. Although it is no panacea for today's social problems, providing today's young people with guidelines for, and practice in, taking responsibility for their personal well-being and contributing to the well-being of others can make a difference in what they value and what choices they make. At least it can plant a seed.

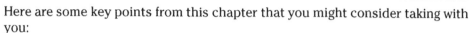

Here are some key points from this chapter that you might consider taking with you:

- For PE or PA professionals, What's worth doing? is perhaps the most important question we can ask ourselves. The question takes on added significance if we cannot provide our youth with developmental experiences in all the goals advocated locally and nationally. The answer is that we can't do everything, so we need to focus on doing something; less is more.

- Although What's worth doing? is the key question in our professional work, it is also important to ask whether what we are doing is working and, eventually, What's possible?

- What's worth doing and what's possible include not only in-school PE but also extended-day PA youth development programs and alternative school programs. This is particularly relevant in the current climate of social problems, which often requires new approaches such as teaching life skills and values and the principles of the youth development movement.

- TPSR was developed as an answer to the question What's worth doing? so that I could make good on my commitment to try to help kids with the social problems they face and to facilitate their personal and social development.

- There are no silver bullets to solve the problems kids face today, and that includes TPSR. The best most of us can do is plant seeds with the kids.

- If these ideas and strategies are worth doing from your point of view, help yourself!

2

A Framework for Teaching Personal and Social Responsibility

You gotta have a system.

—Eddie Robinson,
former Grambling football coach

■ ■ ■ ■ ■

In chapter 1, I briefly told the story of how TPSR came into being, in part to highlight a few of the basic ideas, but more important, to show what a human and therefore flawed process the development of this approach has been. It amounted to taking a few values and beliefs (less is more) and some physical activities into a teaching situation with kids who didn't exactly roll out the red carpet. What followed was all trial and error (mostly error) and a heavy dose of the three Rs—reflection, reflection, and reflection—which is why I call it a working theory-in-practice. That's just a fancy way of saying I made it up and continue to do so! The rest of chapter 1 discussed the rationale for TPSR in greater depth and explored promising developments for PE and PA programs in youth development, alternative schools, and after-school programs as possible answers to the questions: What's worth doing? and What's possible?

In his first year of coaching, renowned Grambling football coach Eddie Robinson attended a clinic and learned that, as a new coach, "You gotta have a system." Taking a cue from Eddie Robinson, I assert that the only way the mix of ideas and values in this book has a chance of being shared is to be at least somewhat systematic, to give it some structure, even though imposing a structure threatens to reduce its humanity by overlooking the idiosyncratic zigzag nature of the educational process. My compromise is to offer a framework—not a rigid structure or blueprint—of basic values, ideas, and implementation strategies that honors the craft of teaching (see figure 2.1). These ideas and strategies are described in depth throughout the book, but first, this chapter offers a guided tour of the framework.

TPSR Framework

- Core values
- Assumptions
- Levels of responsibility
- Program leader responsibilities
- Daily program format
- Suggested embedding strategies
- Problem solving
- Assessment

FIGURE 2.1 TPSR is shared through a flexible framework.

CORE VALUES

Although the purpose of TPSR can be summarized as teaching kids to take personal and social responsibility through physical activity, which implies a values orientation, a small set of core values underlie this purpose (see figure 2.2). Values fall outside the boundaries of science; they are *not* derived from data-based findings anchored in rigorous research methods.

In essence, the core value of TPSR is "putting kids first" (Hellison et al., 2000, p. 36) and being "youth-centered" (McLaughlin, 2000, p. 9). Although this sounds like one of those slogans such as "sport builds character" that can be interpreted in many different ways, at least it tells us what it is not. It is not putting physical activity or an active lifestyle or sport or fitness first and certainly not putting oneself first (as in focusing on one's win–loss record). But what is it? Borrowing from Fraser-Thomas, Cote, and Deakin (2005), it is simply to help kids become better people. That includes promoting human decency and positive relationships with others. In this world we need to help each other more than compete against each other, whenever possible supporting acts of kindness and negotiation instead of acts of war, and controlling our inclination to put ourselves first.

A complementary core value is holistic self-development. Physical development must take place side by side with emotional, social, and cognitive development in TPSR. As Noddings pointed out, these basic dimensions of being human may be separated for convenience but cannot be separated in practice. Viewing our

Core Values

- Putting kids first
- Human decency
- Holistic self-development
- A way of being

FIGURE 2.2 The core values of TPSR.

job as helping the whole person puts kids first. Every time I try to help some student with her temper or ask some young man with basketball stars in his eyes whether he'd like help improving his grades and why that might matter to him "when the air goes out of the ball" (as Jimmy Jones, coach and professor at Henderson State College, told his students), I am trying to promote holistic self-development.

Later in this chapter, and more fully in chapter 3, the five levels of responsibility are described. Level V, transfer to other aspects of one's life, which is unfortunately ignored by many TPSR users, is really the essence of the core values. In my view, this is truly what's worth doing.

Core values also involve a process. Nick Forsberg called TPSR not a way of teaching but "a way of being." First and foremost it needs to be a way of being for us as program leaders! To the extent that we are able, it needs to be who we are, the values that we live as we work with kids, the values we hope they seriously consider as potential guidelines for their lives. (See chapter 7 for more on living our values.)

Two examples provide another way to understand these core values. John Hichwa's wonderful book, *Right Fielders Are People Too* (1998) is not based on TPSR, but John is a kindred spirit. Closer to home (my home), Amy and Rob Castenada direct Beyond the Ball, a cluster of related programs for kids in a low-income Latino community in Chicago. Beyond the Ball is not based on TPSR. Instead, it is based primarily on Amy and Rob's personal values and intuition, informed to some extent by their visit to the New York City playgrounds and their observations of some of the influential program leaders involved at those playgrounds. When I talk with John, Amy, and Rob, I would not even begin to suggest that they change anything, because they embrace what I believe are the core values of TPSR. It is simply what's worth doing for Amy and Rob, for John, and for me and others as well.

ASSUMPTIONS

Assumptions bring to our attention those often-hidden beliefs and values that provide a foundation for our programs. Here are three assumptions that have particular relevance for TPSR:

- PE and PA programs offer unique personal and social development opportunities, but it takes more than rhetorical claims to turn these opportunities into realities. Personal and social development is not automatic: progress requires responsibility-based goals, strategies, and teacher qualities.

- If PE and PA programs are to be truly developmental and holistic, they need to be focused as well. Following Sizer's (1992) less-is-more guideline, a program with a few goals will have more effect on kids than one with many goals.

- If physical activities are central to our programs, we must be competent at teaching and coaching them, even if we are also teaching TPSR. That is, we must embed TPSR ideas and strategies in the PA content knowledge, pedagogical skills, and activities we teach and coach.

Assumptions by definition are those ideas and concepts we take for granted. By making TPSR assumptions explicit, we can compare them to our current practices to be certain they are indeed providing guidance.

LEVELS OF RESPONSIBILITY

When I visit gyms of PE and PA professionals who tell me they are teaching their students to take personal and social responsibility, I am often greeted by a wall chart announcing the levels of responsibility followed by four numbered descriptions of specific behaviors. My knee-jerk reaction is to wince, not because of what the program leader is doing with students—I don't know what he or she is doing—but because the simplicity of a four-concept wall chart does not truly represent TPSR and omits a key responsibility.

To be fair, program leaders, especially those who work in public schools rather than after-school programs or alternative schools, typically face large classes and lots of students every week. Unless the school uses some form of block scheduling or other structure to add depth to the classes, shortcuts are necessary. Wall charts meet that need. Moreover, I started the same way. I created and then whittled seven unwieldy levels down to four, later adding Level V and many of the other ideas and strategies described in this book as I learned more from working with kids (more making it up!). As my understanding of the complexity of TPSR grew, I thought perhaps I had created a monster.

I continue to learn more about what becoming personally and socially (and morally) responsible entails, which then informs and gradually transforms my teaching practices, a process similar to that of other veteran TPSR users. In this way, TPSR becomes a more robust theory-in-practice. However, even if program leaders who work under severe constraints understand the complexity of TPSR, they can only do what is possible in their settings. Depending on the setting, they may be able to successfully lobby for structural changes (such as block scheduling) or else restructure their own classes as John Hichwa (1998) did when he created three mini-classes within his middle school class of 30 students. Fortunately, teachers' personal testimonies (Mrugala, 2002) revealed that some who adopted what they thought was an approach to reduce discipline problems became more sensitive and holistic teachers as they used the first four levels, even though that wasn't their intention. Because TPSR makes teaching less adversarial, they also benefitted from having fewer problems with kids.

Wall charts listing the levels of responsibility are often helpful to students, but both teacher educators and practitioners need to somehow communicate that the true essence of TPSR is more than a wall chart. Table 2.1 provides a more expanded and nuanced conception than figure 1.1. It is followed by an overview of the other TPSR framework components to emphasize that TPSR is more than just levels of responsibility.

Table 2.1 helps kids focus on what they need to take responsibility for. Although taking responsibility for one's own development and well-being and for contributing to the well-being of others is the purpose of TPSR, the five levels give students specific responsibilities, specific targets to shoot for, within the broader purpose. Chapter 3 explains each of these goals more fully. The point here is to introduce a more authentic version than that shown in figure 1.1.

Table 2.1 Components of the Levels of Responsibility

Level	Components
I: Respecting the rights and feelings of others	Self-control
	Right to peaceful conflict resolution
	Right to be included and to have cooperative peers
II: Effort and cooperation	Self-motivation
	Exploration of effort and new tasks
	Getting along with others
III: Self-direction	On-task independence
	Goal-setting progression
	Courage to resist peer pressure
IV: Helping others and leadership	Caring and compassion
	Sensitivity and responsiveness
	Inner strength
V: Transfer outside the gym	Trying these ideas in other areas of life
	Being a positive role model for others, especially younger kids

These goals are often referred to as levels because they represent a loose teaching and learning progression from I to V. Although students don't always progress in a linear fashion, the levels provide specific steps to keep in mind when planning lessons and making personal plans for individual students.

The first two levels, respect and effort, including cooperation as a dimension of effort (as in a team effort), can be viewed as the beginning stage of responsibility development; both are essential to establishing a positive learning environment. Respect can be traced back to the core value of human decency, whereas effort is an important component for improving oneself and others in just about everything. The next two levels, self-direction and helping, extend the learning environment by encouraging independent work, helping roles, and leadership roles, thereby freeing program leaders to work with kids who need more help while at the same time contributing to a more positive experience for all students. Both also represent more advanced examples of human decency and holistic development. Transfer outside the gym is the most advanced stage; it involves exploring the previous four responsibilities in school, at home, with friends, and so on, to evaluate whether they work better than what the student has been doing. Because transferring positive behaviors outside the gym was the original impetus for developing TPSR, it is unfortunate that program leaders often exclude this goal.

PE teachers in particular often stress the behavioral nature of the levels. That makes sense because they deal with behaviors all the time, and some of them interfere with teaching and learning. But TPSR encompasses more than observable behaviors; it also includes attitudes, beliefs, values, and intentions. In other words, it takes into account the inside self as well as the outside self. Focusing exclusively on behaviors, although easier, addresses only the tip of the iceberg. Fortunately, strategies are available to make the inside self more accessible (see, for example, the discussions of group meetings and reflection time in the Daily Program Format section).

A number of goal modifications are available to suit a variety of teaching situations and perspectives, including the cumulative levels, which are especially popular with PE teachers. Cumulative levels are described in chapter 3 as part of an in-depth treatment of TPSR student goals.

PROGRAM LEADER RESPONSIBILITIES

Although the levels of responsibility occupy center stage for some, and perhaps many, TPSR program leaders, the true essence of TPSR is both broader and more nuanced. For those of us who base our programs on TPSR, daily themes are essential to guide an authentic day-to-day implementation process. After the first few weeks, the point is to try to make the themes a constant presence. If the levels of responsibility are the kids' responsibilities, the themes—empowerment, self-reflection, integration, transfer, and our relationships with the kids—are the program leader's responsibilities (see figure 2.3).

Program Leader Responsibilities

- Gradual empowerment
- Self-reflection
- Embedding TPSR in the physical activities
- Transfer
- Being relational with kids

FIGURE 2.3 The TPSR program leader's responsibilities.

Gradual Empowerment (Shifting Responsibility to the Kids)

Lickona (n.d.) captured the essence of empowerment:

> Choices determine our quality of life. You get to choose: how to treat other people, how much you'll learn, how you'll handle adversity, your character—the kind of person you'll become. It's an inside job. (p. 2)

I would add only that circumstances, including socialization and peer pressure, enhance or restrict an individual's ability to choose. With effort and guidance some hurdles can be overcome, as the resiliency literature demonstrates. But freedom of choice is not unrestrained.

TPSR really stands for *taking* personal and social responsibility. That's why I often use terms such as **self**-control, **self**-motivation, and **self**-direction when referring to the levels. The implication is that these are the kids' responsibilities. The program leader's role is to facilitate the empowerment process, gradually shifting responsibility to students until they are doing more and adults in charge are doing less. In actuality, this role gradually shifts from direct instruction to guidance as necessary, somewhat similar to Mosston's now-classic spectrum of teaching styles (Mosston and Ashworth, 1994). Facilitating and providing guidance means helping students learn to make wise personal and social–moral decisions and giving them opportunities to do so, accompanied by self-reflection.

Of course, nothing is simple when it comes to dealing with the complexity of human beings, as Joe McDonald (1992) so eloquently pointed out in his book *Teaching: Making Sense of an Uncertain Craft.* Empowerment is an uneven process. Kids in our programs may take on considerable responsibility one day and regress the next. They may show little interest for several weeks (or months) and then suddenly show signs of controlling their temper, learning independently, or even stepping up to leadership roles.

A number of strategies are available to help program participants make their way through the empowerment process. Later chapters describe these approaches, but a specific example might help in understanding how empowerment might be implemented. The program leader can adjust the extent of responsibility given to an individual student, a small group working together, or everyone in the program based on how they handle their responsibilities.

My rule of thumb is to gradually empower the whole class and build this idea into my planning. At the same time I know that some students can move along the empowerment continuum faster than others—for example, by working on their own at a station or by providing peer leadership for a drill. I also know that some won't be ready to assume the extent of responsibility I'm asking of the group; they need a more structured situation. Reducing empowerment sometimes becomes an issue—for example, when I replace student leaders who have slacked off. They don't always want to hear the reasons, but that too is part of their responsibility (and part of the negotiation process described in chapter 6). Confrontations come with the territory. This process of loosening and tightening control based on how much responsibility each youth can handle reminded me of playing an accordion (although I've never touched one), so I call it the accordion principle.

Schilling, Martinek, and Tan (2001) use the following developmental continuum for youth empowerment:

1. Students share their ideas and thoughts in the group meeting.
2. Students make decisions within the physical activity program.
3. Students engage in peer teaching and coaching.
4. Students take on leadership roles with younger kids—that is, become cross-age teachers or leaders.

Self-Reflection

When Socrates reportedly said, "The unexamined life is not worth living," he was referring to self-reflection. Self-reflection is also central to professional development. What's worth doing? and its companion questions Is it working? and What's possible? require deep and critical self-reflection. Is this approach and content relevant to students' lives? To my sense of purpose as a professional? Whether it's worth doing or not, is it working? Are students interacting with TPSR ideas and strategies, learning from them, and raising questions about them? What's

TPSR *in Action*

A program called the Youth Leader Corps allows youths who are veteran members of an elementary and middle school sport club (called Project Effort) to plan and lead other kids through values-based physical activity instruction. The youth leaders create lessons that incorporate both sport skills and the TPSR goals. They teach them to preschool children (Head Start) and elementary age children from various segments of the Greensboro community. The Youth Leader Corps runs one day each week during the entire school year. In addition, six undergraduate and graduate students assist the leaders in planning and teaching. They also play a vital role in evaluating the leaders' performance.

Recently, the Youth Leader Corps has been extended to include a community service project. The Youth Leader Corps members set up a homeless shelter on the campus of the University of North Carolina at Greensboro. The shelter was part of larger program called the Guilford Interfaith Hospitality Network (GIHN). GIHN seeks out agencies (mainly churches) to house and feed homeless families on one-week rotations. The Youth Leader Corps is now part of this network. Leaders provide activities for the children, help to set up rooms for sleeping, and provide dinner and breakfast for three families. This experience provides the leaders with opportunities to expand their leadership skills to a broader community. More important, it fortifies my effort to interface leadership skills with the spirit of helping and serving others.

Tom Martinek, University of North Carolina at Greensboro

possible in my situation with these kids? Am I helping them reach beyond what they think is possible for themselves? Am I doing the same for myself?

All of these questions and more require us as professionals to learn how to critically self-reflect. This task is made more difficult by our ability to use defense mechanisms such as rationalization and denial to avoid being self-critical. These same questions, adjusted to match kids' perspective, maturity, and circumstances, are relevant as well, including the issue of defense mechanisms.

Self-reflection is a companion skill to empowerment. Making decisions and choices requires thoughtfulness. Whom does this help? Whom does this harm? What am I trying to accomplish? Is it a worthwhile goal? Will this really help me achieve my vision for these kids? (One of my many eye-openers from kids: When I mentioned contributing to the group, a middle school student asked, "What does *contribute* mean?" Language and word definitions matter!)

Just as sport skills require practice, so does self-reflection. To ensure that self-reflection is practiced on a regular basis, it is built into the daily program format (discussed later).

Embedding

To be most effective, the TPSR levels and strategies should be embedded in the physical activities of the daily (lesson) plan rather than taught separately. Those of us doing this work therefore must be competent not only in teaching physical activities but also in teaching students to become more personally and socially responsible—and in integrating the two sets of content.

A popular but insufficient substitute for embedding, called the add-on, does not tamper with the game or activity. The game is played in the usual way, whatever that is. But afterward, the program leader tries to teach fair play, teamwork, or some other strategy that promotes the way the game ought to be played. But by separating the activity from the lesson, the game continues to be played the same way, and the lessons are truly "academic." Another type of add-on gives information about the game or activity (e.g., a geography lesson to show where the game originated or where it is popular).

Transfer

After using TPSR in my teaching for several years and being mindful of the less-is-more guideline, I hesitated to add a fifth level. But when I realized that transfer is really my ultimate goal in teaching kids to take personal and social responsibility, I had to build it into the goals or else leave it to chance. All along, my sense of purpose, my vision, my passion has been to help kids lead better lives. But their lives don't end when they leave the gym. Kids can learn to take responsibility in PE and PA programs, but transferring those behaviors from the activity setting to other arenas of life such as other places in school, the playground, the street (if possible), and home is not automatic. It must be taught just as surely as respect for others must be taught. At the same time, the provisional nature of transfer must be honored. It cannot be a top-down dictate. Instead, kids need to be empowered to explore possibilities and make choices about whether to put TPSR ideas into practice in their lives—no easy task in many settings.

There are many ways to teach for transfer. For example, program leaders can talk with a classroom teacher about one or more of their students who are in the TPSR program. They can ask how they are doing with self-control or effort. Then they can tell the kids that their teachers are sometimes asked how responsible they have been in class. They can also ask their students by a show of hands how responsible they have been in class or on the playground. Better yet, students can be asked to volunteer how they were responsible outside the gym.

Being Relational With Kids

None of the other ideas matter if a certain kind of relationship with kids is not developed. Although much has been written about this issue (e.g., McDonald, 1992; Noddings, 1992; Tom, 1984), it is still too often perceived as either a mixture of artistry and charisma or, in contrast, a set of concrete pedagogical skills. Chapter 7 expands this discussion, but the key in my experience is to be able to recognize and respect the strengths, individuality, voice, and decision-making capabilities of our students (imagine these qualities entering the door to the gym).

KID QUOTES

"The talks were good so everything doesn't get chaotic."—High school sophomore

"I'm very grateful he has you in his life."—Mother of a high school sophomore

---

Strengths

Each student has strengths, not just deficiencies that need to be fixed. (Who wants to be fixed?) Sure, we all need work to be better human beings, but by recognizing and building on strengths, program leaders can help kids be open to working on their issues, such as making fun of others, getting angry when things don't go their way, or being good team members.

Individuality

Each student is an individual and wants to be recognized as such, despite the uniformity of attire, slang, gestures, and so on. Gender matters, of course, and so does race and ethnicity. (Whoever said, "It doesn't matter to me if they are green or blue" just didn't get it.) I've never met a kid who wanted to be known as a category. She may be proud of being a girl or a Mexican American, but that's not all she is. And kids are not just a bundle of behaviors. They have an inside self that contains feelings, dreams and fears, values, intentions. Of course, most kids don't want to stand out in ways that they or their peers judge to be uncool (although those seeking attention are another matter), but they do want to be recognized and respected for who they are. That's where recognizing kids' strengths and potentials comes in.

Voice

Each student knows things the teacher does not; each has a voice, an opinion, a side that needs to be heard, whether we agree or not. When I first got the idea to listen to what kids think, I only had in mind to convey to them that I cared about their thoughts. What I found was that they know things I don't know and often evaluate things differently than I do. Listening to them made me a better program leader (and person)!

Decision Making

Each student has the capacity, if not the experience, to make good decisions. Often, they just need practice, as they do in learning a motor skill. If given the opportunity, they will make mistakes, but that's an important part of the process. Self-reflection is needed to accompany decision making; it is built into the daily program format to help students become more reflective about the choices they make.

Putting It All Together

If we want to treat kids with dignity and promote self-development, working from a strengths perspective shifts the focus from their inadequacies and incompleteness to their positive qualities, providing a base from which to work. Recognizing and respecting their individuality conveys to them that everyone starts in a different place and has unique strengths, capacities, needs, and interests. As Walt Manning, former professor at Portland State University in Oregon, used to say, "You gotta treat them unequal but fair." Honoring differences among students is what individuality is all about. Giving them a voice in the process and gradually turning some choices and decisions over to them are central to the process of taking responsibility. And what better way is there to treat kids with dignity?

A caveat needs to be attached to this issue of being relational (as well as most of the ideas in this book). None of these qualities—recognizing strengths, listening, treating kids as individuals, and so on—means caving in to everything kids want or demand. It is absolutely crucial for TPSR users to have the courage to stand up for its core values and principles and to confront kids when necessary. However (and this is a big however), the way we confront reflects how relational we really want to be. The kids we are confronting still need to be respected and valued for what they contribute positively to others and to their own development. They still have a "side" that needs to be acknowledged and negotiated. Here is one line I've drawn on multiple times: "What you did is not okay; the question is not whether you did it, but what you are going to do about it." That leaves room for negotiation (which is still relational). In my experience, kids don't like being confronted, but in the long run, they come to understand that being relational means something other than the program leader being a pal or a pushover.

DAILY PROGRAM FORMAT

To ensure that my responsibilities truly became themes throughout the program, I found it necessary to create and use a daily program format—which is a daily curricular or programmatic structure for TPSR programs (see figure 2.4). It consists of five flexible components, each intended to address one or more of the themes, and all of them are intended to reinforce the role of the levels in the program.

Relational time takes place before the program begins or sometimes during or after the program, during which the program leader can interact briefly with

Daily Program Format

- Relational time
- Awareness talk
- Physical activity plan
- Group meeting
- Self-reflection time

FIGURE 2.4   The daily curricular structure for TPSR programs.

some of the kids, just to recognize them, say their names, and maybe mention something special about them (maybe just a new pair of shoes). Problems that occurred in the last meeting can sometimes be addressed as well.

The awareness talk more formally opens the meeting, although sometimes it helps to conduct a quick activity such as a warm-up or an icebreaker (or a shoot-around in invasion sports) before the awareness talk. If the group isn't too large, students can sit in a circle with the program leader. The purpose is to emphasize the importance of taking responsibility in this program, that it is the first step in putting responsibility into practice (i.e., know and then do). Levels come in handy as a way to discuss being responsible. This talk should be very brief, at first perhaps only describing Level I or Levels I and II or sometimes just broader concepts, such as, "Today let's really focus on not causing problems for anyone." As soon as possible, kids should be invited to volunteer what they think the program is really about (in their own words) as they understand the basic concept. Simply choose one or two to share a sentence describing what this program is really about. If they are even vaguely "in the zone," thank them and go on to the physical activity lesson.

The physical activity plan by far takes up most of the time. The principles of TPSR such as the levels and themes need to be embedded in the physical activities during this time.

Near the end of the program, students gather in a circle again for the group meeting to discuss how the program went that day. The discussion should include deciding who made positive contributions and giving advice to the teacher about what worked and what didn't (but not all in one session).

Reflection time, in the same circle, is really a time for self-evaluation. The levels can be a way for each student to assess his or her responsibilities that day.

OTHER ASPECTS OF THE TPSR FRAMEWORK

Perhaps the most difficult task for a rookie TPSR user involves embedding TPSR values and principles in the physical activity content. That's because it requires discarding old beliefs and habits about how to teach and trying things that one physical educator called "turning teaching on its head." As already stated, it requires knowing two sets of content, TPSR and the knowledge and pedagogy of specific physical activities, and then integrating the two. The suggested integration strategies consist of the unique contributions of different physical activities, a strategies progression, and strategy suggestions for each of the levels. These aspects of embedding TPSR values are explained in detail in chapter 5.

Lesson and program planning are often emphasized in professional preparation programs, but what if something unexpected happens? What if a student says, "That's stupid; I'm not doing it"? Problem solving and preparing for unanticipated occurrences are an integral part of effective instruction and of the TPSR framework and are addressed in chapter 6.

Assessment, the final piece of the TPSR framework, focuses on two questions: Do the program activities and interactions reflect the program framework and associated activities (fidelity)? and, Is the program being evaluated for what is working and what isn't in relation to the impact on students? Chapter 11 offers a toolbox of assessment ideas for evaluating these questions in TPSR programs.

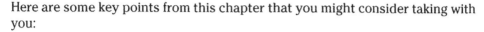

TAKE-AWAYS

Here are some key points from this chapter that you might consider taking with you:

- A set of core values underlies the purpose of teaching personal and social responsibility through physical activity. But unless daily interactions with students embody and demonstrate the principles of TPSR, the program will not succeed as planned.

- Although TPSR is often interpreted as "the levels," the levels are just one part of the TPSR framework or building blocks (or principles) of TPSR. The building blocks consist of a few ideas and a number of suggested strategies and themes. To ignore these is to risk missing the point of TPSR.

- Basic TPSR ideas include the core values, a few assumptions, the levels of responsibility, and five responsibilities of program leaders (i.e., program themes). Suggested strategies include a five-part daily program format, integration strategies for physical activity time, problem-solving strategies, and assessment tools that address program fidelity and impact.

- If responsibilities are not gradually shifted to the participants, taking personal and social responsibility becomes a slogan without meaning.

- Unless TPSR is integrated into the physical activity lesson, the lesson is not likely to teach kids to take responsibility.

- If transfer to life outside the gym is ignored, the original purpose of TPSR will not be fulfilled.

3

Levels of Responsibility

No philosophy, theory, or theorist can possibly capture
the idiosyncratic reality of your own experiences
as a teacher.

—S.D. Brookfield

■ ■ ■ ■ ■

Although teaching certainly has a "technology," a "here's how" to teach physical activities, it also ought to possess a spirit—a moral compass, a sense of purpose, a passion. TPSR is an attempt to provide that kind of vision so that interested PE and PA professionals can help kids progress in a series of loose, zigzag quasi-sequential steps, or levels. Table 2.1 (see page 21) describes these sequential steps without depicting the zigs and zags.

The primary purpose of TPSR is to help kids take more personal and social responsibility by embedding TPSR ideas and strategies in physical activity programs. The five levels facilitate this process by giving both the program leader (i.e., PE or PA professional) and program participants a loose progression of specific goals to work toward. Because kids develop at their own pace—for example, while some struggle with respecting others, others begin to take on leadership roles quickly—the levels can be individualized by making brief personal plans for individual students as necessary.

TPSR encompasses more than observable behaviors; it also includes attitudes, beliefs, values, and intentions as mentioned earlier. The levels were formulated to

- reflect the core values of TPSR,
- be few in number,
- balance personal and social responsibility,
- indicate a progression (though not a strict one), and
- be provisional.

The term *provisional* in this context means that the values offered in TPSR are not etched in granite. Ultimately, students are free to accept, reject, or modify them. That's the way it must be if they are to take responsibility for themselves. Program leaders also have these options; rejecting a TPSR value simply means that they prefer to base their programs on other values. It does not mean that they have somehow gone astray.

PROGRESSION OF LEVELS

Having some sense of what to do first, second, and so on, is helpful not only in program planning but also in teaching values to kids. Respect for the rights and feelings of others often is necessary before much else can be addressed. Participation and effort, along with cooperation, are obviously important in a physical activity–based program, so they too need to be addressed early on. Self-direction, which involves working independently and eventually making and achieving personal goals, comes next in the sequence because it is more difficult for many kids to do. Genuinely caring about and helping others is often even more difficult because it involves going beyond one's self-interest and becoming less egocentric. (However, some practitioners point out that helping others is sometimes easier for kids to carry out than self-direction.) Most difficult of all is transferring these values and skills outside the gym, where the environment is often less supportive.

Respect for the rights and feelings of others is perhaps the least each of us can do for others, just as putting effort into the tasks we take on is perhaps the least we can do for ourselves. Becoming self-directed is even more helpful to personal growth, and appropriately caring about and helping others is arguably the most we can do for others (and perhaps ourselves as well).

A less rigid way to present the levels is as a sequence of three categories: beginning, advanced, and most advanced (see table 3.1). The first two levels, respect and effort with cooperation, can be viewed as the beginning stage of responsibility development; both are essential to establishing a positive developmental environment. The next two, self-direction and helping, extend the learning environment by encouraging independent work and helping and leadership roles, thereby freeing the program leader to work with kids who need more help and, at the same time, contributing to a more positive experience for all students.

Transfer outside the gym is the most advanced stage and the primary goal of TPSR (at least in the originator's "grand plan"). It involves exploring the use of the previous four responsibilities in the classroom, at home, with friends, and so on to evaluate whether they work better than what students have been doing. Unfortunately, this goal is often excluded in TPSR programs.

The order of the levels attempts to take into account both a loose teaching–learning progression and a hierarchy of values. When Williamson and Georgiadis (1992) worked with kids from the notorious Cabrini Green Housing Project, they needed to spend the first few weeks exclusively on Level I to deal with issues of violence and abuse. Respect was a minimal value that required immediate attention and therefore needed to be the first step in their instructional plan.

Table 3.1 Cumulative Levels

Category	Levels
Beginning	Level I—Respect Level II—Effort
Advanced	Level III—Self-direction Level IV—Helping
Most advanced	Level V—Outside the gym

KID QUOTES

"The levels were good. They let you know if you were acting like a fool or whatever."—High school student

"In your class you could always learn something . . . about how to deal and cope with everyday life and reality. Although your class was PE, I learned a great deal more . . . made me take pride in myself . . . and not be quick to judge other people. (PS If you can find time between push-ups and sit-ups, drop me a letter.)"—Letter from a former high school student

---

The progression, although loose, is open to question. For example, Shields and Bredemeier (1995) suggested moving caring to Level II and reconceptualizing Level III as group direction. Their aim was to de-emphasize what they perceived to be the egocentrism of the levels (see the next paragraph for a broader interpretation). The Saskatchewan, Canada, provincial curriculum guide inverted the levels so that what the committee thought was the most important level, caring about and helping others, came first.

The appropriate caveat is to use the progression in the way that makes the most sense in individual situations and with individual dispositions, and to be flexible. If it becomes a rigid, dogmatic structure into which all kids must fit, whether they really do or not, or if it is used as a weapon to punish kids when they don't conform, then the intention underlying the levels has been lost. If the levels language doesn't work very well, program leaders shouldn't use it. Some just refer to the levels as "your responsibilities."

Although a balance between personal and social–moral responsibility is reflected in the progression, the primary focus of the levels is on the individual rather than the group taking responsibility, as Shields and Bredemeier pointed out. However, the daily program format (see chapter 4) does address group interaction and decision making in the daily group meeting. This is an excellent example of how incomplete the levels are in fully representing TPSR.

CUMULATIVE LEVELS

When I was in survival mode as a high school PE teacher in the early 1970s, I began to teach the levels as a cumulative progression, as shown in figure 3.1. Used this way, students learn that each level builds on and encompasses all lower levels. A new level, Level Zero, represents irresponsible attitudes and behaviors.

Level I becomes respect for others' rights and feelings without much participation in the lesson's activities (and without self-direction or caring about others). Students at Level I show minimal social responsibility by not being disruptive but little personal responsibility (assuming participation is a worthwhile and not contraindicated educational experience). Level II describes a participant who participates under supervision, is cooperative, and respects other kids' rights and feelings. Level III represents someone who is respectful, participates, and is

Level IV, Caring

Students at Level IV, in addition to respecting others, participating, and being self-directed, are motivated to extend their sense of responsibility beyond themselves by cooperating, giving support, showing concern, and helping.

Level III, Self-Direction

Students at Level III not only show respect and participation but also are able to work without direct supervision. They can identify their own needs and begin to plan and carry out their physical education programs.

Level II, Participation

Students at Level II not only show at least minimal respect for others but also willingly play, accept challenges, practice motor skills, and train for fitness under the teacher's supervision.

Level I, Respect

Students at Level I may not participate in daily activities or show much mastery or improvement, but they are able to control their behavior enough that they don't interfere with the other students' right to learn or the teacher's right to teach. They do this without much prompting by the teacher and without constant supervision.

Level Zero, Irresponsibility

Students who operate at Level Zero make excuses, blame others for their behavior, and deny personal responsibility for what they do or fail to do.

FIGURE 3.1 The levels presented as a cumulative progression.

Adapted, by permission, from D. Hellison, 1985, *Goals and strategies for teaching physical education* (Champaign, IL: Human Kinetics), 6-7.

self-directed. Level IV adds helping and leadership to the traits of Levels II and III, and Level V—when it is used—signifies that a student is practicing Levels II, III, and IV outside the gym.

The cumulative approach has the advantage of simplicity, especially with large classes, which is why, with 30 to 40 kids in the urban high schools I worked in, I created it. Students can quickly set goals for themselves, such as to achieve Level III or Level IV, and they can quickly evaluate themselves—for example, by saying, "I was mostly at Level II today." The disadvantage is that during the course of one lesson, students are often at several levels. They may call someone a name but then help someone later; they may be off task at one moment and self-directed the next.

Some teachers have created rules for self-evaluation. For example, students who were at more than one level that class period must evaluate themselves at the lowest of these levels. Using that rule, any student displaying any Level Zero behavior should be self-evaluated as Level Zero for the lesson. Students in one of my programs invented a scoring system of their own to deal with this problem. Each student averaged the levels they perceived themselves to be on that particular day and came up with a cumulative level (e.g., two and a half) to represent their various attitudes and behaviors for the day.

The cumulative approach has other disadvantages as well. Most cumulative level users completely ignore Level V. Its inclusion does raise issues—students need to provide evidence from outside the gym—but ignoring it minimizes the importance of life lessons in TPSR. The other disadvantage involves the temptation to use the cumulative levels to label students. It's almost too easy—one number will do the trick. But the point of empowerment is for kids to evaluate themselves. Our role is to raise questions when necessary and share our evaluations when appropriate but not to force our judgments on students. They are the only ones who can change themselves (Boyes-Watson, 2001).

FIVE LEVELS

When I began to teach in small alternative schools with small classes that served "wayward" youth, teaching became less about management and more about building relationships. Later, in extended-day programs, again with small numbers, I was able to continue more relational and less managerial program leadership. In the process, I abandoned the cumulative levels. However, it remains a popular choice for many program leaders, especially PE teachers who have large classes and see many students each day, despite its shortcomings. By necessity, it becomes TPSR Lite.

As I dug deeper into each of the levels and began to appreciate their nuances, it seemed best, at least in my situation, to treat each separately within a loose progression. Some kids have great difficulty working on their own but are competent leaders. Others have major temper issues, but when they manage to be temporarily under control, they are model citizens. And so it goes.

An extended description of each level without the cumulative level structure follows. To minimize the chance of getting lost in these details, it may help to remember that the essence of Levels I and IV is human decency, just as the essence of Levels II and III is holistic self-development, two core values of TPSR.

Level I

Level I, respect for the rights and feelings of others, is intended to provide a psychologically and physically safe place for students, to respect their right to participate without being hassled, and to confront those who need to deal with issues of self-control and respect. Major issues include the following:

- Verbal and physical abuse, such as name calling and making fun of others
- Intimidation, bullying, and hogging equipment or space
- Inability to control one's temper or to resolve conflicts peacefully
- Disrupting the work and play of others

Kids who struggle at Level I often deny personal responsibility and make excuses or blame others for their own abusive behaviors (e.g., the other guy is the problem). They sometimes acknowledge being abusive or manipulative but argue

TPSR *in Action*

The power of TPSR hit me during my second semester in my doctoral program when I organized and ran an after-school Youth Sport Club for refugee boys. There were kids from various countries who had come to America at different ages, so I designed the club to be as welcoming and inclusive as possible. There was one young student who did not speak, so we adapted our program to incorporate skits, written words, and body language into the awareness talk, group meeting, and reflection time. I and two undergraduate interns believed that these adaptations could help the young refugees feel comfortable in the Youth Sport Club. During the group meeting in our ninth session, as we were pointing to our list of activities for the day to see what each student liked the best, our silent student suddenly blurted out, "Basketball!!" Instead of waiting for us to point to his favorite activity and nod, he found his voice in our circle. And judging by the shocked look on the interns' faces, they had truly grasped the impact they can have as mentors and the difference our program can make in these kids' lives.

Meredith Whitley, Michigan State University

that the behavior is justified in a survival-of-the-fittest world. Interestingly, both affluent and street kids use this kind of explanation on occasion. It is important to listen to students' explanations to better understand and to problem-solve, but it is also important to say, "That's not okay" when abusive attitudes and behaviors are involved, followed by, "What are you going to do to fix this?" (See chapter 6.) Because being adversarial is often a protective device for urban kids, being responsive to the context is an important skill, something called code-switching, when the setting shifts from the street to the school (or the reverse).

Level I has three related components (see table 2.1 on p. 21). The first, self-control, means controlling one's attitude and behavior in a way that respects the rights and feelings of others. I tell kids that it means controlling your temper and your mouth, two of their major problems in my programs. Moreover, the goal is for kids to control themselves without supervision (or policing). Self-control is an external behavior that may not be matched by the internal value of respecting others, a crucial but often overlooked distinction. To learn respect for others, students can start by trying to control selfish behaviors while they struggle to become internally more sensitive to others' feelings and needs, prompted by a climate that supports and expects kids to get along with others and eventually to demonstrate leadership qualities. The relational time, group meeting, and reflection time processes described in chapter 4 facilitate this process.

Self-control means not being controlled by what others say. It does not mean giving away one's rights—for example, as a response to bullying or intimidation. When someone's behavior does not deserve respect, the student may be able to confront the person without creating a scene or to walk away (which sometimes really takes self-control). Self-defense is the last resort in standing up for one's self, but most kids, especially those who are picked on, need basic training. If nothing else, training can elevate their confidence enough to help them avoid acting like victims. In many cases, the program leader will not have the training and either needs to enroll in a self-defense or martial arts program, or else be knowledgeable enough to refer individual students to a legitimate neighborhood martial arts program.

Walter Mosley's fictional detective Easy Rawlins offered this advice in the novel *White Butterfly:* "I want you to promise me that you won't never fight unless somebody hits you or tries to hit you. 'Cause you know that some man can control you if he can drive you to fight over some [garbage] he talks" (p. 181). I've seen students attempt to retaliate in the face of a verbal attack, only to be further humiliated. Retaliation encourages more retaliation. Where does it end? All too often these days, it ends in injury or even death.

The second component of Level I, the right to peaceful conflict resolution, encourages negotiation and recognizes that legitimate differences of opinion can sometimes make rights difficult to determine. This component helps students learn the value of resolving conflicts peacefully and democratically (see chapter 6).

The third component specifies that everyone has the right to be included. All participants deserve turns and playing time, whether or not they are skilled and regardless of gender, race, ethnicity, or sexual preference. On teams, they deserve to have the ball or puck passed to them. That, in turn, also requires at least minimal cooperation from everyone, an essential ingredient in group interaction as well as game play.

Like the other levels, Level I is not an either–or, yes–no proposition. A continuum exists between having no respect for others to having full, internalized respect. Students are present all along this continuum, and their attitudes may fluctuate from day to day. Socialization into either elitist or street values becomes a barrier to the development of Level I. In my experience, however, all kids (or almost all) can make progress on this continuum and improve their day-to-day consistency. If progress is not possible, the right to exit the program (or referral to a specialist in cases of genetic or behavioral disorders) should be available. A developmental perspective that views kids as works in progress makes these last-resort courses of action less likely.

Level I can be viewed as the least any of us can do for others, whereas Level IV, caring, can be seen as the most that we can do for others. Empathy, taking the perspective of another, begins at Level I and develops further at Level IV.

Level II

Just as Level I attempts to counter socially destructive attitudes, values, and behaviors, Level II, effort and cooperation, is intended to help kids positively experience program content, which includes learning to get along with others, some of whom, as one high school student told me, "aren't so easy to get along with." Effort counters self-defeating attitudes and behaviors, such as the passivity of "cruisin' in neutral," learned helplessness (Martinek and Griffith, 1993), and attempts to discredit anything that appears to have meaning (Maddi, Kobasa, and Hoover, 1979). Level II is also intended to help students better understand the role of effort in improving themselves not only in physical activity but also in life (a dash of Level V).

The first component of Level II is self-motivation because the intention of Level II is to help students take responsibility for their own motivation. Embedding small student responsibilities in skill drills and fitness activities, such as moving to the next station on their own when they have finished a task, can assist in the development of self-motivation. Cooperation is also needed so that participants can be self-motivated. Being hassled, made fun of, or criticized by peers severely hampers self-motivation except in the most confident kids.

The next component of Level II is exploring effort and trying out new tasks. This could be called "Try it, you might like it!" Simply going through the motions of participation is a first step past nonparticipation. Gradually, the concepts of training and practice can be introduced, leading to development in such things as motor skills and game play as well as physical health, physical appearance, and strength. Tom Martinek explains effort at Level II by saying, "Try your best and don't give up."

Exploration at Level II also needs to include introduction to a variety of personal definitions of success. By being exposed to the concept that success can have a variety of definitions, students can eventually develop internal self-standards that work for them. Competitive achievement is initially the most popular definition of success as well as the most discouraging for some, but improvement, achievement of personal goals, or even effort can define success. John Nicholls' (1989) theory of task versus ego involvement sheds light on this component of Level II. A task-involved person defines success in terms of participation, improvement, and mastery in a specific task, whereas an ego-involved person defines success as being superior to others. With task involvement, success depends primarily on one's own effort (although there are other factors such as ability and task difficulty), whereas in ego involvement, success depends on how others do. One is under the individual's control; the other is not. Kids need to understand their options and be able to put them into practice.

Level III

Level III, self-direction, is intended to help students go beyond the lessons of Level II as they learn to take more responsibility for their well-being. Level III celebrates the diversity of student talents, needs, and interests by encouraging reflective choice. Level III promotes a "complementarity of excellences" (Norton, 1976) by treating all responsible, self-direction goals as equal rather than favoring culturally popular activities, one gender over another, or the motor elite. Alternative school PE teacher Mike Reeder reminded me that I had written about this a long time ago (Hellison, 1978). That book, based on a year with a class of high-school kids, described the Level III question I posed to my students: Who can I be? They were given a little homemade booklet of personal options: health (e.g., cardiovascular, weight control), physical safety (e.g., learn to swim, self-defense), appearance (e.g., muscular development, weight control), and achievement (e.g., being competitive, improving skills and performance).

The first step at Level III is to move from the more teacher-directed confines of Level II to on-task independence, such as by working at a station without supervision. The next step is to begin a goal-setting progression that will depend on age, self-motivation, and understanding of the goal-setting process.

TPSR *in Action*

"On belay." "Belay's on." "Climbing." "Climb on." These calls can be heard echoing off canyon walls at any rock climbing mecca as skilled climbers make their way up sheer rock faces. But this is not a climbing mecca and these are not skilled climbers. They are 12 year olds (1/4 of whom sport ankle bracelets) from an alternative middle school at an indoor climbing wall. This is the Climbing Club!

Our charge: develop a physical education program for these students. After a few dismal failures we decided to choose content that was "risky" (in their eyes), leveled the playing field (no previous experience), brought them into a new environment (the university), and allowed us to teach more than skill. Indoor climbing was it! The youth practiced responsibility while learning to climb. To make the "levels" more meaningful and relevant to climbing we translated into climbing terms. Level I was the same—respecting the rights and feelings of others. They "tied in" (Level II) by doing such things as persevering through challenging parts of a climb. Such things as properly tying their own knots and climbing with good technique without prompting comprised Level III, "climbing." Level IV, "on belay", included assisting others with knots and harnesses and belaying with a back-up. "Leading out", Level V, meant being able to belay another climber without assistance; thus taking someone's life into their hands.

The year always ended with a day trip to a real climbing mecca where their voices were heard echoing across the rock face.

Melissa Parker, University of Northern Colorado

Ken Hansen, California Polytechnic University, Pomona

Goal-setting principles are a staple of sport psychology (Weinberg and Gould, 1999) and include helping kids set goals that are realistic and under their control. They should also record their progress. One way to start (unless it is too elementary) is by asking them what a goal is and whether they have any personal goals. Some goals might be suggested until they grasp the idea. I've had success asking students at the beginning of class if anyone has either a personal (e.g., attitude, behavior) or sport or fitness goal for the day and then following up in reflection time by asking if anyone actually practiced his or her goal (assuming that at least a few kids chose goals). Eventually, they should be able to make and carry out personal physical activity plans. However, to set, achieve, and evaluate personal goals require self-knowledge (What do I need to improve?) and conceptual knowledge (such as the role of feedback in motor skill improvement). These needs can be integrated into the program using examples and one-liners. Once again, one of my most systematic efforts to implement goal setting was back in 1978 (Hellison, 1978), but I had to employ behavior modification to make it work, which reduced its appeal for me. As I've worked with goal setting over time, my approach has loosened up, making adjustments a lot easier.

Level III also involves working toward an understanding of one's needs, not just one's interests. Setting goals and self-standards and developing one's uniqueness (e.g., by developing a physical activity specialty) are aspects of this process. Of course, having fun, being with friends, celebrating, and even managing stress are important too. Although most kids are oriented to the present, learning to choose and stay with activities that meet both long- and short-term interests and needs in some balance is one of the hallmarks of mature self-direction.

To accomplish the kind of independence required for true self-direction, kids must develop the courage to look inside themselves. Some of this is sensitive work, especially for adolescents. If they can be convinced to bring perceived weaknesses out into the open, at least to themselves, they can address the need to look good or seek approval by making personal plans to strengthen those weak points. Many students would feel better about themselves if they confronted their issues and made a plan to resolve them. One way to address these issues is self-acceptance—accepting limitations that make them less popular or less part of the mainstream while emphasizing being themselves and developing their unique talents. Another way is self-image actualizing (Lyon, 1971), which involves making and carrying out a plan to improve skills, game play, strength, endurance, appearance, or whatever is necessary to feel better about themselves.

Among the most difficult aspects of striving against external forces (deCharms, 1976) is being able to stand up for personal rights. Creating a truly personal plan derived from one's own needs and interests is no easy task for kids who need peer approval. The importance of making a plan that is truly one's own can be addressed in awareness talks, group meetings, or relational time. Having identified their needs as something distinct from the opinions of others, students also need to learn how to stand up for their independence and protect themselves. A plan to do so may take the form of learning how to be appropriately assertive and practicing such assertiveness in the physical activity setting (Banks and Smith-Fee, 1989) or even learning self-defense skills as suggested earlier. Outward Bound creator Kurt Hahn often talked about making the brave gentle and the gentle brave (Richards, 1982). From an empowerment perspective, the goal would not be to "make" kids anything but instead to assist them in taking charge of these goals to the extent that they are perceived to be relevant (unless their actions threaten to harm others). The levels attempt to meet these needs, especially Levels I, III, and IV.

Questions have been raised about whether Level III is relevant for children. My experience with primary and elementary school teachers is that although some of the ideas described here are advanced, children can often do more than we expect. Such things as goal setting may be relevant if adjusted for age—for example, by introducing the idea or giving some choices with reflection afterward. However, program leaders who work with young kids have a better idea than I do of what they can handle. My only suggestion is to experiment a bit before dismissing this level.

Level IV

Level IV, like Level III (and all levels), needs to be adjusted for age. Mature Level IV students possess the interpersonal skills of sensitivity and responsiveness to act out of caring and compassion for others (a process started at Level I), contribute to their community, and do so without expectations of extrinsic rewards. Working at Level IV is easier said than done. It requires the following:

- Interpersonal relations skills of listening and responding without being judgmental or dogmatic
- An ability to help without being arrogant
- An understanding of the importance of helping only when the other person wants the help
- Not becoming a rescuer
- An ability to help others resolve differences peacefully and democratically

Students at Level IV recognize that others have needs and feelings just as they do, and they learn to see and feel things from the viewpoints of others. This is a very tall order for those of us who do this work, let alone for kids! A first step that reflects the spirit of Level IV might be to ask them to contribute however they can to everyone having a positive experience during the program. The complexity of helping others and taking on leadership roles convinced Tom Martinek (Martinek and Hellison, 2009) to develop and employ a four-stage youth leadership development process, beginning with learning to take responsibility and progressing to leadership awareness, cross-age leadership, and self-actualized leadership beyond the gym.

Despite the emphasis on sensitivity and compassion in Level IV, interpreting it as being soft would be a mistake. Level IV requires inner strength—the courage to resist peer pressure and an egocentric agenda, to step up as a leader, to represent what's right for the group. Leadership requires not only the skills and qualities mentioned earlier but also the ability to give to others without losing sight of one's own individual needs and interests. It requires confidence but not arrogance as well as the ability to strive against external forces (deCharms, 1976) when necessary, including the strength to stand up for TPSR leadership principles without being defensive or overbearing.

Interpersonal skills aside, Level IV may be a difficult achievement for young people these days. Thanks to the electronic media, celebrities have kids' attention more than ever before. One teacher who includes a hero unit in her curriculum has said that it is becoming harder to teach the unit because kids can't distinguish between a hero and a celebrity (Lickona, 1991). From a Level IV perspective, a hero is someone who shows extraordinary courage and compassion in contributing to society. Perhaps the late Kirby Puckett, who played for the Minnesota Twins (in a subpar indoor stadium) his entire career, declined offers of more money from other teams, and acknowledged that winning the Branch Rickey Award for community service meant more to him than anything he had done in baseball, clarifies the difference between celebrity and hero. Many other well-known athletes have contributed to society not by their physical performance but by doing genuinely good deeds. The work of Drew Brees in New Orleans is a more up-to-date example of a hero who also happens to be a great football player. (I have a file stuffed with such examples from *Sports Illustrated* and other sources.)

Whether Level IV really extends beyond self-interest in its broadest sense is a matter of debate. Not at issue, however, is the importance of being a contributing member of the community and society. William James argued that kids need to find "a moral equivalent to war" as their sense of purpose (Richards, 1982, p. 24). Kurt Hahn (Richards, 1982) and others (notably, Berman, 1990) have suggested offering students opportunities to make social contributions as this moral equivalent.

Level I and Level IV attempt to counter ego- and ethnocentrism, the me-first and us-first orientation that inspires all the "isms"—racism, sexism, motor elitism, handicappism, and ageism (Siedentop, 1980). Level I teaches doing no harm and being at least minimally cooperative; Level IV teaches making a positive contribution. The emphasis of Level IV on contributing to the well-being of others balances the self-centered goals often chosen in Level III (although some kids do choose social goals).

Level V

Level V refers to exploring the application of the four other levels outside the program—on the playground, in the classroom, at home, on the street. A wall chart of cumulative levels developed by Michigan elementary PE teacher Linda Masser (1990) addressed the transfer issue by showing students how the cumulative levels might apply to various settings in their lives (see figure 3.2).

If kids are to become responsible for their own well-being as well as that of others, they need to be the ones to decide whether and in what situations to use the levels. This is the provisional caveat introduced in chapter 2. Level V makes students aware of the possibility of transfer and encourages them to discuss and experiment with it. For example, Gene Washington, a basketball player who assisted me in an inner-city program, told the kids that self-direction helps improve both their individual basketball skills and their schoolwork.

Level V is the place to discuss the reality of life outside the gym. Within the program, the levels contribute to a climate of respect, effort, autonomy, and community, but these qualities are not often valued on the street and sometimes not at home or in school (especially in the halls, in the lunchroom, and on the playground). It is one thing to work on TPSR principles in a safe setting where everyone is respected and has a say, but what if the group is not respectful or is downright out of control? What if the adult leader or leaders (e.g., teachers, coaches) do not support making decisions or are abusive adults (or just one adult who has authority)? What if peers ridicule someone's efforts because others are more skilled or because the group doesn't value doing homework, or just because someone doesn't go along with the crowd?

Level V can't solve these problems, but strategies suggested in Levels I and III can help. Level I can, for example, provide skills and guidance so that weaker kids can stand up for their rights on the playground. However, to address Level V, program leaders can facilitate brief discussions of these issues during awareness talks, group meetings, and relational time, thereby giving kids a chance to think about the relevance of the levels for their lives outside the gym. What small steps would it take to begin to put them into practice? Is it worth the effort? The students can also volunteer examples, perhaps about how they took responsibility in specific situations.

Level V ultimately means being a role model for others. This, in fact, is the essence of Level V! Charles Barkley caused quite a stir several years ago when he said that professional athletes are not role models. Sorry, Sir Charles, but they

What's Your Level?

Level 0: Irresponsibility

Home: Blaming brothers or sisters for problems
Playground: Calling other students names
Classroom: Talking to friends when teacher is giving instructions
Physical education: Pushing and shoving others when selecting equipment

Level 1: Self-Control

Home: Keeping self from hitting brother even though really mad at him
Playground: Standing and watching others play
Classroom: Waiting until appropriate time to talk with friends
Physical education: Practicing but not all the time

Level 2: Involvement

Home: Helping to clean up supper dishes
Playground: Playing with others
Classroom: Listening and doing class work
Physical education: Trying new things without complaining and saying I can't

Level 3: Self-Responsibility

Home: Cleaning room without being asked
Playground: Returning equipment during recess
Classroom: Doing a science project not as part of an assignment
Physical education: Undertaking to learn a new skill through resources outside the physical education class

Level 4: Caring

Home: Helping take care of a pet or younger child
Playground: Asking others (not just friends) to join in play
Classroom: Helping another student with a math problem
Physical education: Willingly working with anyone in the class

---

FIGURE 3.2 Linda Masser's application of the four cumulative levels.

Adapted, by permission, from L. Masser, 1990, "Teaching for affective learning in physical education," *Journal of Physical Education, Recreation, and Dance* 61: 19.

are widely admired and looked up to by kids, whether you think they should be or not. And some are exemplary role models—like David Robinson for his good works in building a unique school, which he refused to allow being called the David Robinson Academy (ho hum, just another humble athlete!), and former NBA all-star Dave Bing for taking on the exceedingly difficult job of being Detroit's mayor. Better yet, program leaders can tell kids that rather than looking for role models, they should be role models themselves. TPSR is one way to give them the tools to do that.

LEVEL MODIFICATIONS

The five levels—respect, participation, self-direction, caring, and transfer outside the program—can be represented in a variety of ways. Missy Parker's fourth-grade Navajo students called Level II "work and try" and Level III "just do it." In a team sport program, the following cumulative level substitutions were used (Hellison and Georgiadis, 1992):

- 0 = Cut from the team
- I = On the bench (no problems but not participating)
- II = Player (under supervision)
- III = Self-coach
- IV = Coach
- V = Outside the gym

Levels can be deleted, rearranged, split apart, or supplemented. Darin Kennedy, a primary school PE teacher in Falconer, New York, uses color-coded levels including yellow for following the Golden Rule and red for having "heart." Curt Hinson (1997; 2001) used three levels in adapting TPSR for recess and playground (see p. 142 in chapter 9).

The Saskatchewan provincial curriculum inverted the levels so that caring and helping was Level I. In basketball I changed Level II, effort, to teamwork, because the kids already showed effort but weren't interested in passing the ball or otherwise cooperating.

Whether other approaches similar to the TPSR levels or based on other values are useful tools in PE and PA professionals' bag of tricks are judgments that need to be based on individual experiences, values, and beliefs. That's what it means to be a professional. John Hichwa's wonderful book on middle school physical education, *Right Fielders Are People Too* (1998), described his three Rs for teaching prosocial behavior:

1. Respect (e.g., consideration of others)
2. Responsibility (e.g., obligation and accountability)
3. Resourcefulness (e.g., having the inner strength to accomplish something)

Hichwa posts the three Rs and discusses them every day. In addition, they are an integral part of his daily lesson plan. For example, two small groups of students play games by themselves, taking responsibility for working independently, calling their own fouls, and including everyone. This frees John up to work more relationally with a third small group, "giving individualized instruction and adding variation to the activity" (p. 41). Such small-group interaction allows him to personalize his teaching, be more relational, and motivate his students. John doesn't use the levels and, in my opinion, shouldn't. What he does works for him and his students and reflects the core values of TPSR (see chapter 2).

The guiding principles for using the levels or some other approach effectively are to make sure that they make sense in the setting in which they are used and that they reflect the program leader's purpose and vision for kids.

LEVELS AND EMPOWERMENT

The levels provide specific targets for student empowerment. Levels II and III are aimed at having students gradually take responsibility for their own well-being, whereas Levels I and IV focus on their contributions to the well-being of others. Level V addresses exploring and making decisions about transfer.

The levels will remain words on a wall chart unless relationships with kids conducive to teaching responsibility are developed. If kids feel that their strengths as well as what needs work are recognized, if they are treated as individuals, and if they are empowered to share their views and make decisions in line with the responsibility they are willing to take, a number of things begin to happen. They are introduced to Level I by being treated with respect and to Level IV by being treated with care, sensitivity, and responsiveness. When program leaders recognize kids' potential for empowerment and hold them accountable, most kids, some perhaps reluctantly, begin to accept the idea of taking responsibility. And by honoring their strengths and individuality, program leaders lay the foundation for Levels II and III.

⟨⟨⟨ TAKE-AWAYS ⟩⟩⟩

Here are some key points from this chapter that you might consider taking with you:

- The levels provide students with specific targets for taking responsibility.
- The levels are intended as a loose progression, both for planning the program and for progressive steps the kids can take.
- Cumulative levels can be helpful to those with large groups because they simplify a complex process. They often omit transfer, however, an especially serious flaw for an approach that aspires to teach life skills and values.
- Empowerment must be linked to the levels so that students evaluate themselves and begin to take responsibility for their own well-being and for contributing to the well-being of others.
- As difficult as this is, the levels should not be reduced to behaviors. They also represent the students' inside selves—their values, intentions, motives, and attitudes.
- The levels are social constructions, which simply means that they can be modified in all kinds of ways as long as the underlying principles of TPSR are honored, including the concept that less is more.

STRATEGIES

TPSR

4

Daily Program Format

Do not go where the path may lead, go instead where there is no
path and leave a trail.

—*Ralph Waldo Emerson*

■ ■ ■ ■ ■

Day-to-day consistency in the use of the program leader's responsibilities (i.e., program themes) and levels of responsibility is an essential feature of the TPSR framework. Consistency is crucial, because kids' understanding and exploration of these ideas grows slowly and unevenly, often with considerable backsliding.

One way to achieve some consistency in using TPSR is to adopt the TPSR daily program format introduced in chapter 2, although as Emerson's quote suggests, this format is not the only way. The format facilitates the integration of TPSR by providing a generic plan, with specifics to be filled in by the program leader, including the age and maturity level of the kids (while keeping in mind that children can often do more than we expect).

Initially, I created the daily program format to hold myself accountable for putting my then-new ideas into practice. Before adopting this format, putting TPSR into practice was a hit-and-miss affair. The format consists of five parts:

- **Relational time** either before or after the lesson or whenever possible
- An **awareness talk** to formally open the session and ensure that the participants understand the true purpose of the program (i.e., taking responsibility)
- The **physical activity plan** with TPSR woven into the physical activities
- A **group meeting** near the end of class so that students can express their opinions about the day's activities and processes and how to make improvements
- A **self-reflection time** to close the class so that students can evaluate how personally and socially responsible they were that day

The daily program format addresses the five program leader responsibilities (i.e., program themes) described in chapter 2:

- To empower kids (or share power with them)
- To help kids self-reflect (e.g., How did you spend your time in the program today? Did you help anyone? Hurt anyone? Waste the time you had?)

- To embed TPSR principles in the physical activities (Did you learn anything about yourself while practicing and playing volleyball?)
- To help kids understand that what they are learning in the gym can transfer to other parts of their lives
- To prioritize relationships with the kids in all aspects of the program

Empowerment is encouraged by having students actively participate in the awareness talk, especially by leading the discussion. Empowerment is also addressed in the physical activity plan whenever students are able to make choices or provide some form of leadership such as coaching a team. Empowerment is also central to participation in the group meeting and reflection time, because kids are asked to share their own evaluations of both the program (group meeting) and themselves (reflection time).

Self-reflection is built into self-reflection time, whereas the group meeting involves group reflection. Embedding TPSR with the activities is a major purpose of the activity plan (or lesson).

Relational time sets aside a specific time for developing relationships and having brief meetings with kids, although a relational culture needs to be nurtured so that relational moments occur across the program.

Transfer from the program to life needs to be built into relational time, the group meeting, and reflection time in a gradual step-by-step process as relationships with the kids develop and they grasp a broader understanding of taking responsibility (i.e., that it includes life outside the program). Relational time should eventually include questions about kids' lives outside of physical activity involvement (e.g., their work in school). Reflection time should evolve to the point that kids can be asked specific outside-the-gym questions such as how their respect for others was in school or at home since the last meeting. Goals can be set as well—for example, giving them the option to choose a personal (nonsport) goal such as, in my kids' case, self-control (a huge issue) or a physical activity goal.

RELATIONAL TIME

Because the relationship with kids is crucial to making TPSR work, connecting one on one is essential. The challenge for those with large classes or groups is doing so with little time. However, regardless of the group size, the effort must be made to convey to each student that he or she

- has strengths as well as things that need work,
- is a unique individual,
- has a voice that matters, and
- has the capacity to make decisions.

The daily program format itself helps to reinforce these qualities—for example, when kids are given opportunities to conduct awareness talks, express opinions in group meetings, and evaluate themselves in reflection time—but nothing substitutes for a quality one-on-one exchange with a caring adult, even if it is brief.

TPSR *in Action*

Dayson never said anything. Even when I asked his closest peers about it, they just said, "Don't worry about it, Coach. He don't talk to no one." What Dayson did was show up. For two years in a twice-a-week program he showed the most consistent attendance of over 100 kids. He worked harder than most but at times seemed disinterested and was very difficult to engage in a group or one on one.

The Team Support advisory program at the Boston English High School uses a somewhat typical TPSR format in which after the activity we sit in a circle and reflect. But during what we call the cool-down in this particular group we adopted something like a Quaker meeting approach in which each person in the circle is afforded a space to say something he is moved by. On the last day Dayson stunned everyone. He opened up about how the program leaders had helped him, what his teammates meant to him, and he even talked about some of his plans for the future!

This episode helped it hit home that the nature of this sort of work is long term. And it reminded us how exhilarating it was to witness a young person beginning to find his voice, especially since we still have another year to work with him before he graduates.

John McCarthy, Institute for Athletic Coach Education, Boston University

Before or after class, a quick sentence or exchange can begin to communicate these things. Raths, Harmin, and Simon (1966) called this a one-legged conference, meaning a quick exchange in passing—"Hey, Deborah, got a new 'do'?" or "Jeremy, remember to pass the ball today, okay?" Conducting relational time after class permits immediate follow-up on individual successes and problems that day.

It is often convenient to conduct relational time when the kids first come in the gym. Some may be playing with equipment that has been set out while others mill around or carry on conversations. This can also be a time to take roll if that is necessary. Elementary school PE teachers often have little time available before or after class, so they need to make brief one-on-one connections at other times, such as during class, at lunchtime, in the halls, or on the playground. Relational time can also be conducted during a scheduled Level III time for all students, when they are working independently at stations, playing games, or working on their personal goals and plans. Even if only five of these contacts are made in a day, not counting kids chronically in trouble, they mount up and make a difference.

In large classes or groups, program leaders should try to keep track of whom they've already talked with so that, in the long run, no one is left out. One year when I took attendance by memory, I found that I never remembered whether this one kid was there or not. So I tried some relational time with him, and, no surprise, he saw right through my feeble effort and walked away in disgust—it was too little too late.

Four Goals of Brief Relational Encounters

In such brief encounters, what can be accomplished? If relational time is to truly reflect TPSR and its core values, it must be about putting kids first—not only what they do (both good and not so good) but also how they feel and their attitudes toward others, including the program leader, as well as toward the program, school, perhaps the police, and other aspects of their lives. Of course, it is possible to get only a glimpse of a few of these things with a few kids in one brief relational encounter, but these snapshots add up and help to guide the relational process. This is a multifaceted undertaking, but the four "recognize and respect" relational goals (recognizing strengths, individuality, voice, and decision-making ability) provide more specific guidance.

Recognizing Strengths

Program leaders can recognize and show respect for students' strengths; mention their talents (especially if these are not generally acknowledged); or comment on recent efforts, improvements, or achievements. Recognizing kids who help to make the gym a more positive place and demonstrate leadership can be especially important. Program leaders should pay attention to outside-the-gym improvements, such as academic progress, positive reports from teachers or parents, or (for kids who tend to get into trouble with the authorities) not getting suspended from school recently.

Recognizing Individuality

Program leaders can recognize and show respect for individuality by paying attention to individual kids in some positive way—for example, by checking in and commenting on a facial expression (smile or grimace) or a new item of clothing. Of course, commenting on their individual strengths, efforts, improvements, and achievements as suggested earlier also recognizes individuality.

Recognizing Voice

To recognize and show respect for students' voice, program leaders can ask authentic open-ended questions (not questions that require a certain answer) and show genuine interest in their answers, comments, and questions. They may have a solution to a problem that has come up in the group meeting or during activity time, whether or not they are involved in the problem (thereby promoting leadership). Students may have thoughts about how to help certain kids manage their anger, how to stop arguments in games, how to improve the group's motivation, or how to get leaders to step up. If a student appears to be abusing or causing problems with others (Level I) or is slacking off (Level II), the program leader can identify the issue but allow the student to tell his or her side of the story and, more important, suggest ways to improve or fix the problem (e.g., a genuine apology sometimes works wonders). Adults too often jump in right away and try to solve the problem for the kids before they have a chance to share their ideas. (I plead guilty, especially in my early years.)

Recognizing Decision-Making Ability

Recognizing and showing respect for students' capacity to make decisions can be done by noticing choices they have made and roles they've taken on, such as player-coach or group leader, and asking them how these choices and roles worked for them. Some may have helpful opinions about solving class problems, as suggested earlier, and those who seem ready can be invited to take on a Level III or IV task that day or in the near future.

Counseling

In previous editions of this book, the relational component of the daily program format was called counseling time, which suggested that we might be therapists in disguise. A TV interviewer once accused me of being a PE shrink trying to get inside kids' heads. I replied that I was just trying to get kids inside their own heads. I like Noddings' (1992) claim that all decent adults should be prepared to educate kids morally, that it is a human responsibility. Alan Tom agreed when he described teaching as a moral craft (1984). I also like this dictum from Quincy Howe (1991): "Social workers can address part of the job, but a teacher can address the entire job" (p. 3). Of course, this responsibility holds true only to a point; professional help must sometimes be sought. If a student's problem runs deep or seems to require specialized skills, a referral is the appropriate choice. So with the support of these expert opinions and a caveat or two, counseling time continues to be an aspect of TPSR, albeit with a "softer" name.

AWARENESS TALK

Relational time formally opens the program, although a shoot-around, icebreaker, or other fun activity might set a positive tone prior to holding a brief awareness talk. The students can stand or sit, whatever works best, as they are reminded that this program is based on taking responsibility. Gradually, the levels of responsibility can be taught, although with older kids (and in some cases with all kids) just informing them of their responsibilities without using the concept of levels works better. In most situations this needs to be done very gradually, starting with respect or respect and effort, and eventually adding self-direction and helping, and even later including transfer outside the gym. The key modifier is *gradually,* a guideline often ignored.

The awareness talk must be brief. A couple of quality minutes of talk are worth far more than blabbering on and on. Program leaders who are long-winded, a characteristic common among rookies, often obscure their message in a torrent of words. Early in my career, I got a wake-up call from one of my students, who wrote, "You talk too much" on an anonymous evaluation form. When students start rolling their eyes or are not paying attention, the awareness talk is over! In professional preparation, I've sometimes invoked the 10-word rule (which I made up), meaning, you've got 10 words to explain the levels. Of course, it may take more than 10 words, but the rule makes the point about brevity.

Another good rule of thumb for the awareness talk (as well as relational time and the group meeting) is to monitor the questions-to-answers ratio. Both rookies and veteran program leaders too often tell rather than ask. Telling is important sometimes, but without genuine questions (versus answers thinly disguised as questions), such interactions are disempowering.

Following the initial talk, the awareness talk is an opportunity to remind kids about their responsibilities that day. The most important part of the awareness talk, however, is to have students volunteer to tell everyone what the levels (or responsibilities) are in their own words, or, said more simply, what this program is about. If allowed to improvise, a participant might offer something like "We all gotta get along" or "Don't act the fool." My response to these kinds of comments might be, "Good idea for when we start the activity, which is right now!" (Less is more! And getting to the activity quickly is important.) As this example shows, students need not describe the levels or mimic the program leader, but whatever they say should indicate a grasp of what TPSR is about in at least a general way. Kids do come up with some doozies. One third-grader said this, without his program leader having ever uttered these words: "This class is about making the world a better place to be!" An inner-city seventh-grader surprised his teacher even more by saying, "It's having a philosophy!" Who knew?

Increasing awareness was the first strategy I used to put the levels into practice. I quickly learned that, in most cases, awareness was insufficient to promote action, but it did provide a rationale for taking responsibility, especially when I curtailed my long-windedness. These simple suggestions came out of my experience:

- Post the levels on the gym wall for easy reference. This is the all-too-familiar wall chart, but it does help.
- Relate their responsibilities to current experiences in the program.
- Follow up, follow up, follow up!
- Develop one-liners (or two-liners) to explain the essence of the levels. Here are some examples of awareness talk one-liners:
  - "The only person you really get to change is yourself" (Boyes-Watson, 2001, p. 18; relevant for all levels, especially Level I).
  - "If one person is out of balance, so too is the community" (Boyes-Watson, 2001, p. 19; Levels I and IV).
  - "If people can get to you with their talk, they can control you" (Level I).
  - "To get better, you have to pay the price" (Level II).
  - "You're about to spend 40 (or whatever) minutes of your life in here; what are you going to do (or what did you do) with that time?" (Levels II and III).
  - "It's your body and your life" (Levels II and III).

- "You can choose what your friends are doing or make up your own mind" (Level III).
- "Good idea, but can you say it more positively?" (Level IV).
- "Let's see if we can help everybody walk out of here today feeling that they had a positive experience" (Level IV).
- To kids whose lives revolve around basketball and dreams of the NBA: "When the air goes out of the ball, what are you going to do?" (Level V).
- "How could you use the levels in your classrooms? At home? On the playground?" (Level V).

Bill White, a Portland, Oregon, high school teacher who, in the early 1970s, was the first professional to try to implement TPSR (and his work is still one of the best!), encouraged Level V awareness in his program by means of a piece of paper taped to the wall. On the paper he had drawn a line with a zero at one end and a 70 at the other, representing ages in the life span. He drew an X on the line to represent the approximate age of his students (about 14), and on the bottom Bill had printed: "It's your trip." Bill referred to this drawing often in his awareness talks to remind his students that they had not gone far in their life trip and that the levels might serve as handy guides from this point onward.

One way to deepen students' awareness of Level I is to ask them to help devise respect rules for the class. How do they want to be treated? How should everyone be treated? Does name calling matter? Should everyone on a team have to be involved during a game? Should mean faces be allowed during a conflict? How would you like to be treated? Students can brainstorm about these issues and perhaps come up with some respect rules they can all agree on. The point is to have them think about the respect issue and give their input. To reduce the hassle of separate respect rules for different classes, Lickona (1991) suggested one set of respect rules for all programs developed from students' input in each of the classes.

Nick Compagnone (1995) extended the awareness talk into the lesson by using finger signals. When one or more students started to show disrespect, he held up one finger as a reminder to get under control. Extending this approach, one could use two fingers to signal being off task, three fingers to remind students to use their independent time more wisely, and four fingers to remind them to be more positive when helping someone.

PHYSICAL ACTIVITY PLAN

Except on special occasions or during emergencies, the majority of program time is spent on the physical activity plan. The purpose of the physical activity plan is to make TPSR ideas come alive by embedding them in the physical activity content. Integration of TPSR with specific physical activities often means changing long-standing patterns of teaching physical activities. Integrating the kids' responsibilities into the lesson will probably make teaching more difficult at first, but when they start to work independently and provide leadership for other students, it frees the program leader to step back, give support, and deal with kids who haven't understood or bought into TPSR yet.

Awareness talk reminders can also be woven into the activity lesson. Bill White was a master at this. He once asked a student to demonstrate the bench press, and when the student had difficulty executing a repetition, several boys laughed. One, however, quietly went over and moved the pin so the demonstrator could complete a repetition. Without missing a beat, Bill asked his students what cumulative level the laughers were at. "Zero," they mumbled. And at what level was the boy who moved the pin? "Four," several said in unison.

Although empowerment is a fundamental theme of TPSR, direct instruction can be useful, particularly while students are still learning to take on some responsibilities in the program. For example, respect for the rights of others involves, among other things, including everyone in the activities. Because the kids with better skills generally get the ball or puck more in team sports, thereby strengthening their skills while ignoring the less skilled, a temporary rule in basketball might be that everyone must handle the basketball on offense before a shot can be taken, or in volleyball that at least two people need to touch the ball before it is sent over the net. The number can be negotiated and will vary with different sports and skill levels. These tactics teach kids not only to include others but also to play as a team, such as getting open to receive a pass or bump-set-hit.

Individual empowerment can be integrated into the lessons in many ways, some simple and some more complex. In all cases kids need to be empowered gradually while applying the accordion principle as needed to enlarge or reduce the extent of choice in relation to their interests and ability to handle it. For example, students can be asked to do as many push-ups as they can instead of performing a set number, a traditional task that does not recognize an individual's developmental needs.

Group empowerment can be included in the activity by calling timeouts during a breakdown in team play or a dispute of some sort to help the group deal with the problem. Lost activity time can be recouped once students begin to put these lessons into practice themselves. For example, they can be taught to call timeouts during games for brief team huddles to deal with problems.

These and many more awareness, direct instruction, individual empowerment, and group empowerment strategies that program leaders have used are described in more detail in chapter 5.

GROUP MEETING

As Clark Power (2002) observed, "We have little experience deliberating in common about the rules and policies that affect our daily lives, and often less experience deliberating about the common good" (p. 134). The group meeting gives students practice in these democratic values and skills.

Near the end of the period, a group meeting is held. The purpose of the group meeting is to give kids the opportunity to express their views about the day's lesson, how their peers as a whole did, and perhaps even how effective the adult leadership was. They can also raise issues and suggest solutions, or the program leader can suggest a solution and ask for advice. Problems that students have with one another can be addressed during relational time or, if handled carefully, during group meetings. I emphasize repeatedly that blaming others is not appropriate for group meetings or in the program, that instead kids need to express how they felt and how what others did affected them. Then the issue can be discussed, and a separate conversation with those implicated can be held. Sometimes humor works. In response to a complaint from a boy about two girls trying to play basketball with him, Nikos Georgiadis responded: "I don't see two girls; I see two basketball players."

If time is limited, it may not be possible to squeeze in many of these group meeting strategies. One possibility is to ask for one or two volunteers to say what they liked or disliked about the class that day, followed by a show of hands of those who agree. In that way at least all students have a chance to share their points of view, and the program leader gets some feedback from the group.

Meeting Purpose

An important purpose of group meetings is to give students practice in the group decision-making process and opportunities to experience the feeling that they can make a difference through a group process. Decision-making abilities improve gradually with practice, so students become more competent at making group decisions, evaluating the program, and coming up with ideas for improvement. When I first asked students how I could improve, they didn't understand the question! But one time I actually got a compliment, and a special one at that: "You don't need to improve because you're improved enough!"

All group meeting strategies could be new to the kids, depending on how adults in their lives treat them. But they probably have the least experience in formally evaluating adults in their lives, especially if the person they are evaluating is requesting the evaluation. As students learn that their input is wanted and that their comments won't be judged as right or wrong, trust will gradually build, and they will feel more comfortable in sharing their true feelings and opinions.

Group meeting strategies primarily focus on Levels I and IV—Level I because the problems addressed usually involve Level I respect issues, such as disruption, conflict, and abuse; and Level IV because the whole process can be viewed as a contribution or service to the group, the program, and the program leader. As one self-centered student complained, "Why do I have to do this? It's not my problem." The process demands a caring perspective, caring about the program and about others in the program. But it is also self-serving, and this point is not lost on kids. If they want things their way, they need to lobby for their interests. This process, often contentious, can lead to their seeing someone else's side of an issue and becoming more empathic, even if only slightly.

Meeting Guidelines

It often helps to have guidelines for participating in group meetings. Although other responsibilities are involved, guidelines are mostly based on respect issues:

- No disrespect in the group—for example, no ganging up on (Meadows, 1992) or blaming others
- Inclusion of everyone in the discussion
- Peaceful resolution of conflicts

After experiencing TPSR for a while, participants ought to have the opportunity to comment on the levels—to suggest modifications, additions, and subtractions. Remember, TPSR ideas are provisional; program leaders as well as kids need to be empowered to think about their validity and applicability and whether having more people who believe in these ideas could influence systemic change in schools and the community, if only by planting seeds. Of course, tradition and experience often intrude when students analyze the levels, which is why these discussions and students' evaluations should come after they have had some experience in TPSR.

For example, one time a group of students decided they wanted to play trash-talk, in-your-face basketball. This decision ignored respecting others' rights and feelings, but we talked about it and voted. Trash talk won by a couple of votes. I agreed that during the next lesson they could split into groups and play basketball their way, but by the end of the session, the groups had called timeout on their own and decided to reinstate Level I. Such a happy conclusion was by no means assured. If they had not made that decision, I would have had to go back to the drawing board. When students are given the opportunity to make decisions that matter, the decisions they make may not support TPSR. This possibility is part of the process. The progression to full decision making, including conflicts between program goals and student goals, is a rocky road full of potholes and barriers and, it must be said, often not achieved. I typically struggle with how much I can push without losing my students (the "what can I get away with" question).

Other Meeting Options

Although Level V, transfer of behaviors outside the gym, is mostly the province of reflection time and relational time, sometimes things come up in the group meeting. The "big picture" questions will be infrequent unless they are raised by an adult, but more immediate issues often pop up, such as an upcoming exam that has a strong bearing on whether students will move on to the next grade (in these test-oriented times), a new dress code, a squabble in the lunchroom, or in-school suspensions. These things are often big deals to kids and need to be acknowledged.

In some programs, teachers use workbooks or journals to give students the opportunity to evaluate the class as well as themselves. Writing in private sometimes elicits opinions that students are reluctant to express with their peers. In our martial arts programs, participants comment on the class, evaluate their responsibilities, and keep track of their fitness and skill progress in a workbook. One classroom teacher has her charges keep journals about class, but if they don't want her to read a particular entry, they can staple the page shut.

Occasionally, when something happens that requires the immediate attention of the whole class, a group meeting can be held on the spot. In most cases, however, holding a group meeting just before reflection time at the end of class is better for sharing perceptions of the class that day.

REFLECTION TIME

Refection time follows the group meeting, usually as a continuation of the group meeting but with the emphasis shifted from program evaluation to self-evaluation. Whereas the group meeting empowers students to evaluate the program, reflection time is designed so that the kids can reflect on and evaluate themselves—that is, how well they respected others' rights and feelings and cooperated with others, the extent of their effort and self-motivation in class activities, their self-direction if they were given the opportunity, their contribution to others and to making the class a positive experience for everyone, and whether they put some of these things into practice outside the program.

Self-Evaluation Methods

A variety of self-evaluation methods are available. The simplest one, if the levels are treated separately instead of cumulatively, is to have students point their thumbs up, down, or sideways for each level. For example, in response to the question, Who didn't make a problem for anybody else since you came into the gym? kids can point their thumbs upward (I didn't cause anyone a problem), sideways (I caused some minor problems), or down (I need to work on this). Before going on to Level II, the program leader should look around to be sure everyone is pointing their thumbs and to get an idea of how the class in general saw themselves that day in relation to that level.

Using hands to indicate yes or no is an even simpler evaluation system, although it is less accurate because the only choices are "good" and "not yet." Brief journal entries permit students to keep their self-evaluations and explanations private (see figure 4.1). To validate the process, however, it is necessary to read their comments and write something back or at least initial their entry, and this takes time. Some PE teachers overloaded with classes have only one class each day write in journals, thereby reducing what they have to read every day yet offering their students the opportunity to express themselves privately once in a while. Checklists provide a written shortcut to journals. Workbooks, which include other self-evaluations such as fitness and skill development, are an effective way of doing reflection time, but again, these require reading students' entries and making comments. Karyn Hartinger in elementary school PE and Jeff Walsh in middle school have used this approach, and so have I. Nick Cutforth and Missy Parker (1996) wrote a useful article on journal writing in physical education, arguing that it doesn't need to take much time and can be beneficial to both teachers and students.

Level III and V Self-Reflection Questions

Level III involves goal setting and requires follow-up to be effective. For example, in the awareness talk, kids can be asked if they have a personal–social goal or a sport–fitness goal that they want to work on that day. Then, in reflection time, those that had a goal could be asked whether they worked on it, and if so, whether they made any progress. Using thumbs, thumbs-up would mean that they worked on their goal, thumbs-sideways that they had a goal but didn't work on it during the program, and thumbs-down that they had no goal. Thumbs-down can be skipped if goal setting is a choice.

Level V, in which students transfer values outside the gym, calls for a slightly different question: Did you do any of the levels outside of class since we met last? If so, how did it work? I've found that the application of the levels outside

Self-Evaluation Form

Name: _____ Date: _____

Self-Control

☐　☐　☐　　How well did you control your temper and mouth today?

Effort

☐　☐　☐　　How hard did you try today?

Self-Coaching

☐　☐　☐　　Did you have a self-improvement or basketball goal and work on it today?

Coaching

☐　☐　☐　　Did you help others, do some positive coaching, or help make this a good experience for everyone today?

Outside the Gym

☐　☐　☐　　Self-control?

☐　☐　☐　　Effort?

☐　☐　☐　　Goal setting?

One Comment About Yourself Today?

_____

_____

_____

FIGURE 4.1 A simple self-evaluation form.

From D. Hellison, 2011, *Teaching personal and social responsibility through physical activity, 3rd edition* (Champaign, IL: Human Kinetics). Courtesy of Tom Martinek.

the gym is often too general for kids to grasp. A better approach is to ask them to volunteer examples of how they have used one or more of the levels in their lives outside PE. One of my students recently answered, "Yeah, I'm not getting suspended so much!" Another way is to ask a specific question, such as one of the following:

- How was your self-control in the classroom so far today?
- How was your self-motivation in doing your homework last night?
- How self-directed were you after school yesterday?
- Did you help anybody to learn something after school yesterday or in school today?

Kids may have difficulty understanding how to transfer the levels to other areas of their lives. After all, the climate in many settings does not approach that of a TPSR gym. As one student exclaimed, "Do this stuff on the street? You've got to be kidding!" So we talked in specifics about whether they could do anything related to the levels anywhere outside the program and to what extent.

For self-reflection to work, students need to be reasonably honest in their responses, which requires trust. If they had a bad day, they need to be able to admit it without being penalized, but they also need to understand that self-reflection includes self-analysis of their excuses, especially when they blame others for things that they did or did not do. They need to examine the reasons for, and consequences of, their attitudes and behaviors. One way to focus their attention on the consequences of their attitudes and actions is to ask, Did what you did today work for you and why or why not? As with the group meeting, such honesty and introspection don't usually happen unless students feel trusted and supported.

Using the Cumulative Levels in Self-Reflection Time

The cumulative levels discussed in chapter 3 provide a simple and convenient self-evaluation system for reflection time. Students choose the cumulative level that most closely represents their attitudes and behaviors for that class period. For example, if a student views herself as having been respectful of others as well as a participant in the activities during the lesson, she would give herself a Level II. If she participated but was verbally abusive to another player, she would not have met the criteria for Level I and so would rate herself at Level Zero. Students can call out their level numbers while sitting in a circle at the end of the lesson or on their way out of the gym. Or they can hold up fingers to show their levels. Another method is to ask them to make journal entries in which they write cumulative levels for the day along with explanations.

Pete Hockett, a PE teacher at an elementary school outside Madison, Wisconsin, painted the levels vertically on his gym wall next to the door. His students simply touched whichever level they had as their goal for that day as they came into the gym and whichever level they achieved during class when they left the gym. Pete only talked with those who, upon entering the gym, touched Levels Zero or I, because that told him that they were having a bad day. He also spoke with those whose self-evaluations at the end of the day didn't quite match his observations; in such a case, he might say, "I didn't notice you helping anyone; what did you do?"

Kit Cody, a PE teacher outside Portland, Oregon, modified Hockett's strategy by displaying the levels in a target. When the target fell off the wall one day, his kids were so used to the routine of "touching in and touching out" that they continued touching the blank wall space where the target used to be!

Tim Kramer created a tag board with pockets for his Reedville, Oregon, elementary school students. He assigned a color to each cumulative level. At the end of class kids put a colored card in their pockets to represent their cumulative level for that day. By looking at the tag board, Kramer could quickly check any discrepancy between the levels students chose and what he observed. He would then discuss this difference of opinion with the students.

Self-Reflection on Demand

Ordinarily, reflection time occurs at the completion of a lesson so that students can evaluate their responsibility for the entire session. Sometimes, however, reflection time is useful during the program when students need to reflect on a particular choice they have made or a particular event that has just occurred. For example, it's easy for kids to make choices but far more difficult to make good choices. Questions such as, Did that choice work for you? and, Would you choose that again? can help students think more deeply about making wise choices.

All this group and self-reflection may be perceived as conflicting with the joy and spontaneity of physical activity, but my experience is that kids still have a lot of fun in TPSR programs, especially if the program leader brings a playful spirit into the culture of the gym (see chapter 7). Moreover, most kids probably need more reflection in their lives, not less, and these two daily bouts of reflection are just a drop in the bucket.

⟪⟪ TAKE-AWAYS ⟫⟫

Here are some key points from this chapter that you might consider taking with you:

- The five-part sequential daily program format provides day-to-day consistency in students' exposure to, and experiences in, taking responsibility.
- Relational time offers a chance for one-on-one interactions.
- The awareness talk sets the stage, and the physical activity plan puts responsibility into practice.
- The lesson closes with a group meeting, which provides opportunities for kids to share their ideas and thoughts, and a reflection time devoted to self-evaluations of the levels of responsibility they achieved that day.

5

Embedding Responsibility in the Physical Activity Content

It is impossible to distinguish between the methodology and the message.

—*John Goodlad*

■ ■ ■ ■ ■

One of the five TPSR themes, embedding personal and social responsibility in the physical activity content, is the focus of this chapter. The empowerment theme, essential to teaching kids how to take personal and social responsibility, is also woven throughout.

Physical activity time is by far the most extensive component of the daily program format. It is also at first the most difficult to do. PE and PA professionals learning to do TPSR seem more able to integrate the awareness talk, group meeting, and reflection time into their programs but less able or willing to embed TPSR principles into the physical activities—for example, how does one embed human decency or empowerment? It is much easier, although much less effective, to teach physical activities pretty much as usual and occasionally talk to the kids about being a decent person or being more responsible.

This chapter expands the brief introduction to the physical activity lesson in chapter 4 by describing specific strategies at each level of responsibility for integrating TPSR into the physical activity lesson plan. First, however, we need to explore the role of the physical activity subject matter itself.

PHYSICAL ACTIVITY CONTENT

Physical activity content is obviously integral to any physical activity program, but I don't want to make the mistake attributed to both John Dewey and Charles Silberman, who claimed that their approaches not only attended to the whole child but were superior ways to learn content. As Nel Noddings (1992) pointed out, their approaches may not result in students' learning content as well as they would with other approaches, but students in programs of the Dewey-Silberman type are more likely to become better people (which is a core value in TPSR).

Having said that, the principles of TPSR often can be seamlessly blended with shooting a basketball, playing a floor hockey game, doing push-ups—the list goes on. But teaching and coaching this way requires practice.

To teach personal and social responsibility effectively in a physical activity setting, program leaders must be competent teachers of physical activity. In my extended-day basketball and martial arts programs, kids don't come to write in journals or hold group meetings; they come to shoot three-pointers or learn a spinning back kick. However, across my career I've had more competence in some activities than others and especially struggled as a PE teacher with the typical three-week units I had to teach. For example, I quickly learned to find a different way to teach gymnastics, given my pathetic performance in the gymnastics course for PE majors. I opened the unit by telling my students how bad I was and then said, "So don't ask me to demonstrate." I then handed out some old copies of a basic gymnastics textbook, opened to the section on floor exercises, grabbed the lightest kid in class, and with book open, tried to maneuver him through the basic routine. Then I told them to pair up and help each other learn this skill. It was a pretty sorry excuse for professional practice, but at least it included helping each other. Surprisingly, the students worked hard, asked questions (answers to which I had to look up in the book), and we made it through the three weeks, culminating with a show in which the kids performed their favorite gymnastics routines.

Not every student cares about competent teaching, especially in mandatory programs (one of the key differences between PE and PA). More than a few in my experience couldn't have cared less about physical activity content, and they were at both ends of the skill spectrum. I remember Cliff, who was repeating his high school PE requirement and could hardly walk across the gym floor without tripping. But once he began to grasp what the program was about—that he was respected and had a say in what went on, that the gym was a safe place to be—he was the first student to show up and the last to leave. He volunteered to put up the volleyball net and, by the end of the year, to do about a hundred other chores. Then there was David, a highly skilled kid who brought a number of problems to the gym. He wrote this in a letter to me years later:

> What I really admired about going to your classes was that if you didn't learn anything physical, you could always learn something mental. Myself, I learned more mental stuff, but that's because I could learn physical stuff whenever I wanted.

Nevertheless, had the instruction not been credible, David might have been less likely to make this statement. Sound physical activity knowledge and pedagogy authenticate TPSR-based experiences. For the Cliffs of the world, and perhaps for some Davids, content is less important than how they are treated and what they learn about life. Yet many others do come for the content, and if they believe it to be poorly taught, TPSR is also weakened.

Depending on the setting, stakeholders—perhaps including board members, parents, administrators, students, and taxpayers—expect the instruction to be competent. A swimming teacher knows that people expect her students to learn how to swim, and a baseball coach is supposed to know how to coach baseball. The PE or PA program leader should be credible to the stakeholders as well, which means delivering competent, knowledgeable instruction even if one goal of the program is teaching kids to take responsibility for themselves and their relationships with others. Of course, reality sometimes gets in the way, as my gymnastics example vividly demonstrates.

KID QUOTES

"We drove by the other day."—Very limited "progress" reported by three high school students one month after they asked for and received a recommendation in the community for continuing their martial arts training

"I learned that it doesn't pay to put on an image of being tough. When you feel down and out and read this letter, it better warm you up or I might have to fly to Chicago to beat some sense into you."—Letter from a former high school student

"Yes!"—An eighth-grader responding to being asked whether he wanted to be me (i.e., run the whole program) the next time our program met

Awareness talks, reflection time, and group meetings take time away from the activity, even if done expeditiously, as do individual and group decisions that students are empowered to make during the activity. These trade-offs are necessary in TPSR, but with careful planning and guidance such as the 10-word rule (see the Awareness Talk section in chapter 4), the trade-off can be minimized.

Do some physical activities facilitate TPSR more than others? The answer is a qualified yes. Different forms of physical activity offer different opportunities. For example, games and scrimmages offer many opportunities for teaching socially responsible behavior such as leadership, teamwork, fair play, and verbal or physical conflict resolution. Fitness activities provide opportunities to develop personal responsibility for one's body, individually and noncompetitively, in an environment that supports helping others. Less feedback is required in fitness than in skill learning, so independent work is more accessible. Volleyball is more cooperative than most other team sports because the bump-set-hit is an integral part of the game. Basketball and football, in which trash talk and an in-your-face attitude have been common, and martial arts, which is sometimes associated with violence and fancy (and fanciful) fight scenes, provide opportunities to confront and discuss these values and choices.

People have challenged me on several occasions about my basketball coaching club (see chapter 9) because, according to them, urban basketball is an extension of street life (anger, violence, egocentric activity, sexism) and perpetuates the social mobility myth of an NBA career. They have suggested cooperative games, adventure education, and other alternative forms of physical activity as substitutes. My response is that these alternative activities may be preferable in some situations, but if an attractive activity can be offered within a TPSR framework, initial interest will be higher, the impact on kids may be greater, and in voluntary programs, attendance may be better. I willingly acknowledge that as concepts such as "over-winning" (i.e., winning is not enough; humiliating the opponent is better) become more ingrained in popular sport, it becomes more difficult to use sport as a vehicle for teaching responsibility.

Despite being PE and PA professionals, most of us are not equally competent at all activities, nor do we always have the luxury of choosing to teach only our favorite activities. I ran basketball programs in Chicago for 17 years (see Coaching

TPSR *in Action*

Shronda was at a crossroads in her young life. Her senior year was quickly coming to a close, and her future beyond high school was unclear. Being a single parent of a two-year-old boy and living independently in a public housing apartment, she had been seriously challenged by the enormous tasks of finishing school and being a good parent. Working nights, receiving no support from an unseen father who was in and out of jail, getting child care to go to school, and squeezing in time to do homework were but a few of the hurdles she faced daily. Remarkably, she managed to navigate through all these obstacles; Shronda was able to graduate.

Shronda was also a veteran member of the Youth Leader Corps. She and eight other high school students served as youth leaders in after-school and summer physical activity programs for younger children. Their role was to run a TPSR sport club to help younger children become personally and socially responsible people. For Shronda, an important by-product in this process was an emerging self-confidence for pursuing possible futures beyond high school. Shronda is now a dental assistant with two more children living in a brand-new Habitat for Humanity home.

Tom Martinek, University of North Carolina at Greensboro

Clubs in chapter 9), for example, because the kids wanted them and would show up, even if I did weird things like make them pass the ball and evaluate their levels of responsibility every time we met. Obviously, I presented myself differently in these programs than does my colleague, Nikos Georgiadis, a former professional basketball player. I have learned a lot from Nikos, but I can't be him. One time a student complained that he wasn't getting to shoot enough because he was required to pass to his teammates. Georgiadis asked whether the best shooter should take all the shots. "Sure," the student replied. So Georgiadis joined the game on his team and proceeded to knock down about 10 shots in a row. The kid didn't get to touch the ball in all this time. "How do you like this idea now?" Georgiadis asked during the group meeting. The student decided that getting everyone involved might be a better option.

All of us in the field must find a personal style of teaching activities. Demonstration by the program leader is not essential; nor must the program leader play with the students. There are other ways to get the points across, as my previous gymnastics example, however pathetic, shows. The point is that those of us who do this work are responsible for knowing as much as possible about the content as well as for finding a personal style that works for us and our kids.

STRATEGY PROGRESSION

TPSR relies on a loose progression of strategies to facilitate the embedding process. This process can be loosened considerably depending on the size and maturity of the group.

The first step is making kids aware that taking responsibility for themselves and their relations with others in the program is the top priority in the program. It is also the first step in the progression of gradually *taking* responsibility.

Direct (top-down) instruction is initially useful to create a climate that supports everyone's right to be involved as well as to introduce the concepts of effort, cooperation, and eventual leadership needed for a TPSR-based program to be successful. Otherwise, the kids tend to choose games and activities that eliminate players, do not require teamwork, and, in general, where the strong get stronger and the weak get weaker. In this early phase, the program leader makes most of these decisions, although with smaller groups—such as in alternative schools, private schools, or after-school programs—this process can be more flexible. In all situations, the goal is to shift more responsibility to the kids as quickly as possible, taking into account variations in their interest in taking charge of various activities in the program and their ability to do so.

At this stage, especially in in-school PE, most of the activity time involves the activity itself interspersed with responsibility reminders and direct instruction. That doesn't mean a lot of talk time! It simply means holding a brief awareness talk followed by one- or two-sentence reminders as needed. Direct instruction can include such strategies as the all-touch rule (all teammates must handle the basketball before it is shot, with modifications for other sports) to promote teamwork and reciprocal coaching (two partners take turns giving each other feedback) to introduce leadership. Kids are minimally empowered at this stage as they learn to respect the rights of others and help others.

Gradually, individual decision making is introduced, consisting of an empowerment progression so that students gradually take more control of, and responsibility for, their decisions, attitudes, and actions in the sport and exercise activities. When problems arise during the activity (e.g., a game, practice, or fitness activity), kids can step up and call timeouts and then conduct brief talks or interactive group meetings (or sometimes one-on-one conversations) to address conflicts and other disruptions. Although the action is temporarily halted, such brief meetings make future interruptions less likely. For this strategy to be successful, the program leader needs to guide the process until kids get the idea and to step in as necessary to solve difficult problems. Sometimes, a bit of specific feedback is all that is necessary.

As the year progresses (or as several years progress, if participants continue beyond a year), more of the program can involve individual and group decision making and leadership with less direct instruction. As always, the accordion principle (described in chapter 6) is available to expand or contract empowerment opportunities as necessary for both individuals and the group.

LEVEL I STRATEGIES

Kids who disrupt the lesson by disrespecting their peers—for example, by name calling, intimidation, or losing their temper—are addressed in chapter 6, which focuses on problems and situations that arise in class.

A different Level I issue, respecting everyone's right to participate, can be treated before a problem arises by changing the rules of the games. For example, one rule that can be changed to reduce student feelings of exclusion ("nobody wants me") is the much-maligned but nonetheless common practice of choosing sides. With so much criticism and so many alternatives available, it is amazing that choosing sides has survived. If I give kids the choice, they go right back to it, but that is driven both by habit and by the most outgoing and confident kids for whom choosing sides works.

I give student coaches the mandate to "make the sides fair." Because they are in a meeting by themselves, they may choose sides or use some other procedure, but at the end, they need to ensure that the sides are fair. If time is short, I arbitrarily group students with comments such as "It doesn't matter" and "If your team isn't as strong, take that as a challenge." If I need to balance the teams, I might ask a couple of kids to switch sides after the game has started, or better yet, they can make those decisions themselves as long as there are no arguments and no emphasis on being less skilled (e.g., who is going to take the less skilled kids). Reminding them to make fair teams, solve problems themselves, and solve them peacefully works wonders. Interestingly, as the program progresses, boys begin to see the point of having girls on their team, a point strengthened by visits from women who are former college basketball players and whose skills are better than those of the most talented boys, with the evidence seen by all.

Another inclusion strategy is to use or adapt games that help students get the idea that everyone has the right to participate. For example, the all-touch rule in basketball means that no one can shoot until everyone on the team has handled the ball. The rule can be modified so that a certain number of players on offense have to receive the ball or puck, depending on the sport or game. One sixth-grade inner-city boy who was required to play with and pass to girls responded in this way to an end-of-year questionnaire that asked if he improved as a person: "I improved because any other time I wouldn't want girls on my team!" (However, a few months later, after a heated argument with his girlfriend, he decided that he didn't want girls on his team anymore. And so it goes.)

To modify volleyball for inclusion, the rules can require at least two hits on a side, and the server can move up if necessary to get the ball over the net. If kids have difficulty returning overhand serves, rules can require underhand serves. In this and other instances, rules can be tightened when students' skills improve.

Softball can be modified so that all fielders (or a certain number of fielders) must touch the ball after the batter hits it. If they can accomplish this before the batter circles the bases and scores, the batter is out (thereby promoting batter fitness as well as cooperation). The rules can be further modified so that every batter has the opportunity to put the ball in play—for example, by giving players who have difficulty hitting a pitch the option of using a tee. If necessary, the program leader or a youth leader can do the pitching to control ball speed and accuracy for different batters.

The media arguments over dodgeball (e.g., the "wussification of PE") in part focus on the quick exit and the subsequent exclusion of players who are less skilled. Dodgeball can be easily modified so that a player who is hit immediately joins the other side. Eventually, one side will have fewer and fewer players, mostly the more skilled ones, who will have their dodging skills tested by balls flying in from all directions. (Softer balls also help.)

For many more game modification ideas, consult Stiehl, Morris, and Sinclair's book, *Teaching Physical Activity: Change, Challenge, and Choice* (2008).

TPSR *in Action*

The physical education leadership class is part of a leadership class whose purpose is to help at-risk students develop skills to lead themselves away from unproductive, maladaptive behavior choices toward choices that help them see that no one else is responsible for their behavior and that life is, in fact, about relationships. We use the physical discomfort and uneasiness inherent in moving and challenging the body to create necessary settings for practicing personal and social responsibility. The unproductive behaviors of the students emerge when they are stressed by such things as initiatives, fitness challenges, and cooperative modified sport games. We problem-solve as needed to relate the activities to responsibility learning.

The class culminates in a weeklong experiential camping trip. The trip begins the process of making the personal and social responsibility link from class to real life, and as in class, we use meetings before and after the day to help make that connection. Experiential challenges through backpacking, canoeing and kayaking, primitive camping—anything that will create physical or emotional apprehension in our students—provide individualized opportunities at whatever responsibility level they are ready to accept. Their reactions to these situations initiate the learning of how to handle the challenges they will experience in their lives.

Mike Reeder, Crossroads Alternative High School, Coon Rapids, Minnesota

LEVEL II STRATEGIES

Level II strategies promote self-motivation as an early step in the empowerment progression, including help for those who are not motivated to participate, try, or attempt new things. Level II also encourages the cooperation necessary for everyone to get turns and full participation in playing time.

Self-Modification of Tasks

In motor skill instruction, rather than using teacher-directed drills, students can be encouraged to modify the task to challenge themselves appropriately—for example, by moving closer to or farther from the basket or by setting the volleyball net higher or lower (Mosston and Ashworth, 1994). Although kids will sometimes do this on their own to increase or decrease task difficulty, direct instruction can help them understand why this is important and get them started.

In fitness activities, the overload principle can be briefly explained, followed by encouraging everyone to overload their abdominal muscles by choosing one of three kinds of sit-ups, each at a different level of difficulty (crunch, feet flat on the floor, or sit-down), and the number of sit-ups that will challenge them. To give a bit of structure to this strategy, the program leader can pick an average number of sit-ups for the group and tell them to either do this number or as many as they can. This empowering approach can also be used with push-ups, aerobic activities (students select distance and pace, monitored by heart rate), and flexibility (students stretch to the limit of their range of motion).

By making individual commitments, students take responsibility for pushing themselves and finding their limits. Some program leaders worry that kids won't push themselves, that it's the program leader's job to set goals for students and make them accomplish these goals—"We are going to do 20 push-ups" or, "Pass and trap the ball back and forth until I tell you to stop." This approach doesn't provide an optimal challenge for almost anyone because of the different developmental stages of the kids, but more to the point, it fails to empower them. A better empowerment strategy is to make them aware that they are in charge of their bodies and that their improvement depends mostly on their commitment and effort. Of course, they can choose not to challenge themselves, going through the motions instead. The section Level II: Teaching by Invitation in chapter 6 can help with this problem.

Self-Paced Challenges

Self-pacing requires sequencing physical activity tasks and instructing participants to move through the progression at their own pace, accomplishing each task in the progression before moving on to the next task. Following are some specific implementation options:

- Create stations with specific goals. When a student completes the goal, he or she moves on to the next station.
- Create a list of gradually more difficult tasks—for example, basketball or soccer dribbling drills with increasingly more difficult obstacles and time limits. When students complete the least difficult task, they move on at their own pace through as much of the rest of the sequence as they can.

A simple example of a task that becomes more difficult gradually, and one I've used with kids and in PE teacher workshops to demonstrate self-pacing, is the volleyball underarm pass progression:

- Bump the ball five times to yourself. Do five in a row if you can; if you can't, do two plus two plus one, or whatever it takes to get five. If you are a rookie, don't hit the ball too high. If you're a pro and can control the ball, hit it almost to the ceiling (versus the typical admonition not to hit the ball to the ceiling!).
- Bump the ball five times to yourself off the wall, using the same guidelines. (This is more difficult than bumping in the air and more game related.)
- Get a partner and bump the ball back and forth 10 times, again trying to do as many in a row as you can.
- When you have completed the tasks, you have free time to relax, volley the ball some more, or have a conversation.

Write the list of gradually more difficult tasks for a variety of skills—for example, dribbling, passing, shooting—on task cards and place them on the wall at different stations or on individual cards that students can carry with them (in their waistbands or socks) as shown in figure 5.1.

Task Card

Modified Handball

Practice hitting the ball to the wall. Allow only one bounce after it hits the wall.

☐ I can hit the ball against the wall 5 times in a row without missing using my strong hand.

☐ I can hit the ball against the wall 10 times in a row without missing using my strong hand.

☐ I can hit the ball against the wall 5 times in a row without missing using my weak hand.

☐ I can hit the ball against the wall 10 times in a row without missing using my weak hand.

☐ I can hit the ball against the wall 10 times in a row without missing using either hand.

FIGURE 5.1 A sample task card for modified handball.

Adapted, by permission, from D. Hellison, 1985, *Goals and strategies for teaching physical education* (Champaign, IL: Human Kinetics), 104.

Task modification can be built into these self-paced activities in several ways. Students can be encouraged to modify some aspect of the task—for example, by completing a certain number of successful trials but being able to adjust the distance if a target is involved or to take as many turns as they need to be successful. The previous volleyball example allows students to modify the challenge of hitting five in a row as well as to choose the height of the ball's flight. Another way to modify the task is to have participants explore the planned progressions and choose either to stay with them or create and perform their own progressions in small groups.

If some kids struggle with these kinds of decisions, give them the choice of belonging to a teacher-directed group, described in chapter 6. In a teacher-directed group, the program leader makes the decisions, not to be punitive but to provide some structure and positive instruction for those students unwilling or incapable of making their own decisions.

Redefining Success

Losing is an important experience for all of us, but a steady diet of failure does no one any good. That's why task modification and self-paced challenges are important. A slightly different approach is to help kids redefine success for themselves so that, with sufficient effort, success is within reach. This doesn't mean eliminating the opportunity to win or lose, and it doesn't mean giving everyone awards. Redefining success means giving students options, including but not limited to the option of trying to be the best or the winner. At the same time, they must learn to respect definitions of success other than their own.

The following strategies can help students redefine success:

- Improvement is one measure of success. Hand out a journal or workbook so that they can record their scores for the number of push-ups done, number of tasks completed, or percentage of time on task. This provides self-reinforcement for their effort and progress. I've found that my urban kids like to write about themselves and keep track of their progress, even though, for many, writing is not one of their favorite activities.

- Use a form of self-grading so that students have the opportunity to build in their own definitions of success.

- Make tournaments optional, especially if they involve eliminating participants, or else offer alternatives, such as a competitive tournament, a less intense recreational game, a cooperative game related to the sport, or sport skill practice.

- In mandatory programs, give them an out for any activity when it makes sense to do so—for example, by offering alternatives to game play such as skill drills, walking or running around the perimeter of the gym, or even a reading assignment. Forcing kids to participate is neither empowering nor motivating, and it can create an adversarial relationship, especially in a required class. And kids who have little to lose will refuse anyway. (In voluntary programs, kids can usually "vote with their feet.") My PE teaching experiences with high school kids convinced me that they already know whether they are "any good" at a particular activity, and unless I can motivate them by using some of the strategies in this chapter, they are better off doing an alternative program or even reading and writing a short report on fitness or sport.

- Create a "crazy station" for expressive activities to emphasize creativity as a legitimate personal goal. Nikos Georgiadis came up with this idea: "It proved to be a popular station, and all sorts of activities were developed, from working on Harlem Globetrotter moves to skipping and singing to a rap beat" (Williamson and Georgiadis, 1992, p. 17).

Intensity Scale

Another empowerment strategy for participation and effort is the intensity scale. Simply ask students to privately assign themselves a number between 10 (all-out effort) and 0 (no effort) that best represents the effort that they are willing to give in the next activity. This number can then be used in several ways:

- Give them the choice of joining one of several activity groups, each of which has a designated minimum and maximum intensity—for example, a group for 8 to 10, a group for 4 to 7, and a group for 1 to 3. This method will bring together kids willing to expend similar effort, reducing conflict over students who "don't try" or "don't want to win" and providing a more supportive environment in all groups. Those who rate their intensity as 0 usually go through the motions and sometimes find out that the task is actually fun! If they need to sit out, that is always an option (ever try to make a kid move?), but sitting out can affect their grades, if they care.

- Ask them to compare their number to the minimum required for game participation—in the preceding example, 8, 4, or 1—to determine whether to participate. In the process, students learn that group activities require a certain effort because others depend on them, whereas giving little effort in an individual task affects only the individual.

- After the activity, ask them to evaluate their actual effort and compare that number to their participation prediction. By reflecting, they begin to learn not only to predict more accurately but also that they sometimes underestimate what they are willing to do. For example, many don't feel motivated until they begin to participate.

LEVEL III STRATEGIES

An empowerment progression does not honor discrete categories such as Level II and Level III. Lines blur because kids (and all of us) are human! Most of us develop in fits and starts with plenty of backsliding (including many PE and PA professionals who attempt to implement TPSR!). The levels are an artificial construct intended to facilitate, not handcuff, a complex developmental process that is further complicated by individual differences. Program leaders who find the categorical nature of the levels problematic can still be a TPSR user in good standing (if they care about that). In other words, modify the ideas in this book as necessary so that they work for you.

Having acknowledged that, the empowerment theme is expressed in Level I mostly as negotiation (see chapter 6), whereas Level II strategies provide limited decision-making opportunities. Level III strategies further expand individual decision making. To fully experience self-direction, kids eventually need the opportunity to create and carry out a personal physical activity plan that addresses their needs (i.e., a plan for development or improvement) and interests (e.g., having fun, being with friends). They may not be able to do this yet depending on their stage of development, but at least they ought to be aware of the existence of an empowerment progression that leads to having a personal plan.

Most program leaders have had some kind of personal plan to develop their sport skills or fitness and to become a teacher, coach, or youth worker. If so, they can share their plan with kids who are old enough to understand (and perhaps let young kids reach a bit). Sharing a plan to improve a personal or social skill can help kids see the point of having a personal plan. It can also make the program leader more human in the eyes of kids! And it dovetails with goal setting (described in chapter 3).

Chapter 6 addresses problems that students have with Level III.

On-Task Independence

The first step toward on-task independence is having students do independent work without direct supervision—for example, offering independent station work in which the physical activity tasks are predetermined by the program leader. The kids can then progress to choosing from several stations with different tasks, depending on their self-identified needs and interests.

The following fitness example, which I've used with students from seventh grade through high school, more specifically describes one way that uses fitness to get started in promoting on-task independence:

1. Start with a 10- to 15-minute (adjusted to the situation) fitness routine using direct instruction. Integrate fitness concepts such as overload and aerobic activity into the routine so that the students' knowledge base becomes sufficient for making Level III personal plans.

2. On a day when they seem ready, ask them to do the fitness routine on their own and at their own pace. Those who can't or won't need to join a teacher-directed group. Most just need a reminder or some encouragement. If necessary, post the routine as a reminder.

3. Encourage them to develop their own fitness routine for the 10- to 15-minute fitness period. They can reorder the exercises, skip those they don't like, or even spend the entire time jogging or performing some other fitness activity that they choose.

The rationale is that by step 3, they know the fitness concepts and have had time to experience fitness over a period of time. If a few still don't see the benefit or don't like some of the activities, that is their choice. Someone usually asks, "Can we spend the entire time stretching?" "Sure," I respond, "as long as you do stretching and not just talking." Just stretching quickly becomes boring for most students. (This is an example of testing the boundaries.)

Goal-Setting Progression

Goal setting follows on-task independence, As kids extend the progression—whether in fitness, motor skills, or something else—they can take on more responsibility for developing personal plans based on their goals. Eventually, they can come up with ways to evaluate themselves, such as the amount of time it takes to accomplish a specific task related to their goal, the number of times they can accomplish a specific task compared to their last self-test, or improvement in their mechanics based on the feedback of someone who knows the correct cues.

Goal setting, as suggested in chapter 3, will depend on kids' ages, maturation levels, self-motivation, and understanding of the goal-setting process:

- Program leaders should make sure students know what a goal is.
- Goals can be set for students until they get the idea, but the goal needs to be important to them or they won't work on it on their own.
- Students should set goals that are under their control and realistic—outdoing others, for example, is not fully within their grasp, whereas improving their percentage of free throws could be.
- Goals should be measurable, whether quantitatively (by counting) or qualitatively (by description).
- Goals should be short term at first and then gradually extended to long term.
- Kids need to receive feedback on their progress. One way is to help them keep track of their progress (e.g., in a workbook), whether using quantitative or qualitative evaluation. Feedback can also be given to individuals, not

only by the program leader but also by student leaders if they are taught how. Some version of reciprocal coaching, which is described later in this chapter, can be used to get peers involved.

- At first, students need assistance to establish and practice strategies that will help them achieve their goals. Eventually, they should be able to make and carry out their own personal physical activity plans.

One way to help students set goals is to have them use the self-report shown in figure 5.2. I have used an expanded version of this self-report that included motor skill development to help students set goals. To set, pursue, and evaluate personal goals, students need self-knowledge (as mentioned earlier) and conceptual knowledge, such as fitness concepts if they are planning their own fitness programs and motor learning concepts such as practice and feedback if

Self-Report

Name: _____ Date: _____

Fitness Area

Desire to Improve

Body fat: I have
☐ too much
☐ enough
☐ too little

☐ Yes   ☐ No   ☐ Don't care

Cardiovascular endurance: I can
☐ run 2 miles in 12 minutes
☐ jog a mile
☐ get out of breath easily

☐ Yes   ☐ No   ☐ Don't care

Flexibility: I can
☐ touch my toes easily
☐ touch my toes barely
☐ not reach my toes
☐ not reach much beyond my knees

☐ Yes   ☐ No   ☐ Don't care

Relaxation: I can
☐ never seem to relax
☐ relax sometimes
☐ relax whenever I want to

☐ Yes   ☐ No   ☐ Don't care

(continued)

FIGURE 5.2   Students can fill out self-reports and then use their new self-knowledge to help them set goals.

From D. Hellison, 2011, *Teaching personal and social responsibility through physical activity,* 3rd edition (Champaign, IL: Human Kinetics). Adapted, by permission, from D. Hellison, 1985, *Goals and strategies for teaching physical education* (Champaign, IL: Human Kinetics), 90-92.

Fitness Area	**Desire to Improve**		
Strength: I am	☐ Yes	☐ No	☐ Don't care
☐ very strong			
☐ strong enough to take care of myself in an emergency			
☐ too weak to take care of myself in an emergency			
Speed: I can run away from trouble	☐ Yes	☐ No	☐ Don't care
☐ if my assailants have broken legs			
☐ in some situations			
☐ usually			
☐ almost always			
Self-defense: My self-defense skills are good enough to	☐ Yes	☐ No	☐ Don't care
☐ get me in deep trouble			
☐ help me a little bit			
☐ help me in most situations			
☐ help me in any situation I can imagine			
Water safety: I can swim, float, and tread water for	☐ Yes	☐ No	☐ Don't care
☐ over an hour			
☐ over 30 minutes			
☐ at least 15 minutes			
☐ glub-glub			
My body is:	☐ Yes	☐ No	☐ Don't care
☐ muscular			
☐ heavy			
☐ soft			
☐ light			
☐ just right			
My posture is:	☐ Yes	☐ No	☐ Don't care
☐ poor			
☐ average			
☐ good			

FIGURE 5.2   *(continued)*

From D. Hellison, 2011, *Teaching personal and social responsibility through physical activity*, 3rd edition (Champaign, IL: Human Kinetics). Adapted, by permission, from D. Hellison, 1985, *Goals and strategies for teaching physical education* (Champaign, IL: Human Kinetics), 90-92.

skill development is their goal. Teaching basic concepts simultaneously with fitness and skill instruction helps prepare them for Level III. If kids know that they must understand the basic concepts before they can work on their own, it is my experience that they'll learn them!

One caveat to all of these guidelines is that shortcuts, although less technical, are often helpful in getting kids started. One shortcut is to ask them if they have personal or sport–fitness goals, and if so, to set aside a little time for them to practice. Then, a little feedback on how to pursue their goal might make more sense to them. Although shortcuts promote "goal setting lite" (or very lite), they can provide a starting point and perhaps more than that—and they are doable. (See the discussion of oral contracts in the next section.)

For more information on goal setting, see chapter 9 by Tom Martinek in Hellison and colleagues (2000) and Weinberg and Gould (1999).

Personal Plan

Goal setting is an important component in the development of a personal physical activity plan. A personal plan can take a variety of forms, depending on the developmental level of individual participants, class size, and the amount of paperwork the program leader can handle. The plan can take several forms:

- Checklists: See figure 5.3 for a sample.
- Oral contracts: A student who told me, "I need to work on shooting and not laughing at others," made progress in both areas without anything other than a reminder here and there.

Checklist of My Personal Goals for Today

Do three of these activities. Check them off, fill in how many you did, and hand this form in to me. I will announce the activity at the instructional station. If you want to do it, come to this station first.

☐ Flexibility exercises: How many different stretches did you do? ___

☐ Push-ups: How many? ___

☐ Laps: How many? ___ 6-second pulse rate ___

☐ Ten free throw attempts: How many baskets? ___

☐ Ten jump shot attempts from same spot: How many baskets? ___

☐ Ten volleyball bumps to self: How many in a row? ___

☐ Ten volleyball sets off the wall: How many in a row? ___

☐ Volleyball sets and bumps in a row with a partner (three tries): How many? ___

☐ Ten soccer passes ___

FIGURE 5.3 A sample personal plan in the form of a checklist.

- Written contracts, or records, as illustrated in figures 5.4 and 5.5.
- Workbook entries

Once Level III (or self-direction) time is introduced, those who are ready should be able to put their plan into practice in the program. This time can be brief at first but can be lengthened as they improve their knowledge base and become more proficient at working on their own, setting goals, and evaluating their progress. If Level III time is offered sporadically, it may not make much of a contribution to the development of self-direction. Level III time should only be suspended for cause on an individual basis, as a logical consequence of, for example, one or more kids with personal plans slacking off or making fun of those who are not on personal plans.

Level III and Children

As with everything, Level III challenges need to be developmentally appropriate. The question is, What's possible? Even first-graders have demonstrated considerable responsibility on occasion—for example, by making and carrying out written Level III contracts in one school and planning a curriculum unit in another. Of course, older students can take on more responsibility, but children can often do more than we expect of them and are sometimes more open to new ideas. As one eighth-grader told me, "We're pretty set in our ways." The safest approach with little kids is to tiptoe into Level III, but give them the chance to spread their wings a bit. Have a little faith in them, and the result may be a pleasant surprise. Alfie Kohn (1993) gave this advice:

> It goes without saying that a 16-year-old can approach a decision in a more sophisticated way than a 6-year-old and therefore can usually be entrusted with more responsibility. But this fact is sometimes used to justify preventing younger children from making choices that are well within their capabilities. Moreover, the idea that we must wait until the children are mature enough to handle responsibilities may set up a vicious circle; after all, it is experience with decision-making that helps children become capable of handling them. (p. 14)

LEVEL IV STRATEGIES

Walt Kelly, football coach and high school PE teacher in Bozeman, Montana, tells his students and players that for all games there is one primary rule: Be at Level IV of the cumulative levels. That means they must cooperate, be trustworthy, support each other, help each other, and assume their share of leadership.

Helping and Leadership Roles

To promote Level IV experiences, program leaders can integrate helping roles into the program. Options range from such strategies as reciprocal coaching to providing leadership outside the gym (Level V), which Tom Martinek called self-actualized leadership (Martinek and Hellison, 2009).

My Personal Plan 1

1. Fitness

Choose at least one.

My flexibility goal is _____.

My strength goal is _____.

My aerobic goal is _____.

Today in fitness I did _____.

2. Motor Skills

Choose at least one skill from one activity.

My basketball goal is _____.

My volleyball goal is _____.

My soccer goal is _____.

My _____ goal is _____.

Today in motor skill development I did _____.

3. Other

Choose one.

The creative/expressive activity I did was _____.

I spent my "pal time" with _____ doing _____.

The stress management activity I did today was _____.

The self-defense activity I did today was _____.

4. During My Level III Time

My respect for others was

_____ good   _____ fair   _____ poor

My effort was

_____ good   _____ fair   _____ poor

My plan was

_____ my own   _____ somewhat my own   _____ not my own

My self-discipline in carrying out my plan was

_____ good   _____ fair   _____ poor

I helped someone else.

_____ yes   _____ a little   _____ no

FIGURE 5.4 A sample personal plan in the form of a written contract.

From D. Hellison, 2011, *Teaching personal and social responsibility through physical activity*, 3rd edition (Champaign, IL: Human Kinetics).

My Personal Plan 2

The First 15 Minutes

My goal: _____

_____

_____

What I will be doing: _____

_____

_____

How I will measure my progress: _____

_____

_____

The Second 15 Minutes

My goal: _____

_____

_____

What I will be doing: _____

_____

_____

How I will measure my progress: _____

_____

_____

FIGURE 5.5 Another sample personal plan in the form of a written contract.

From D. Hellison, 2011, *Teaching personal and social responsibility through physical activity, 3rd edition* (Champaign, IL: Human Kinetics).

Reciprocal Coaching

Reciprocal coaching (adapted from Mosston and Ashworth, 1994) gives every participant a chance to take the first step toward youth leadership by learning how to give appropriate feedback to a peer when both are practicing a specific motor skill. One of the pair coaches first, which means that she observes her partner in relation to three specific cues (e.g., in soccer: kick with the shoelaces, not the toe). After a few turns, they switch roles. When both have taken their coaching turns, they get together and share how well the other person coached them. Did she say anything? Was she positive? Was she helpful? Note that they talk about the other person's performance as a coach, not as a player. This strategy needs to be set up carefully to ensure that kids know the relevant cues and are able to give positive feedback.

Peer Teaching and Coaching

Peer teaching and coaching roles expand the Level IV concept of helping others to include youth leadership. Traditionally in in-school PE classes, assigned leadership roles have been limited mostly to athletes or highly skilled kids who lead exercise routines familiar to the students in class. Being a good athlete isn't enough, though. It may help if the student leader brings to the experience relevant sport knowledge or if kids have high regard for those who are athletes or are highly skilled, but these things aren't necessary. What is necessary, depending on the developmental level of the kids, is at least some beginning signs of the following:

- Caring and compassion, which refers to the youth leader's intrinsic interest in helping a peer, in truly caring about his or her well-being and development
- Sensitivity and responsiveness, which refers to the youth leader's ability to size up what other students need and can handle, and being responsive to these needs
- Inner strength, which is necessary because youth leaders' decisions and actions will not always be popular (e.g., leaders need to be able to confront kids who are fooling around and help them to focus)

Although these criteria are not precisely measurable (which is often the case with the qualities we most prize), the kids need to understand what it takes to become a successful leader. Doing this serves the following purposes:

- Makes it clear that everyone, not just the physically or socially elite kids, can become leaders
- Helps students more fully understand what Level IV is all about
- Positively reinforces the preceding qualities in youths as leaders

Drill and Exercise Leadership

Kids can also provide leadership during skill drills and fitness exercises, first by following direct instructions, and later, after being given the responsibility, by making some decisions about what and how to teach. Leaders can be called together to receive instructions while the others have a brief free play period (or some activity they can do without instruction such as walking and running around the perimeter of the gym). Brief written instructions for the leaders offer reminders or prompts during their leadership experience, a strategy developed and used as homework by Jay Nacu in his martial arts program with fourth-through eighth-graders (see figure 5.6). These leadership meetings will take more time at first but much less later on. Eventually, handing leaders a card may be enough to get them started, and as they acquire experience and begin making some decisions, they won't even need that.

Student Leader Cues for Martial Arts

Front Kick With Back Leg

- Left foot forward fighting stance
- Keep your guard up
- Front knee bent
- Back leg comes up in front with knee to chest

- Extend kicking leg
- Kick with ball-of-foot/toes
- Snap back kicking leg
- Step back with kicking leg

Do the same with right leg forward

Roundhouse Kick With Back Leg

- Left foot forward fighting stance
- Keep your guard up
- Front knee bent
- Back leg comes up to the side
- Pivot on front foot

- Extend kicking leg
- Kick with shoelaces/instep
- Snap back kicking leg
- Step back with kicking leg

Do the same with right leg forward

Side Kick With Back Leg

- Left foot forward fighting stance
- Keep your guard up
- Front knee bent
- Back leg comes up in front with knee to chest

- Pivot on stationary foot
- Extend kicking leg
- Kick with side edge of foot
- Snap back kicking leg
- Step back with kicking leg

Do the same with right leg forward

Jab-Cross Combination

- Left foot forward fighting stance
- Keep your guard up
- Front knee bent

- Lead hand extends with a fist
- Back hand extends with a fist while pivoting off the back foot

Do the same with right leg forward

Front Kick With Front Leg: Jab Kick

- Left foot forward fighting stance
- Keep your guard up
- Front knee bent
- Shift weight to back leg
- Front leg comes up in front with knee to chest

- Extend kicking leg
- Kick with ball-of-foot/toes
- Snap back kicking leg
- Step down with kicking leg

Do the same with right leg forward

FIGURE 5.6 Written cues for leaders can help them during their leadership experience.

Reprinted, by permission, from Jay Nacu.

Roundhouse Kick With Front Leg

- Left foot forward fighting stance
- Keep your guard up
- Front knee bent
- Shift weight to back leg
- Front leg comes up

- Pivot on back foot
- Extend kicking leg
- Kick with shoelaces/instep
- Snap back kicking leg
- Step down with kicking leg

Do the same with right leg forward

Side Kick Stepping Behind Front Foot

- Left foot forward fighting stance
- Keep your guard up
- Front knee bent
- Back foot steps behind front foot
- Front leg comes up in front with knee to chest

- Extend kicking leg
- Kick with side edge of foot
- Snap back kicking leg
- Kicking leg comes down
- Step back with back leg

Do the same with right leg forward

FIGURE 5.6 *(continued)*

Reprinted, by permission, from Jay Nacu.

Player-Coaches

Kids can also assume coaching roles as player-coaches during team practices as well as in the game, as popularized by sport education (Siedentop, 1994), with an alternative model, the coaching club, described in chapter 9. Again, a progression will be needed beginning with specific instructions for the practice (e.g., drills, offensive plays, defensive formations), supplemented by cards (which become coaching cards) to give prompts to coaches. The practice can be scripted, at least at first, but leadership in a game is much more fluid and therefore more difficult to coach. My early strategies for developing coach-leaders were so loose that often kids were bewildered. I gradually added structure in trial-and-error fashion, but I learned a lot from my graduate students, especially Dave Walsh, who saw the need for more clarity in teaching leadership and created some specific strategies. (My graduate students have always been very good at nudging me to pick up the pace!)

Other Leadership Roles

More recently, I added other leadership roles. Kids who want to coach (sometimes as early as fourth grade) but don't know enough about the sport or how to step up and lead can be assistant coaches (another strategy first introduced by Dave Walsh). If they are assigned a specific drill to teach and the participants already know the drill, it is easy for the assistant coach to be successful. I also created a coach mentor role for skilled coaches who wanted to teach others how to coach.

Having students be me (i.e., take over my job as program leader for one or more sessions) is something I did recently for the first time. At first, Michael didn't understand what I was asking. When he got it, he responded with a broad grin followed by a loud "Yes!" Afterward, when I asked him to evaluate his performance as me, he said, "I was terrible" and admitted that he was scared. He wanted to try again and nailed it on his second attempt. In the process, he learned that if he planned better, he could take over the program, and I learned that I should have started doing this a long time ago! In this experience I was once again outgunned, this time by colleague Tom Martinek, who had earlier developed and implemented a detailed step-by-step progression for youth leadership development (Martinek and Hellison, 2009).

One way coaches can show leadership is by calling timeouts to solve offensive and defensive problems and issues that arise such as arguments, bad attitudes, or selfish play. Nikos Georgiadis developed a strategy based on the two-tier system of timeouts used in professional basketball (NBA) whereby student coaches can call either a 20-second timeout for small problems (by touching their shoulders) or a full timeout (by making a T with their hands) for big problems, whether the sport is basketball or another activity.

Although the coaches are in charge, anyone can call a timeout at any time. Sometimes a teammate steps up when the student coach has problems coaching. However, sometimes a teammate may take over even if the coach does not need help, requiring intervention by the program leader. To help kids get the idea, the program leader can call the timeouts at first and take the lead in helping them solve problems, while explaining that players have the right and the responsibility to call timeouts to help solve these problems. Before every game I tell coaches that if I have to step in, they aren't doing their jobs. Some fourth-graders have shown the ability to call timeouts in my programs and have enough skill to handle team meetings, especially with some on-the-job training. Eventually, student coaches may be able to head off problems such as angry outbursts, verbal abuse, and low motivation by noticing the first signs of trouble.

Tom Martinek (Veal et al., 2002) used this helping-leadership progression for kids:

1. Help someone one on one.
2. Provide leadership for a few students.
3. Coach a team in class.
4. Teach new students in the program the levels and class procedures.
5. Teach younger kids an activity using the levels and daily program format (cross-age teaching).

Group Goals

Nikos Georgiadis and Bobby Lifka, when they were graduate students with me, used group goals to promote Level IV experience. In this strategy, kids are divided into small groups that decide on a group goal for the activity—for example, number of sit-ups, amount of rope-skipping time, or number of volleyball sets off the wall. Then they attempt to attain their group goal, each contributing what he or she can during the activity. In rope skipping, for example, if the group sets a three-minute goal, at least one person in the group needs to be skipping rope at all times during the three-minute period. If the goal is 60 sit-ups, group members do what they can, and then each volunteers to do more until the group reaches the goal.

Giraffe Club

I have never done this, but creating a Giraffe Club for those "who stick their necks out for the common good" has been used to reinforce elementary school children who have demonstrated Level IV on a regular basis (Lickona, 1991, p. 309). The presence of a Giraffe Club focuses attention on the value of Level IV and those students who practice it. To add a group empowerment dimension to this strategy, students can participate in the selection of giraffes. They can also be included in conversations about the benefits and drawbacks of starting a Giraffe Club.

LEVEL V STRATEGIES

Although Level V is intended to focus students' attention on becoming responsible outside the gym, in-class cross-age teaching and service projects do promote Level V involvement. Cross-age teaching, in which experienced student leaders teach small groups of younger children what they have learned, is a powerful Level IV experience that provides a service to younger kids regardless of setting. My eighth-grade and high school students (as well as a few younger kids) have demonstrated the ability to conduct awareness talks, lessons, group meetings, and reflection time with 10-year-olds.

I have an unfortunately deserved reputation for just throwing designated leaders in there and then working through the many issues raised by the situation as well as the kids (both older and younger). My more successful cross-age teaching experiences, as well as those of Tom Martinek (who is much more organized), have involved providing specific daily or weekly cross-age leadership training for a semester or more. Tom has recently expanded his program to include Level V service projects for advanced leaders, which involve Head Start kids and other outside-the-gym activities.

I have also conducted a quasi–student-teacher experience to prepare high school students at an alternative school to teach elementary kids. This involved students first practicing teaching with each other, followed by one or more teaching experiences with an invited class of younger children. (Using video is great because it allows them to see themselves teach.) I've done this a number of times, and even when the student teachers had only one experience teaching a group of younger kids, they talked about being teachers after class. ("Fourth grade is just right for me 'cause they are still fun to teach," remarked one student who struggled to graduate from high school.) Such experiences reflect at least a fleeting glimmer of Level V as well as a Level IV experience.

There are many other examples of service-based youth leadership. For example, Nick Cutforth has had success inviting former middle school students to come back and provide leadership in their former classes (Hellison et al., 2000). Any service project the group takes on that attempts to make a social contribution qualifies as a Level V experience. Recently, a group of seventh- and eighth-grade students under the leadership of Stein Garcia made a martial arts video that promoted self-control and nonviolence, and they showed it to administrators, teachers, and other students in the school.

The strategies in this chapter are intended to help integrate TPSR into physical activities. During the program, however, problems and situations arise that these strategies do not address. Chapter 6 does.

⟪⟪ TAKE-AWAYS ⟫⟫

Here are some key points from this chapter that you might consider taking with you:

- Integration of responsibility-based strategies into the physical activity lesson is perhaps the most difficult aspect of TPSR implementation, because many of us think we already know how to teach skills and fitness development and are reluctant to try something new and different.
- Competent physical activity instruction matters, even in a TPSR program!
- Different physical activities (e.g., soccer, dance, fitness) offer somewhat different TPSR integration opportunities.
- A physical activity progression that gradually moves from direct instruction to empowerment can facilitate embedding TPSR principles into sport and exercise activities.
- Each level, including Level V, has a range of possible integration strategies that need to be tailored to the situations of interested PE and PA professionals.
- Younger kids are not exempt from the empowerment process, although the process needs to be modified to fit their stage of development.

CHAPTER

6

Strategies for Specific Problems and Situations

My goal is to be morally strong, and I fail at every turn. But every now and then I have a moment where there's a little something.

—Actor Ken Howard, who played an
inner-city high school basketball coach
on the TV show The White Shadow

■ ■ ■ ■ ■

In PE and PA youth programs, guidelines for everyday practice can be drawn from the program's purpose, its curricular or programmatic goals and themes, and a daily format or routine, all of which should reflect the program leader's beliefs and values (unless trumped by institutional priorities). But what happens when something unplanned occurs, a surprising and unusual problem or situation? Even with something that has been faced before, the solution that worked the first time may not work again. Three general strategies can help:

- Self-reflection (Hellison and Templin, 1991) and problem setting (Lawson, 1984)
- Reflection-in-action (Schon, 1987), including a solutions bank (Orlick, 1980)
- Fattening one's bag of tricks

SELF-REFLECTION

Self-reflection is central to planning, carrying out, and evaluating a program. Lawson (1984) suggested that to solve problems effectively, the first step is to problem-set—that is, to clearly identify the problem to be solved. It sounds simple, but in my experience, this step is often overlooked. My suggested questions—What's worth doing? Is it working? and What's possible? (see chapter 1)—are attempts to problem-set.

What's worth doing in my professional life? This question is about the heart and soul of the program leader's professional practice—the personal convictions and sense of purpose that provide motivation and drive programs. Whether the program works well or not, is it the kind of contribution the program leader wants to make? The second question, Is it working?, refers to what ideas and strategies are working, which ones aren't, why or why not, and what is needed to improve practice.

The third question, What's possible?, explores ideas and strategies seemingly beyond the reach of the kids in the context of the program. It asks program leaders to imagine a more ideal situation, an alternative vision, and then explore ways that can head the program in that direction.

Self-reflection is particularly useful after a day of working with kids (that is, if any energy is left to do it). Keeping a journal formalizes the process and may provide a small measure of accountability. Critically reflecting on how unplanned problems and situations were dealt with and what might have worked better sharpens one's ability to solve problems. The solutions bank described in the next section is a variation of this approach. These strategies encourage alternative ways of thinking and in the process fatten our bag of tricks. Howe (1991) derived an important insight from his ability to reflect on his experiences with hostile at-risk kids:

> A lot of horseplay . . . verges on a full-fledged fight, but seldom becomes one. . . . [Students] take their stand and then allow one another to back down with dignity (p. 24). . . . They do not really want to get hurt, so if they must provoke a fight, they will choose the most protective environment, which is the school. (p. 30)

Self-assessment is closely aligned with self-reflection, as Camino (2002, p. 40) made clear:

- Self-assessment is a process of self-discovery.
- Self-assessment should lead to critical self-reflection and discussion, and then to action—otherwise, it is an empty exercise.
- Self-assessment and continuous improvement are not one-time occurrences. Each is an ongoing process—strengthening what works or is promising, stopping what doesn't, and making information-based decisions that both youth and adults have contributed to.

Unfortunately, self-assessment receives less attention than both in-school student assessment and funded program evaluation in the recent educational and youth development landscape. This often means less attention to the program leader's skills and qualities, although as chapter 7 shows, "who's doing it" (i.e., the program leader) is perhaps the most important piece of the puzzle, even if it is difficult to measure or impossible to quantify. (See chapter 11 for specific self-assessment instruments.)

REFLECTION-IN-ACTION

Because working with kids is "an uncertain craft" (McDonald, 1992), self-reflection and problem setting need to be included in PE and PA professionals' bag of tricks. This is especially true of TPSR. Reflection-in-action is a special form of self-reflection. Both reflection practices (self-reflection and problem setting) can lead to important insights but do not produce rigid formulas for decision making or for unplanned incidents.

TPSR *in Action*

I have used the TPSR model in a school for kids with emotional and behavioral problems. I explained to the kids that there were certain expectations for behavior. I knew these expectations, at the time, as levels, but I did not want the kids to think that one expectation was better than another. Don encourages users to adapt and modify the approach based on the students and the setting. Sometimes, respect, identified as sitting and watching and not bothering or fighting with someone else, was the best a child could give me that day and might even be considered a caring behavior. I did not want to create any more sense of not being as good as somebody else. I explained the expectations as being on a continuum rather than hierarchical levels. This enabled the students and me to identify concrete behaviors that could be used during the day's activities to demonstrate the expectations. The affective domain behaviors identified became the critical elements of the expectation, and those behaviors could be practiced, just like the critical elements of throwing. For example, kids were asked to replay a social interaction using the correct critical element.

Gene White, East Stroudsburg University/Wordsworth Academy

Reflection-in-action is a much less contemplative process than self-reflection and self-assessment; it's more like making a snap judgment of what to do right now based on a quick analysis of the situation. Even if the same situation has been faced before, this time a different solution may be required. Schon (1987) argued that reflection-in-action is different from knowing-in-action:

> [Knowing-in-action means we] have learned how to do something, we can execute smooth sequences of activity, recognition, decision, and adjustment without having, as we say, to "think about it." . . . [Reflection-in-action, on the other hand, refers to a brief period of time] during which we can still make a difference to the situation at hand—our thinking serves to reshape what we are doing while we are doing it. (p. 26)

Schon described reflection-in-action as beginning with a surprise, something unexpected, which leads to questioning the assumptions of knowing-in-action and culminates in an on-the-spot experiment. Reflective problem solving—for example, by keeping a self-reflection journal as described earlier—can help to develop reflection-in-action skills. Solutions banks can also be helpful.

The solutions bank is an example of using self-reflection before working with the kids rather than after. Learning to prepare lesson plans is a staple of PE teacher education programs, but preservice PE teachers rarely gain sufficient experience in preparing solutions banks. PA professionals have a much less uniform and structured preparation, but from what I can tell, solutions banks, at least in this form, are seldom part of their training either.

A solutions bank is simply a list of ifs and thens—as in, "If such-and-such happens, then I'll try this." For example, if two students start screaming at each other while tempers soar, one solution might be to separate them, let them cool down, and then bring them together to get the issue handled or dropped. The point is not that a particular strategy will always work; nothing always works! Instead, thinking about possible problems and situations as well as possible solutions is mental preparation for these possible occurrences. It is a warm-up, a practice session for reflection-in-action before the action. Being unprepared leaves only one option: to spontaneously shoot from the hip and hope for the best.

FATTENING OUR BAG OF TRICKS

Developing skill at reflection-in-action as well as self-reflection can help in dealing more effectively with problems and situations that crop up from time to time. Although these general approaches are useful, having some TPSR strategies for specific scenarios in one's "bag of tricks" provides more detailed preparation for tough situations (see table 6.1). However, having a fat bag of tricks does not guarantee that the right one will be chosen for the situation at hand. Self-reflection coupled with experience can provide important insights but will not yield hard-and-fast rules for what to use and when to use it. This is one reason that, after 40 years, I still don't feel that I ever have all (or even most) of the answers when working with kids.

Table 6.1 TPSR Strategies by Level

Level	Strategies
Level I: Individual discipline problems	Accordion principle
	Logical consequences
	Negotiation
	Sit-out progression
	No plan, no play
	Grandma's law
	Teacher-directed group
	Five clean days
	Referral
Level I: Conflict resolution	Sport court
	Self-officiating
	Talking bench
	Emergency plan
	Making new rules
Level II	Teaching by invitation
Level III	Strategies for facilitating empowerment
	Courage to resist peer pressure
Level IV	Enforcing appropriate helping and leader qualities
Level V	Dealing with responsibility issues outside the gym

LEVEL I: INDIVIDUAL DISCIPLINE PROBLEMS

The discipline policy of elementary school principal Peggy Pastor (2002) could easily have been written for TPSR:

> What is it about schools that takes responsibility away from our students and brings many of them to an "us against them" attitude by the time they reach high school? . . . Discipline is not a matter of keeping things under control by making choices for students . . . it is a matter of helping students learn to make good choices and to be responsible for those choices. [Although] we no longer believe that all children learn to read in the same way . . . in matters of . . . discipline we still seem to think and act as if one size fits all. (p. 659)

Pastor told the story of Robby, who was referred to her countless times for fighting on the playground. Nothing seemed to work, so she told him that she wanted to help him but didn't know how. He offered to help and came up with several ideas, some of which he immediately rejected as he talked, but three of which he thought might work. He picked one and wrote it down. They both signed it, and Robby—although he was still a difficult child in a number of ways—never again got into a fight on the playground.

Despite the work of Pastor and others, "Teachers tend to think of discipline dichotomously, as being either authoritarian or permissive, and to think of being democratic as being permissive" (Power, 2002, p. 135). The TPSR version of responsibility is neither "Do what I say and you're being responsible" nor "Do whatever you please." It walks the fine line between personal choice and social–moral responsibility, relying on dialogue, negotiation, self-reflection, accountability, and logical consequences as described by Dreikurs and Soltz (1964). In the process, it promotes a less adversarial relationship with the kids.

Accordion Principle and Logical Consequences

Many Level I problems happen during game play, although any situation from standing in line to doing fitness activities (including interaction in the locker room if there is one) is fair game for disruption and abuse. A common strategy is to expand and reduce the time allotted for game play in relation to the amount of abusive or disruptive behavior. This is called the accordion principle, and although it certainly sounds like behavior modification, it is also an example of using a logical consequence—that is, what logically ought to happen.

If a couple of students are off task during Level III time, the logical consequence is to temporarily reduce or withdraw Level III time for those two students. It would not be logical to punish the whole group or to ignore the irresponsible behavior. It would also not be logical to give prizes to those who were not off task because that would be an artificial rather than logical consequence. The logical consequence to a bullying episode might be a public apology by the bully or a brief follow-up during relational time with both the bully and the bullied to reach a decision agreeable to both sides over the next few weeks. One-shot meetings are not very helpful, because bullying is not usually a single incident. It involves a pattern and therefore requires multiple meetings to hopefully modify the bullying, at least as far as this one student is concerned but hopefully with some carry-over to other victims.

Negotiation; Sit-Out Progression; and No Plan, No Play

Peggy Pastor's story about Robby is a lesson in negotiation as well as self-reflection, accountability, and logical consequences. TPSR is often viewed as being soft on kids, but there is nothing soft about confronting kids who violate Level 1. However, adding negotiation to confrontation sends two messages: (1) you are out of line, and (2) *we* need to work it out. The sit-out progression addresses confrontation, negotiation, self-reflection, accountability, and logical consequences.

The sit-out progression is designed for kids who "get an attitude," lose their temper, or argue a lot. These attitudes and behaviors most commonly emerge during game play, although they do occur elsewhere as well (and the same strategies apply). Wherever they occur, negotiation, a key component of the empowerment theme, must be built in to the sit-out progression. In brief, this progression is as follows:

1. Choosing to sit out or get under control (stop being abusive)
2. Sitting out with the choice of returning when ready to put Level I into practice
3. Sitting out until a plan can be negotiated with the program leader
4. Negotiating a different plan if the first one doesn't work
5. Being referred for special help as a last resort

In the first step, sitting out can be treated as a choice if the incident is not violent. When my students put on a mean face to show their anger, I ask them to change their face or sit out until they can do so. Many incidents can be handled this way unless the disrespect is flagrant or the same problem occurs repeatedly (which means that the sit-out option didn't work). When confronted with the option, some students choose to sit out for several minutes, even when playing their beloved game of basketball, but many students will never choose to sit out. If they choose not to sit out and fail to change their disruptive or abusive behavior, the logical consequence is to have them sit out whether they want to or not, but they can come back in on their own when they are ready to participate responsibly. Note that even at this stage they still retain some empowerment by having the choice of coming back in whenever they are ready. If this doesn't work, a plan needs to be negotiated before they can reenter the activity.

The steps for negotiating this plan are as follows (Glasser, 1965, 1977; Raffini, 1980):

1. Agree on the problem and the student's role in it. Level I problems of self-control such as intimidating or making fun of others or losing one's temper are often compounded by blaming others or in some cases totally deny-ing the behavior. If possible, try to get the student to understand that he harmed or caused a problem for someone else. Agreeing on the problem may take some work and some listening on both sides. Others may be

implicated during this process, but try to focus on the individual's role. If an agreement cannot be reached—for example, if the student denies any involvement even though clearly implicated—move on to step 2 anyway. ("The question is not, Did you do this? The question is, What are you going to do about it?")

2. Negotiate and agree on a plan to solve the problem. Any plan that addresses the problem and doesn't cause a new problem for someone else is okay. If the student refuses to participate in this process (which is common if the problem has not been agreed upon), suggest some plans and attempt to get the student to agree to one. I often suggest some kind of restitution if abuse toward other students is involved. It is amazing how quickly they come up with an alternative plan if they don't like mine!

3. Follow up to ensure compliance with the plan. The plan may need to be in writing and signed to strengthen the commitment. Whether written or not, without follow-through, the process breaks down.

4. If the plan is not followed, make a new and different plan. Don't repeat a plan that hasn't worked. Glasser (1977) suggested using progressive separation from the group, meaning that plans need to begin to isolate the student from those she is hassling. This does not necessarily mean sitting out; for example, she can still do fitness exercises or some sport skill drills alone at a station.

5. As a last resort, refer the student for special help. He should have a right to exit a program that doesn't work for him or for the rest of the class because of him.

"No plan, no play" is a shorthand variation of the sit-out progression (DeLine, 1991). The culprit is not allowed back into the game unless she comes up with a plan to change the behavior that resulted in the suspension. The no plan, no play strategy can also be used when two kids are involved (see the section Level I: Conflict Resolution Strategies).

The negotiation process, like everything else in this book, is only a suggestion. It offers some guidance by providing specific steps. But depending on the situation, time might not be available to do all these steps, or they may be inappropriate for the situation. The key, based on the TPSR themes of empowerment and being relational, is to involve participants as much as possible in the process. Involvement will vary from student to student and from meeting to meeting, but the goal is always the same: to give kids a say in their life in the gym.

TPSR *in Action*

Two sport stations were set up for kids to practice either by themselves or with a partner. One group was to practice basketball skills; and the other, soccer. Daniel, a 10-year-old club member, wanted nothing to do with the station. Daniel also had a very short fuse, and when he found out that he was assigned to the soccer station, he refused to participate. Out came the street face, with arms folded. He proceeded to sit underneath a table not saying a thing while kicking the table legs. Nudging him to participate was going nowhere, and he was ready to "go off." I could see that this was a battle that neither of us was going to win. Grandma's law to the rescue.

"Daniel," I said, "I will make a deal with you." When he heard the word *deal*, he looked straight up at me. I said, "If you give me 10 quality minutes at the soccer station, I will let you go over to basketball." He looked at me for a while and, without saying a word, went over to the soccer station. The kids had organized a small-sided game and Daniel joined, first reluctantly, then enthusiastically. After 10 minutes were up, I went to him and said, "You can go to your basketball station, now." "I think I'll stay here," he said. Thanks, Grandma!

Tom Martinek, University of North Carolina at Greensboro

Grandma's Law

If the kids display disinterest in or disdain for an activity, one approach to encourage them to try something different or challenging is Grandma's law. Grandma's law states that the kids must eat dinner before going out to play. Although it is important to listen to students' feelings about having to do the activity, a mandatory introductory experience sometimes wins them over. I've experienced this several times, most recently in volleyball. "That's for girls," the boys, freshly out of juvenile detention, told me. They were in no mood for a group meeting, so I just used Grandma's law spontaneously: "If you can do volleyball without griping, we'll do basketball afterward." Within a month they were choosing to play volleyball! I also used it in teaching yoga to urban high school students followed by basketball, but without the same level of success. They did the yoga without protest, but only one student chose to do yoga when given a choice.

Teacher-Directed Group

One way to handle problems of disruption and abuse (Level I), which also works for kids not motivated to participate (not at Level II) or unwilling or unable to work on their own (not at Level III), is to create two groups, a teacher-directed group and a self-directed group, whenever it is Level III time (e.g., during individual station work). This strategy meets the need of those who want to individualize but can't figure out a way to do so. If some kids routinely need more structure, a teacher-directed group can be built into the plan for the day, as long as they are allowed to become self-directed when they are ready.

Jeff Walsh, a Portland, Oregon, middle school teacher, gave his students a choice of three activity stations (e.g., weightlifting, volleyball, or soccer). But students who were disruptive, abusive, or off task joined a teacher-directed group and followed Jeff as he went from station to station. He stopped activity at each station when he arrived to teach a mini-lesson, and the teacher-directed group became students at this station. When the mini-lesson was over, the teacher-directed group followed Jeff to the next station, while the Level III group went back to doing their own program at the station. To graduate to the self-directed group and thereby be able to choose to concentrate on one activity and station, students had to demonstrate that they could function at Level III.

Five Clean Days

Early in my career, after several weeks of frustrating attempts to introduce TPSR to my inner-city high school PE students (Hellison, 1978), I created a "five clean days" strategy. Students could earn the right to devise and carry out a personal plan for a day if they successfully completed five days in a row at Levels I and II (or what I could get away with, which included at least going through the motions). (Of course, it could be any number of days; we met daily, so a week of clean days made sense.) By experiencing Levels I and II, they earned Level III.

At first, Level III was simple: Be on task in a physical activity of their choice (provided space was available). Soon, however, it was evident that they could take on much more responsibility. They wrote and put into practice detailed contracts, eventually including an evaluation plan. This was a very thinly disguised form of behavior modification, but as in the other behavior modification strategies, a logical consequence—permission to make some choices and work on one's own—was contingent on being under control and motivated to participate. To move away from this system and toward empowerment, I used open negotiation in the second semester, which permitted all students to make and implement personal plans provided they kept a record of their work and negotiated all Level I, II, and III problems with me.

Referral

Does everyone live happily ever after if all these things are put into practice? Those who have been working with kids for any length of time already know the answer to that. Some kids are on medication or have experienced inappropriate prenatal care or are dealing with any of a hundred other problems. Affluent kids bring their own problems as well. Not all of these young people can be reached; maybe someone else will, maybe not. Perhaps most frustrating are those young people who harm others and show no remorse. They are usually hard-core cases who require long-term specialized counseling and perhaps placement in alternative programs if they are to have a chance of becoming positive members of society. Despite weak referral systems in many schools, a few students should have the right to exit programs that just don't work for them. Also worth considering is the fact that their presence reduces the effectiveness of the program for others. They need special help, and it would best serve them, their peers, and PE and PA professionals if they got that help.

Referral works differently in PE programs than it does in PA programs. Teachers cannot just ask students to leave until they can "get their act together," nor can they unilaterally suspend a student for a determined period of time. They are at the mercy of school policy and decisions made at higher levels. PA professionals, on the other hand, often have discretion in these matters. Some kids in both PE and PA programs need special help to reverse their downhill spirals. Whether such a referral system is in place, especially a competent one (i.e., trained professionals with a reasonable caseload), often depends on available funds and the priorities of the organization. Kids in low-income communities are often underserved in a number of ways, including the availability of specialists who can address special needs.

LEVEL I: CONFLICT RESOLUTION STRATEGIES

Sometimes, conflicts can be negotiated during the group meeting, but often it is difficult to solve an issue with the whole class chiming in. Additionally, many conflicts are potentially too volatile to negotiate in that setting.

Sport Court

When issues come up in class or in the group meeting, individuals can make suggestions, and sometimes a show of hands will resolve the issue, but if the problem requires extended discussion, a small team of kids may be able to discuss it and come to a decision more easily. A sport court is such a group.

Sport court consists of three students elected by the students to make decisions on difficult issues referred by the program leader. Sport court was created when I spent a year working in a PA-based program at a day treatment center for severely emotionally disturbed kids ages 6 to 17. The sport court seemed to function swiftly, fairly, and effectively. You could hear a pin drop when the sport court announced its verdict, which was almost always tougher than what I would have done. As an example, one of the kids' classroom teachers tried to assert his authority during our PE program, and the kids protested that they got to make decisions in this program. The teacher was seething, but I turned it over to the sport court. They debated in private for maybe 10 minutes before coming back with a unanimous rejection of the teacher's demands, accompanied by their rationale. Pretty gutsy, I thought.

Self-Officiating

In games, the job of officials is to ensure that players follow the rules and to resolve disputes. Self-officiating students are responsible for resolving conflicts themselves rather than just trying to avoid being caught by an official. But monitoring oneself and pointing out one's own mistakes are no easy tasks for most kids (or adults for that matter). Struggling through this process, while time-consuming and sometimes rancorous, does teach kids how to solve conflicts. Who last touched the ball? Was she safe or out? Was there a foul on that play? Does that deserve time in the penalty box? These aren't world-changing issues, but they matter to the players. Working them out promotes a more democratic climate. (The coaching club described in chapter 9 used a form of self-officiating.)

When I used self-officiating in the coaching club, the student player-coaches were primarily responsible for solving problems during games. The rules were simple:

- Handle it!
- Do it without anger or disrespect.
- Listen to all sides.

If I have to get involved, that means you had difficulty solving the issue or managing the process.

Don Andersen, an elementary school PE teacher in the Chicago area, created a variation of this policy. He doesn't officiate, but if he sees a student commit an obvious rule violation and not make the call, that student is required to give up the ball and sit out for 30 seconds, leaving the team shorthanded. This is behavior modification, but it is at least a partially logical consequence of failing to call a rules violation on oneself. It is also a wake-up call to start self-officiating.

Talking Bench

The talking bench strategy (Horrocks, 1978) addresses the conflict resolution component of Level I. To resolve a conflict between two kids, the program leader sends them to an area, such as a bench, designated for settling disputes. They resolve the problem and report back to the program leader that the problem is resolved (perhaps by saying, "It's over") before returning to the activity. They are not required to report details. As in other conflicts, the rules were simple: Show respect, listen to both sides, and resolve it.

One teacher requires students to "come up with one story of what happened" (Lickona, 1991, p. 296). Participants may need help in this process, but the program leader cannot act as a referee, which is unfortunately a common practice, because that removes responsibility from the students for solving their problem. Mike DeBusk reported hearing the conversation of two fourth-grade boys who were heading to the talking bench. One said, "Let's tell him it's over," and the other agreed. They pivoted and came back to Mike, told him they had handled it, and he said, "Okay." As he explained, they did end the dispute.

Emergency Plan

California elementary physical education teacher Rudy Benton's idea of creating an emergency plan at a group meeting before games empowers students to determine a generic method for handling conflicts during the game. The group may decide, for example, to flip a coin to decide disputes. In my experience, however, when a dispute arises, students are often reluctant to put their emergency plan into practice; they would rather argue! Reminders help.

Making New Rules

A variation of the emergency plan is to ask participants to make rules to help solve the problems they are having. This technique can also be used to head off Level I problems by asking students to make "respect rules." They know how they would like to be treated; they can share these things and then create some rules for class.

Conflicts sometimes occur at stations where a handful of students are involved in doing task sheets, a drill, a team practice, a game, or some other activity. A challenging example from my experience involved a trampoline station (it's an old story!), where serious safety considerations as well as issues surrounding taking turns and the length of a turn caused one problem after another. I reminded the students about using the levels in resolving problems. Nevertheless, they complained incessantly. I required that they make station rules. The rules they made didn't work, so they made new rules. And then more new rules. Then they requested that I police them. I did that for a little while and then asked them to try again. They got better—safer, happier—but it was a (very) gradual progress with considerable backsliding.

LEVEL II: TEACHING BY INVITATION

The Level II strategies described in chapter 5 promote self-motivation and extend the empowerment process begun with negotiation at Level I. They were developed especially for required PE, with its mandated units that some students don't want to do, although sometimes in after-school programs kids balk at participating for one reason or another. One of my students in a before-school program did not want to be on a team that included his brother. I told him that team players don't have that option. He replied that no one else has a brother in the program. I said good point and changed the teams! But experiencing a new activity or one in which some have had little success in the past is a serious issue that may have to begin with an invitation to these students to go through the motions.

In fitness activities I have invited reluctant participants to try a couple of sit-ups or just walk to get them started. I accompany the invitation with a description of what they need to do to get some benefit out of the activity. I also state my belief that effort is the first step in taking personal responsibility. Another invitation that I've had some success with is to say, "Try it my way for a week" (or for a certain number of days). This invitation is really a negotiated deal: If students still don't want to do the activities after a week of participation, I have to come up with something else for them to do. Fortunately, despite having many students who often feel defeated or alienated by their experiences in PE or sport, only a few have taken me up on my deal. When they do, we make a verbal contract—for example, a fitness routine that includes some stretching, sit-ups, push-ups, and run-walking.

LEVEL III: STRUGGLES WITH EMPOWERMENT

At each step in the empowerment progression, some students seem to have trouble. In the preceding fitness example, some have trouble doing the fitness routine they have learned, and I need to take them through it again. Others can do the posted routine on their own but then get stuck when they have to make their own plan. Fortunately, at least some get unstuck when asked if they need help. "Just getting started," they reply with a smile. Still others race ahead, developing and putting into practice a full-scale fitness program. In one of my programs, students progressed from less than 2 minutes to 15 minutes of Level III time without any problems, in martial arts no less!

Strategies for Facilitating Empowerment

Sometimes a relational time conversation helps kids get back on track. If a few students have trouble creating or carrying out a personal plan, they can be given more structure. Sometimes it takes just a slight adjustment, a push, or some support. I had one student who needed me to tell him what he was supposed to do even though he had written out a step-by-step plan! So I went down the list and said, "Do this; then do this . . . ." The reason? During the year he had been moved three times to the homes of different relatives and wanted some interaction with an adult who showed an interest in him rather than more independence. If the entire group is struggling, address the issue in a group meeting; maybe they don't understand what is expected or maybe there are other hidden issues.

Kids sometimes try to get out of doing the plan they chose or devised. When they whine about their plan, I might say, "Sure, change it and write up your change," while gently and then more forcefully reminding them that the point is to stick with something so they can progress toward their goals. Sometimes they want to achieve the goal—for example, to lose weight—but they also want to do what their friends are doing or what they perceive to be fun at the moment. "Change the goal," I say. "Can I do both losing weight and having fun?" one high school student asked. "Make the plan," I said. She did. Her plan was to run and then do what her friends were doing. Weeks later she asked, "Do I still have to do this running in my plan?" "No," I replied. "Write down the changes in your goal and your plan." "I think I'll run instead!" she said, and off she went.

Kids don't necessarily choose activities they are weak in. Choosing to work on one's strengths is acceptable; in fact, developing one's uniqueness in the form of a specialization is part of the definition of Level III. But it is also important to address weaknesses and problems, especially those that affect one's self-image. To "be like Mike" (Michael Jordan) requires dribbling and shooting with the nondominant hand, yet few kids who love basketball choose to practice any skill that would make them appear awkward or unskilled. It sometimes helps to discuss this one on one in relational time or in the awareness talk to pick out some of the more common weaknesses that could improve their game and suggest a goal-setting strategy. Sometimes just a quick reminder helps.

The accordion principle can be used to adjust the amount of Level III time in relation to the responsibility of individual students or the group, as explained earlier in the section Level I: Individual Discipline Problems.

Courage to Resist Peer Pressure

Self-development requires that students engage in sufficient self-reflection to set goals that reflect their unique needs and interests and, as they get older, their possible futures (McLaughlin and Heath, 1993; Walsh, 2008). But self-reflection, as difficult as that sometimes is, pales in comparison to pursuing one's goals in the face of what's popular with other kids. Subcultural and cultural influences are hard to sidestep, especially advertising in our electronic age.

I know of no way to place a moratorium on cultural and peer pressure. In physical activity programs in particular, what kids do is visible to others and therefore more open to criticism. Creating a TPSR climate in the gym helps, but the climate must be consistently respected, first on the part of the program leader and then, with help, by the kids. It is sometimes difficult to consistently support a policy that makes TPSR sense but is not popular in the kids' environment, such as choosing not to play a contact sport or not to promote winning over playing as well as you can. Invoking self-control can help ("Learn to control your mouth!"), and so can talking about peer pressure. Program leaders should bring peer pressure up directly and challenge students to rise above it. In general, being consistent in promoting team (group) meetings, self-reflection, and gradual empowerment coupled with logical consequences goes a long way toward creating a TPSR climate in the gym and on the playing field.

One time I gave fifth-graders in a track-and-field unit three choices: a competitive track meet, a personal-best track meet, and jogging. Before they chose, I simply said, "If the way you choose is to go with your friends, that's fine with me as long as you understand that you're not making your own choice." You could hear a pin drop as they went off to their choices! Sometimes a reminder is all it takes.

LEVEL IV: HELPING AND LEADERSHIP PROBLEMS

Helping others can be motivated by less-than-honorable intentions. For one thing, it can be characterized by arrogance. Some students, feeling superior, "wipe their help" on others, whether they want the help or not. Others view helping as a way to please the program leader or earn an extrinsic reward. That's why Level IV stresses caring, compassion, sensitivity, and responsiveness. Caring and compassion come from inside oneself; they are different motives than receiving some external reward or operating from feelings of superiority. Only someone who is sensitive to others' needs and wants can be responsive to them. Such youth leaders do not "wipe their help" on anyone.

Caring, compassion, sensitivity, and responsiveness can be built into any lesson that includes helping or leadership roles, but youth leaders must be carefully selected, especially at first when everyone is watching the process closely. Otherwise, problems will arise. Some PE and PA professionals place shy or troubled kids in leadership roles because they believe it will help them. Instead, it often creates new problems, such as derogatory comments by those being led, the need to counsel or even replace the ineffective leader, and the development of negative attitudes toward the youth leadership program. One girl refused to participate unless she could be the coach, so I promised that she could coach once she learned how to be a team member (no small feat). Amazingly, she shaped up very quickly, so I let her coach the next time we met. As I suspected, she had trouble handling the more skilled boys, although she really tried. Chaos ensued, and I was left to pick up the pieces—angry boys, a very sad (and angry) girl, and a leadership program at risk.

Another issue involves youth leaders who have demonstrated leadership abilities but as time passes begin to slack off. The accordion principle can be used in this situation, but reducing a student leader's responsibility in the middle of the session could exacerbate the problem. Sometimes standing behind the leader and quietly giving him one-sentence feedback (e.g., "Be more positive") can correct the problem. Sometimes calling the student aside for some quick feedback works. Letting these issues slide is easy, but helpers and leaders who abuse their responsibility can harm others and set another kind of bad role model example. At times a youth leader needs to be temporarily relieved of leadership responsibilities, sometimes accompanied by making a plan to improve.

Some believe that behavior precedes beliefs, that practicing being a helper or leader, even for the wrong reasons, is okay as long as helping takes place, because the belief will follow. My only concern is that the true meaning of Level IV might be lost unless emphasis on the importance of caring, sensitivity, and responsiveness is included. At the very least, program leaders should keep a watchful eye out for abuses.

LEVEL V: SPECIFIC PROBLEMS OUTSIDE THE GYM

Level V problems do not interrupt the smooth implementation of TPSR nearly as much as problems at the other levels. However, Level V problems can intrude. Here are some examples:

- A student is suspended for involvement in outside-the-gym activities, such as a fight.
- One of the kids is the target of complaints by other staff.
- A parent says that her child is not taking any responsibility at home (e.g., taking out the garbage without being asked).

In these examples, one-on-one relational time might help the student talk about the issue, tell her side, and perhaps set specific goals. These incidents can also be brought up in the awareness talk or group meeting (without names) to remind all the kids of their Level V responsibility. I have met with my students' classroom teachers as a group to get feedback on their classroom progress. My students knew about these meetings, and I reported back in general what their teachers said about how responsible they were in class. Of course, teachers don't always respect students' rights and feelings, which tends to invalidate their comments. That kind of behavior sometimes leads to teacher–student conflicts, which students never win. It's not fair, but they need to learn that confrontation with authority figures in school doesn't work. It often leads to suspension, which sets them back in school and may contribute to a reputation as a troublemaker.

◀◀◀ TAKE-AWAYS ▶▶▶

Here are some key points from this chapter that you might consider taking with you:

- Self-reflection and self-assessment are of paramount importance in fattening the bag of tricks of those who do this work to better address problems and situations that crop up in the program.
- Reflection-in-action augments self-reflection by cultivating the ability to react immediately to new and unexpected problems in the program. Making solutions banks is one practical way to improve reflection-in-action.
- Level I problems and situations include a variety of discipline as well as conflict resolution issues. To help program leaders address these problems

successfully, a continuum of strategies is available, from one-on-one negotiation to the implementation of behavior modification as a last resort.

- Teaching by invitation can sometimes solve Level II problems.
- At Level III, strategies are available to help kids who struggle with independence or with the courage to make their own decisions rather than succumb to peer pressure.
- Helping others and leadership roles require specific skills as well as compassion for, and sensitivity and responsiveness to, others. When students don't possess these skills and affective qualities, problems can arise. Awareness of what is required facilitates the kids' development of Level IV.
- Even Level V issues sometimes need to be addressed in class.

7

Being Relational With Kids

It's not what you do that matters most, but who you are.
And who you are is about relationships.

—Dave Dravecky

■ ■ ■ ■ ■

Dave Dravecky pitched for the San Francisco Giants. In 1989, his career ended abruptly when cancer, diagnosed earlier, had spread and required amputation of his pitching arm and shoulder. He now gives motivational speeches based on the preceding quote, which is also the theme of this chapter.

Of the four TPSR program leader responsibilities described in chapter 2, being relational with kids is the most influential. Without a certain kind of relationship, nothing else—not integrating personal and social responsibility into PE and PA, not empowerment, not transfer to the wider world—will work very well. "Show me a good curriculum with a mediocre teacher," I've often said, "and I'll show you a mediocre program."

FOUR RELATIONAL QUALITIES

Being relational is a pervasive, never-ending series of interactions among human beings characterized by feelings, subjective perceptions, and a whole host of other factors. In short, it is a complex human process, difficult to grasp let alone do effectively, full of soft truths that are difficult to measure. Some interpret this relationship as a mixture of artistry and charisma; others argue that it requires specific pedagogical skills.

In an effort to highlight the most important relational values and skills needed for TPSR, chapter 2 described four student qualities that the program leader must recognize and respect. They are repeated here in abbreviated form:

- Each student has strengths, not just deficiencies that need to be fixed. By recognizing and building on strengths, kids are more likely to be open to working on their issues, such as getting angry when things don't go their way.
- Each student is an individual and wants to be recognized as such, despite the uniformity of attire, slang, gestures, and so on. Gender matters, of course, and so does race and ethnicity, but they want to be recognized and respected for their individual strengths and potentials. In short, "teach individuals, not classes [or groups]" (Dill, 1998, p. 66).

TPSR *in Action*

The use of TPSR in the Project Guard to Make a Splash program is what helps the program to make a unique "splash." The American Red Cross has attempted to develop lifeguards for years, while stressing the importance of swimming in minority communities. Programs such as this one have been in place but have only provided participants with swimming skills. Our program has taken something old and added something new, TPSR, producing participants who have found meaning both in physical activity and within themselves. That is what TPSR has done! As an instructor, I have become more reflective with regard to my own pedagogical approach. I have learned to let go and allow students to get involved in the process that is making an impact on their lives! That makes sense, but trained physical educators are not often taught that way.

Using TPSR in the aquatic medium with students helps them to understand the value of behaving in a professional manner and the importance of being responsible for themselves and others in an aquatic environment. Students are taught caring and leadership skills within their daily lessons and can see the impact of being safe in an aquatic environment and how that can save a life. As an instructor, I am able to help them connect those positive decisions to their everyday lives and the opportunity for guaranteed employment as a lifeguard that could open their minds to multiple possibilities.

Angela Beale, Department of Health Studies, Physical Education, and Human Performance Science, Adelphi University, Garden City, New York

- Each student knows things the program leader does not; each has a voice, an opinion, a side that needs to be heard. A colleague once asked me, "What happened to the old-fashioned idea that teachers know something?" It's not that kids know more; it's that they have views and perceptions about a lot of things that can inform PE and PA professionals. Listening makes adults a bit wiser. Of course, listening and complying are two different things, but listening can offer some insights and sometimes lead to making changes.
- Each student has the capacity, if not the experience, to make good decisions; often, they just need practice, as they do in learning a motor skill. If given the opportunity, they will make mistakes, but that's an important part of the process. Self-reflection needs to accompany decision making to help kids become more reflective about the choices they make.

Working from kids' strengths shifts the focus from how incomplete and inadequate they are to a positive base from which to work. All kids (as well as ourselves) have flaws, and some of those flaws do need to be addressed, but focusing on kids' deficits first sets up an immediate negative relationship. A more relational approach is to recognize and respect their individuality, which conveys to them that everyone starts in a unique place and has unique strengths, capacities, needs, and interests. Giving kids a voice in the process and turning some choices and decisions over to them are positive gestures that promote empowerment and responsibility. All of these relational behaviors—treating kids with dignity, modeling human decency, and promoting holistic self-development—lay the foundation for developing personal and social responsibility.

Noddings (1992) argued that "formulaic approaches [to caring are] hopeless," that caring is an "ethic of relation" (p. 120). Although there is justification for warning against formulaic approaches, temporarily reducing the complexity of the relational process to recognizing and respecting the preceding four qualities has several benefits:

- It reduces to some extent the mystery of "being relational" without losing the human qualities involved.
- Treating kids this ways creates a respectful climate in the gym that is essential for TPSR to thrive.
- Program leaders who genuinely treat their students this way eventually find that they return the favor, but they won't necessarily treat their peers the same way. That's why Level I is needed.
- Although honoring these four qualities in students does not mean that TPSR's relational qualities have been mastered, it does provide opportunities to develop these and other qualities and skills that will enhance relationships and kids' lives.

HAVING THE COURAGE TO CONFRONT

None of this talk about being relational means being touchy-feely or some kind of rescuer driven by a messiah complex, however well intentioned! As Walt Schafer (1992), quoting T.J. Hurley, wrote:

> Being tender-hearted does not mean being soft-hearted. . . . Creative altruists work in the most challenging situations. Those they serve—youth at risk, addicts and drug abusers, juvenile delinquents, the mentally ill, the homeless—are unimpressed by do-gooders and bleeding-heart liberals. But their lives are transformed by the pragmatic intelligence and unconditional support they encounter in creative altruists. (p. 488)

Hal Adams, who works with adults in Chicago inner-city communities, added that respect for those with whom one works is essential, that no one can be successful with the attitude that "you've got problems and I'm here to fix them."

One of the most difficult tasks for some of us attracted to TPSR (including me) is having the courage to confront. None of these relational values and skills—treating kids from a strength-based approach, honoring their individuality and their voice, and recognizing their potential to make independent and smart decisions—will prevent kids from bringing their own values, behavior patterns, and developmental needs into the gym. There will still be arguments, fights, negative attitudes, and the like. The trick, after deciding that confrontation is necessary, is knowing how to confront. Kids should still have a voice to tell their side and be part of finding a solution, which may require restitution or personal changes in attitude or behavior. (For further explanations, see the discussion of Level I in chapter 3 and the strategies to deal with problems in chapter 6.)

RELATIONAL QUALITIES AND RELATIONAL TIME

Relational time (described more fully in chapter 4) is a specific time set aside to connect one on one with kids. I have found relational time particularly valuable because there are many barriers between me and my students, and each one makes our relationship harder. Differences in age, gender, education, socioeconomic status, race, and ethnicity combine to form a high wall between us. I try to poke little holes in that wall by talking to each student individually for a few seconds as often as I can during a designated relational time or whenever I have the opportunity. I tell them that it's nice to have them here today or ask how they are doing or if everything is okay, or I simply shake hands with them. I mention something particular to them if I can, such as, "Been practicing your jump shot?" or, "That's a good-looking shirt." In all cases my intention is to welcome them, to treat them as worthy of personal attention, and to show that I care about them as individuals.

Of course, this strategy works only if I do, in fact, care, do perceive each student as worthwhile, and am sensitive enough to say something that dignifies him or her. Students don't always respond, and sometimes they look away. But so far no one has ever outright rejected one of my personal welcomes or walked away while I was talking, unless I deserved it (which I certainly did in the example on page 51). A bit of courage is necessary to keep offering this gesture if a student isn't responsive. It helps to seek feedback to be certain that kids perceive these interactions in the way they are intended. Specific strategies such as group meetings, reflection time, and anonymous program evaluations provide feedback so that program leaders can calibrate their perceptions.

PROGRAM LEADER QUALITIES AND SKILLS

Honoring the four relational qualities is fundamental to TPSR, but these four qualities do not fully characterize the complexities of being relational. Let's explore this complexity a bit further.

The Person of the Program Leader

The program plan put into practice by PE and PA professionals, whether TPSR based or not, is certainly important and often difficult, but it won't matter much if relationships with kids are flawed. In this era of subject matter standards and accountability, Bill Ayers (1989) reminded us how important the teacher is:

> [T]here is no clear line delineating the person and the teacher. Rather, there is a seamless web between teaching and being, between teacher and person. Teaching is not simply what one does, it is who one is. (p. 130)

A sign seen at a teacher's conference reaffirms this notion: "We teach who we are" (Lickona, 1991, p. 71). David Denton (1972, p. 74) shared a similar idea: "Teaching is you, as you embody history, embody mathematics. . . . The question is not *what* to teach. The question is not *how* to teach. The question is *who* is teaching?"

KID QUOTES

"You're proof that white men can't jump!"—Sixth-grader to Don

"You ain't doin' the exercises!"—High school junior to Don

Are Ayers, Lickona, and Denton right? Partly, I think. Take the core values of TPSR, for example. One cannot preach about putting kids first or about the importance of human decency; one has to live (or embody) these values. What and how we teach matters too, but as Nel Noddings (1992) wrote, "Educational research . . . has made the error of supposing that method can be substituted for individuals" (p. 8). Larry Cuban (1993) argued that curriculum reformers always get it wrong, because they do not understand that "at the heart of teaching is the personal relationship between [teacher] and students that develops over matters of content" (p. 184). My view is that who's doing TPSR matters a lot. A strong program plan in the hands of a weak program leader will reduce the program's effectiveness considerably. A strong program leader with a weak program plan will fare better in my experience, but the best option is both an able leader and a solid program plan.

So the answer to the question, What kind of a person should TPSR program leaders aspire to be? is that they need to live the levels and themes, to embody TPSR, as Denton advised, to treat TPSR as a way of being, as Nick Forsberg does. This embodiment has a number of dimensions, most of which support or reinforce the four relational qualities mentioned earlier.

Sense of Purpose

Some teachers and youth workers I've known seem to go through the motions without much apparent passion. They may have lost the fire. My years of involvement with preservice and in-service PE and PA professionals suggest that intrinsic interest in working with kids varies with them as well. I call this intrinsic interest, this passion, one's "sense of purpose." Those who have it, whether working directly with kids or in professional preparation programs, also have answers to the questions What's worth doing? and What kind of contribution do I want to make? Those answers are the essence of their motivation, the source of their passion. For those who possess this sense of purpose, caring about and connecting with the kids or pre- and in-service professionals with whom they work brings them "fulfillment through satisfaction, through the knowledge that [they have] been true to [their] value of enhancing others, whether or not others express their appreciation or indebtedness" (Schafer, 1992, p. 488).

Professionally, a sense of purpose is what matters most, what is most meaningful. It describes our vision and our primary values and beliefs. It's the "moral intention to develop a certain kind of human being" (Goodlad, 1988, p. 109). It's what we believe in and cherish (Greene, 1986). Only those who believe in and cherish the core values of TPSR as the moral vision for kids can truly embody it (see chapter 2).

TPSR *in Action*

Felicia has been working at Hospice where she, in her words, "helps the patients and their families during a tough time." Thirteen years ago she was a teenager in our alternative school's Leadership Mentor Program. The program's aim was to take TPSR into a novel setting—the outdoors. Through experiences such as rock climbing and winter camping, students quickly realized that, when facing the challenges of an unfamiliar natural environment, many of their usual coping skills were inadequate. They had to make important choices with sometimes weighty consequences. They learned new problem-solving skills as well as valuable social competencies such as caring and effective communication. Journal entries included: *I control my language better; I like working together; I respect everyone's differences; I kept trying even when I didn't meet my goal the first time;* and *I trust everyone in our group.*

Of course, you're never certain whether these and other outcomes will endure. But, almost all of the Leadership Mentor students have remained in town, are raising families, and are contributing members of our community. Felicia's parting comment the other day was, "I remember you telling me that it's my attitude that makes the difference. That one stuck for me. Thank you."

And thank you, too, Felicia.

Julie Trujillo, University of Northern Colorado

Listening and Caring

But sense of purpose is not enough. Kids also need to be respected as unique individuals who have their own values, perceptions, fears, and aspirations and who deserve to be acknowledged, listened to, negotiated with—in short, to be cared about and treated with dignity. Gordon (1999) put it this way: "Effective . . . teachers want to be partners with their students" (p. 305).

Listening is an important way to care and to treat kids with dignity. When we listen, students feel as if they count, and we learn some things (which is especially important when our backgrounds are different). One of the things we can learn is what John Nicholls (Nicholls and Hazzard, 1993) calls the kids' theories of curriculum—for example, that physical education ought to be for playing—which often conflict with professional theories, such as the TPSR theory-in-action. Listening is also a necessary skill for engaging in individual decision making and group meeting discussions, both of which require interaction.

In one inner-city junior high, students said that the teachers who helped them were those who noticed them and asked about them, listened to them, respected them, and gave them chances (Schlosser, 1992). Quincy Howe (1991, pp. 84, 86), who works with low-income minority adolescents in a special education residential setting, put it this way: "A child must be convinced that the adult can be counted on to act in his best interest. This turns out to be an enormous and daunting piece of work. . . . At issue are his doubts, both as to whether he can do the job and whether I will continue to believe in his abilities." Ennis and her colleagues (1999) conducted extensive interviews with "disruptive and disengaged students" in PE and concluded that they "are unwilling to learn when teachers remain aloof . . . and refuse to spend time with students or express interest in their lives" (p. 167).

Bill Rose says to his secondary school students, "If at any time in class you feel you're being abused by me, or I'm embarrassing you in front of the whole class, you have to let me know. I don't know how everybody feels" (Lickona, 1991, p. 73). Rose's admission that he doesn't know everything, that he needs some help, encourages his students to share their thoughts with him. It also shows his desire to listen to them, to try to understand their side of things. He wants to know how his students are feeling, but they need to help him do so. When my students do or say something I don't understand, I am often afraid to ask for fear of being perceived as living in the dark ages (which may be close to the truth!). Yet when I do, I usually learn something and am probably a more sensitive program leader as a result. And the kids don't seem to mind.

McLaughlin (2000) described an incident involving a youth who blatantly broke the community program's rules but was not reprimanded by a nearby staff member who witnessed the violation. When asked, the staff member said there is violence in the young man's home and he needed to "get it out. We'll talk about it later" (p. 15). That staff member paid attention, listened, and responded appropriately.

In different ways, all of these stories highlight the necessity of listening, caring, and being patient. In addition, Rose's story also introduces one way to be genuine and vulnerable when working with kids.

Genuineness and Vulnerability

Caring about kids requires more than talking and listening. It also requires being genuine with them. Being genuine does not mean trying to be cool or being nasty if one is in a bad mood or sharing details about one's love affair. To me it means being oneself (to a point), personalizing one's beliefs rather than turning them into generic mandates for everyone. It also means expressing one's humanity in appropriate ways. I am not always right. I don't live in the gym; I have another life. I am not always upbeat. Most of all, being genuine requires caring sincerely about students and believing in their essential dignity and worth. Otherwise, talking and listening to kids is an empty gesture.

Genuineness also means being vulnerable. Telling kids "I blew it," whether referring to receiving a volleyball serve or an attempt to solve some problem, is an admission that I don't get everything right every time. Students who are potential discipline problems may at first see vulnerability as a weakness that they can exploit. Yet when dealing with someone who is out of control and being disruptive or abusive, I have found that asking, "Am I the problem?" calms things down and gets us into the issue (which may be about me but often is not).

Being vulnerable works well in a one-to-one relational meeting where there is no audience to play to, but it can also work in group meetings. The kids may be confused at first (adults don't share vulnerabilities), but it has never backfired in my experience. After one lesson in which the kids were off task and argumentative with each other, I asked what I was doing wrong. "You need to be tougher on us," one boy said. Another added, "Make us do push-ups when we're bad." (I bet some PE teacher or coach planted that idea.) So we talked about my style, the purpose of the program (i.e., that getting tough on themselves is their job in TPSR), and how we might compromise.

Of course, it is important to be ready for the constant scrutiny of students once they become aware of the genuineness factor. During a fitness session, one kid yelled to me, "You ain't doin' the exercises!" My response? I dropped down and started doing push-ups!

Vulnerability, like other things, makes sense to a point. Martin Buber told Carl Rogers that Rogers was wrong about teachers and students being equal. According to Buber, that relationship is unequal by its very nature. The student comes to the teacher for help. "You are able, more or less, to help him. . . . you see him. . . . he cannot, by far, see you" (quoted in Noddings, 1992, p. 107). To balance vulnerability, the program leader must be able to confront students, to call them on their abusiveness, their argumentativeness, their lack of effort, their lack of self-direction, their egocentrism, and so on. "What they really need is a teacher who will face them, seek eye contact, deflect their jibes and evasions, and tell them what they need to know" (Howe, 1991, p, 66). Vulnerability and confrontation cannot be substituted for each other. Both are needed.

Unfortunately, TPSR is sometimes interpreted as a touchy-feely approach that's soft on discipline and belongs to the genre characterized by "a Disneyized view of emotional life with happy slogans and easy answers" (Divoky, 1975, p. 25). Yet any TPSR practitioner who has had to confront a hostile kid, especially one who's taller and heavier, can attest to the absence of any touchy-feely attitude or happy, easy answers. In the same way, kids need to learn not only self-control but also how to stand up for their rights (see chapter 3).

Intuition and Self-Reflection

Another piece of the relational puzzle is intuition, which Rubin (1985) described as recognizing and acting on clues. *Intuition* seems to me to be a fancy word for sizing up kids when they come in the door. What is their collective mood? What individual issues are noticeable? For everything I plan, no matter what it is, I need to ask the question, What can I get away with? That is, How much of TPSR can I try to have these kids experience today? How much can I push or challenge them? What will they put up with before rebelling or shutting down? I try to sense the receptivity of the group, the rhythm of the lesson. Then I apply the accordion principle, giving more or less responsibility, longer or shorter awareness talks, and so on.

Intuition needs to be reinforced with perseverance. I need to outlast the kids! By that I mean that students (and other stakeholders) may resist the notion of a program based on personal and social responsibility. They come in asking, "What are we going to play today?" Self-direction? Caring? A choice of whether to compete or improve? No referees? Talking and writing? Relational time? To these things, they may reply, "Give us a break!" New ideas, although sometimes attractive, are almost never easy to implement, especially with older kids. To be successful, program leaders must resolve to hang in there, not give up, and continue to pursue their sense of purpose. One of my ninth-grade students, a reasonably skilled performer who was used to being able to play the whole PE period, wrote an essay about my program for his English class titled "PE Makes

You Hate." Ouch! Teaching anything new is provocative. Inner strength, sometimes in short supply, really helps!

Without the ability to size up individuals and groups to determine how much they can handle or the ability to persevere—that is, retain one's sense of purpose—the implementation of TPSR is often derailed. Sizing up is part of the larger habit of self-reflection, which is discussed in chapter 6 on problems that arise in the program. Here's a sample list of questions PE and PA professionals can ask themselves as they self-reflect:

- What is my mood today?

- What relational or pedagogical shortcomings do I need to shore up?

- How can I exhort students to be more reflective or responsible if I am unreflective and irresponsible?

- How can I encourage students to become more responsible if I'm not very responsible?

- How strong is my self-control (Level I)? My self-motivation (Level II)? My self-direction (Level III)? My sensitivity and responsiveness to students' rights, feelings, and needs (Levels I and IV)?

Cultivating the habit of professional self-reflection by keeping a daily journal, by being open to criticism, and by making and evaluating personal change is perhaps the single most effective method for improving all these qualities.

I like to talk to teachers and youth workers about their chaos threshold, by which I mean how much chaos they can tolerate in a session. Some need to tiptoe into the empowerment strategies. If student freedom makes them nervous, I say, "No problem. Don't exceed your chaos threshold, but try to nudge the boundaries a bit." Reflection helps us to recognize such problems in ourselves, to think about solutions, and to evaluate these solutions in practice.

Georgiadis' (1990) struggles to reconcile the values he learned as a professional basketball player with the values that underlie TPSR provide an excellent example of the often painful process of self-reflection. In an early experience with high-needs youth in an after-school basketball program, he found himself screaming at the referees (who were volunteering their time), playing only the most talented kids, and making all the decisions. His students rebelled, and he found himself sunk in a deeply personal struggle of conflicting values. He found that to make TPSR work, he needed to shift some decisions to the students and listen to their input. These strategies conflicted with the professional sport model, so it was an agonizing process that took persistent self-reflection to resolve.

Sense of Humor and a Playful Spirit

Attempting to be a caring, genuine, empathetic, intuitive program leader has its price. When I watched Robin Williams as a teacher in the film *Dead Poets Society,* I thought, "Oh, to be able to teach like that." But could a Robin Williams do that period after period and day after day? Howe (1991) said no: "The trouble is that such [teaching] performances are enormously draining and I am good for only one or two a day" (p. 67). He found after four years of teaching in a residential home that his willingness to share his breaks with students was "not what it used to be" (p. 143).

A sense of humor and a playful spirit are effective guards against burnout. Keeping kids focused on responsibility is hard work for program leaders and for kids as well. A light touch goes a long way toward offsetting the demands of TPSR. The essence of a healthy sense of humor is an attitude that sees the humor in everyday life without, as kids often do, needing someone to bear the brunt of the joke. The most important aspect of humor is to be able to laugh at oneself. Howe (1991) often turned a serious situation into something humorously self-critical. For example, to a student who exclaimed that she was bored, he said, "I once had a student die of boredom in my class" (p. 27). A playful spirit involves many things, including being upbeat and enthusiastic within one's personality, having fun with the kids, and celebrating with high fives or low fives or whatever the latest fad is. Sometimes, it is necessary to fake it. Sarah Doolittle advised a PE intern working with kids to have fun, or at least "look like you're having fun."

TEACHING STUDENTS WITH DIFFERENT CULTURAL BACKGROUNDS

More attention is being paid to recruiting and retaining staff whose backgrounds resemble those of high-needs urban youth. However, many teachers (and at least some urban youth workers) are white and middle class, unlike their students. As a white male who has been a program leader in urban minority and multiracial/multiethnic settings for 40 years, I can attest to the difficulty of navigating in this terrain.

One thing I learned early on is that I will never fully understand what these kids are going through. That insight helped me focus on what I might be able to contribute and realize that I had to be open to negotiation and that my ideas had to be negotiable. PE and PA professionals who grew up in these neighborhoods (and sometimes got into trouble) bring more knowledge and often more insights than those of us without these experiences. One exemplar is "Charles," the sport director of a Boys and Girls Club in Chicago, whose work with urban adolescents Hirsch described in detail in his excellent book, *A Place to Call Home* (2005). "Charles," who earned a PhD in the streets (McLaughlin, 2000), understood the kids' experiences, met them where they were, talked to them in their language about issues important to them and to the community, and was supportive but demanding, particularly about how they dealt with themselves and others.

Don't Try to Be Cool

Being oneself, being genuine, is crucial. Kids quickly spot a phony. I have found it best not to worry about doing fancy handshakes or using street language. Some of these things evolve with time, but they aren't important. A program leader's sincere concern for the kids and respect for them and their culture are far more important. Howe (1991) was the only staff member to wear a coat and tie in a school for at-risk kids, rendering him a high-profile target for student humor. He persisted—it is his natural style—and the humorous jabs disappeared with time.

A number of years ago I supervised two student teachers in an urban high school, one a heavyweight wrestler, the other a skinny guy with a funny haircut and black tennis shoes (very uncool at the time). The kids were very respectful in dealing with the wrestler but ran all over the skinny guy. However, after a month or so, the kids began to call the wrestler disrespectful names, just loud enough for him to hear, and he would fly into a rage. Meanwhile, "Skinny" seemed to ignore all the abuse he was getting and just persevered. By the end of the semester, one PE class looked like a model program, whereas the other was in shambles. Guess which was which!

Not trying to be popular is difficult. The fear of not being liked is always lurking in the back of my mind, but I try not to let it take control. The best antidote I've found is having successful experiences with kids when I am myself. But that takes time.

Learn About and Respect the Culture

Being oneself has limits. Having at least a general knowledge of the culture is helpful. Delpit (1988, p. 93) compared a caring white parent who says to her child, "Isn't it time for your bath?" with a caring African American parent who says, "Get your rusty behind in that bathtub!" Being prepared for and being able to accept cultural differences is essential in becoming an effective program leader of students whose backgrounds differ from one's own. It is one thing to accept cultural differences but quite another to try to emulate those differences. Yelling at kids (as seen through my white eyes) seems to be part of the culture I have worked in for years, although this is certainly not true of all parents, teachers, and youth workers. But yelling isn't my style, and the kids don't seem to expect it from me.

Those of us who work with kids must be wary of cultural preconceptions and stereotypes, even those that seem sympathetic. For example, research suggests that self-concept among African American youth is not lower than that of white youth, though their perception of empowerment may be (Murray, Smith, and West, 1989). As another example, some whites would be surprised to learn that the traditional American work ethic enjoys substantial support among low-income African Americans (personal observation). Bredemeier's (1988) study of urban minority teachers shows that although they recognize existing social problems, they have not wavered from teaching hard work, perseverance, self-responsibility, and orientation to the future. In addition, though it is regrettable, the criminal sector often does a better job of harnessing the energy of inner-city youth than mainstream society does, such as in the case of drug trafficking.

On the other hand, program leaders must be prepared to understand behaviors that do not reflect white, middle-class norms. Foster (1974) described some of these characteristics among inner-city high school students in the 1970s, which are still around at least to some extent in my experience: style and flare as part of the student's performance; physical aggression and impregnating a female as signs of manhood; and such skills as manipulating, taunting, and verbal assault as requirements for street survival. Howe's (1991) description of the difference between his low-income male and female students is another example. The male model is the "rigid jaw and unmoist eye . . . [and a] playful and evasive way of dealing with experience," whereas females are "more tempestuous, more ungoverned" and tend to "make full disclosure of the intensity of their feelings" (p. 32).

Importance of Respect

Respect for the culture and especially for the kids is key to accepting differences. I always try to remember that I am an outsider, that I'll never experience what the kids I've worked with go through every day. But I can recognize my students' strengths and individual selves and give them opportunities to express their views and make decisions. The approach I have found most useful is to listen to my students. I begin to learn their theories of PE and PA, their perceptions of life and school, and something of their cultures. Group meetings and relational time can help here, but an openness to ideas and perceptions different from my own is fundamental to making these strategies work.

I sometimes need to remind myself that the in-the-moment mentality of adolescents allows them to see the humor and pathos of the moment, whereas my focus on what needs to be done gets in the way of sharing their observations and insights. Other times I laugh in spite of myself.

≪≪ TAKE-AWAYS ≫≫

Here are some key points from this chapter that you might consider taking with you:

- Recognizing and respecting students' strengths, individuality, voice, and capacity for decision making reduces the complexity of the relational process and creates a climate in which TPSR can grow.

- A set-aside relational time facilitates brief one-on-one meetings to express recognition of and respect for the preceding four qualities in kids.

- Specific skills and qualities that further facilitate the relational process include having a sense of purpose, listening and caring, being genuine and vulnerable, being intuitive (sizing things up from clues), being self-reflective, and having a sense of humor.

- Teaching students with different cultural backgrounds requires the same skills and qualities needed to teach students with similar backgrounds, especially recognizing and respecting the four student qualities. Those who work with students with different cultural backgrounds need to be themselves while at the same time knowing what they don't know, being open to unfamiliar values and customs, and learning as much as possible about the cultures represented in their programs.

IMPLEMENTATION

TPSR

8

TPSR in PE Teacher Education: One Teacher's Explorations

Sarah Doolittle

In the previous editions of this book, teaching with TPSR was presented as an alternative to conventional pedagogy that an individual experienced teacher might choose if it seemed to be "worth doing." Currently, however, TPSR has become a regular part of comprehensive teacher education in physical education and is now becoming a standard model for the professional preparation of other physical activity professionals and youth workers. Teacher educators, however, have discovered that it is not a simple matter to educate other professionals to "do" TPSR. Beyond the superficial structures of the levels and teaching strategies, teacher educators may also want their students to share the fundamental values and the personal commitment to underserved youth that are the heart of this approach. This chapter presents one teacher educator's story of exploring ways of educating others to Teach for Personal and Social Responsibility through physical activity.

■ ■ ■ ■ ■

TPSR has been a regular topic in my curriculum and secondary methods courses for the past 20 years, but I continually question whether students actually learn more than the superficial outlines of the approach. I used to take satisfaction from seeing my former students, now teachers, display the levels on a poster in the gym, or refer to levels as a behavior management strategy in classes. I was teaching TPSR as a theoretical model, and a few students were using parts of it, but the predominant structure of physical education that I saw in my former students' classes was traditional teacher-centered sports as recreation. Their loftiest goals for personal and social responsibility seemed to be students' willingness to follow directions without complaining. When finally teaching, too many of my former students lived with the expectation that their students weren't interested in traditional physical education classes; the major instructional problems were encapsulated in the students' "lack of motivation." Their students went through the motions in their classes, especially in high school, and too many teachers gradually gave up trying to make a difference for students, focusing their attention on after-school sports or sidelines unrelated to physical education.

My interest in TPSR took on increased significance when I began working seriously with middle and high school teachers in low-income and minority (i.e., high-needs) schools. My former students and their colleagues in these schools were clear in stating that their primary goal for physical education was for students to show positive social behavior and responsibility during physical activities and in their daily lives. They were disillusioned with the traditional physical education goals, and with teaching methods that suggested they should be able to teach sport skills to large classes in poorly equipped gymnasiums, in programs where their colleagues weren't teaching, and where administrators seemed not to care whether students participated, let alone learned anything new. Too many teachers in high-needs schools were exhausted and discouraged with trying to teach students in schools where physical education really didn't seem to matter, resulting too often in previously altruistic people acting like prison wardens.

My observations and teachers' complaints made me question how well I had prepared my preservice teachers. Did they leave our programs with ideas, skills, and the self-confidence necessary to design and teach secondary physical education humanely, in a way middle and high school students might value, even in schools with budget constraints? If not, what should I change?

I had been teaching the recommended alternatives—sport education, adventure education, fitness education, and TPSR—but too few of my students developed the teaching skills and confidence to change the status quo in middle and high school physical education. While still meeting my obligations for our NCATE-accredited program, I began to search for changes that might better provide new teachers with skills and ideas for a physical education program that responds to middle and high school students in 21st-century schools, especially in high-needs schools where physical education could make a genuine contribution to their lives. TPSR seemed an obvious approach. My problem became how to incorporate TPSR into PE teacher education so that graduates could use it in their first teaching jobs.

TEACHING TPSR IN PE TEACHER EDUCATION

My first changes came about as a result of seeing that traditional secondary teacher education squandered too much course time hammering home effective planning and direct instruction teaching skills for psychomotor competency suitable for a rigid, traditional 40-minute time structure. This emphasis seemed to prepare new teachers for failure and disillusionment when they were hired into middle and high schools where neither their more experienced colleagues nor their students valued PE classes or what they might learn there. Once I realized that neither affluent nor low-income middle and high school students were responding positively to even competently taught traditional PE programs, I began to eliminate some of the time-honored content of my secondary methods course work.

My initial course changes focused on presenting alternative curriculum choices that had a better chance of success. I began stressing only a few principles of effective teaching so as to have enough time to take the alternatives seriously, and then I began concentrating on only one or two alternative curriculum approaches (TPSR and sport education). By aiming to teach only one or two things well, I thought my students might "get it"—understand the problem with the status quo, feel more expert in an unfamiliar alternative, and develop more commitment to offering something different in their secondary school jobs.

I also decided that traditional lecture and peer teaching were not a good use of course time. Instead, I focused on designing value-added field experiences, experiential learning, and service learning assignments to provide more powerful experiences with essential principles in schools and to create opportunities for novices to be successful with these principles. For example, requiring students to design and deliver a service project in their field experience schools taught them the real politics of innovation and change in ways that could not be taught in an on-campus lecture. (This assignment had the added benefit of giving students something interesting to talk about in subsequent job interviews.)

I also began seeking out and developing relationships with schools where my students could work with real students while practicing teaching techniques and other less familiar strategies. Doing this kind of course work in the field was far more interesting for students and provided me, as teacher educator, with real problems and issues to consider through a theoretical lens. As I continue to explore and refine assignments and experiences for field-based courses, I am also beginning to appreciate how important noncurricular time is to meeting the goals of physical education. Physical education teacher education (PETE) students are now seeing the value of teaching physical education outside of the standard school time by completing a late afternoon secondary methods course that takes place in a physical activity–based youth development program.

TPSR was my entry point for this shift in emphasis. But the way I had been teaching it wasn't making enough of a difference. I needed to make alternative approaches more important, to convince students to acknowledge that too often conventional physical education wasn't working in either high-needs or more affluent schools and to recognize the need for an alternative approach. I wanted to convey the message that effective teachers do not ignore personal and social development in favor of motor skill and fitness development, that often it is necessary to reverse the usual priority of physical education *of* the physical (i.e., prioritizing skill and fitness development as the main learning goal) to physical education *through* the physical (i.e., prioritizing personal and social development through the vehicle of physical activity).

Although the TPSR ideas were compelling to me and an obvious solution to some of the problems I hoped to address, finding a way to teach TPSR so that students understood more than the superficial aspects required a nontraditional course design. The literature in PETE offers some guidance, but there was little practical advice on redesigning teacher education to prepare teachers to recognize the value of physical activity programs in helping kids take control of their lives. The TPSR literature and communications with Don Hellison and his colleagues led me to believe that the best TPSR teachers were those who had apprenticed at the master's knee: most were graduate students, friends, or

PETE professors on leave who had taught with Hellison in Chicago for at least a semester, and some for many years. Their depth of understanding, commitment to kids, and skills of observation and on-the-spot problem solving were unmatched by any typical PETE TPSR teacher education program. But there had to be a way to scale up from an apprenticeship model to a larger required methods class.

This chapter presents nine descriptions of teacher education approaches I have used, and some others I have heard about, that help novice physical education teachers and youth workers to learn TPSR (see figure 8.1). These approaches are presented in the hope that teacher educators might help the next generation move beyond seeing TPSR as just a theoretical add-on to traditional approaches.

Nine Ways to Teach TPSR

1. Apprenticeship
2. Site-based practicum or internship
3. Conference workshop or short course
4. One-week intensive elective
5. Semester-long elective
6. Within a required activity course
7. Within a required on-site undergraduate methods course
8. Required methods course in an after-school program
9. Framework for a teacher education program

FIGURE 8.1 Nine approaches for teaching TPSR to physical education teachers and youth workers.

APPRENTICESHIP

Don Hellison has taught graduate students, teachers and youth workers, and visiting professors by inviting them to his university and into his site-based kids' programs. Apprentices participate directly in Don's kids' programs, gradually taking on responsibility for leading various parts of the lesson, until they can take over entire lessons. Apprentices are quickly encouraged to begin their own groups within programs or to establish new programs in other venues with supervision and one-on-one debriefing with Don or advanced doctoral students. Some of these apprenticeships exist for a semester; others, for several years.

Observations, coteaching, and extensive in-depth planning and debriefing conversations with Don and other apprentices are the pedagogical method. The advantages are similar to those of all master teacher–directed study approaches: focused and personal attention to shared, specific goals, problems, and issues; help in applying the model with fidelity; opportunities to develop capacity and commitment; the opportunity to share with Don new ideas for developing and extending the model and designing new ways to use TPSR in the future. The primary disadvantage is that of scale: there's only one master teacher, and one-on-one directed study cannot produce a large number of teachers capable of doing TPSR.

SITE-BASED PRACTICUM OR INTERNSHIP

Dave Walsh, Missy Parker, Paul Wright, and Tom Martinek have been among Don's apprentices in Chicago who have moved on to produce the next generations of TPSR leaders, repeating this one-on-one teaching approach. These second-generation master teachers keep the fundamental TPSR principles intact, while also developing their own new patterns and possibilities for professional preparation. For example, Dave Walsh has established a variety of TPSR apprenticeship options for undergraduate and graduate students; Missy Parker combines TPSR with programs for rock climbing and outdoor challenges; Paul Wright has collaborated with his masters' students to conduct several research projects on his site-based programs for underserved youth; and Tom Martinek has developed three programs to professionally prepare university students in sport-based youth development with a focus on TPSR for underserved youth: an undergraduate specialization, a master's program, and a doctoral program. He also developed and currently runs an array of TPSR-based programs for low-income North Carolina kids of all ages.

These new TPSR master teachers and others have educated novice teachers about TPSR through direct apprenticeship in their sport and outdoor activity clubs for kids. The next generation of TPSR teacher educators is carrying on this tradition. For example, Angela Beale coteaches a Red Cross Learn to Swim/Lifeguard Certification course in a high-needs high school using TPSR as the daily class structure. She invites Red Cross–qualified PETE students from her program to teach with her. She takes advantage of required pre-student teaching school-based internships to provide apprentices.

Through optional teacher education program electives, interested novice teachers and other preprofessionals learn TPSR, practice using the goals and strategies under the watchful eye of a more experienced colleague, and get involved with students served by the programs. They also begin to notice contrasts between the TPSR program groups and standard PE offerings, perhaps seeing the advantages of "intermediate space" (Noam, Biancarosa, and Dechausay, 2003) programs over PE classes, with their large sizes, 40-minute time blocks, and deep-seated culture.

The major advantage of offering a site-based TPSR apprenticeship is the ability to bridge traditional professional preparation (e.g., Red Cross Water Safety Instructor Training, sport or martial arts instruction) with TPSR instructional methods in a real setting with kids, in a way that facilitates focused, in-depth discourse, authentic problem solving, planning, and debriefing. Also, experiencing PE in after-school, summer, and alternative youth development programs provides the opportunity to consider possibilities for future physical activity programming at schools and camps. Again, the primary disadvantage is the limited number of prospective teachers who can become apprentices.

TPSR *in Action*

It was 10 minutes before the start of the lesson as I walked across to the gym with Sarah, a local physical education teacher who had been working with the TPSR model for a number of months. Sarah had developed a fitness program based around students making choices to meet their individual needs. As we arrived, one of the year 10 (14-year-old) girls ran up to say that the walking group was leaving. Because the fitness activities were limited to the first 15 minutes of the lesson, this group had organized to get changed during recess so they could leave before class and get an additional 10 minutes of walking. A second group, predominantly boys, began a strength program in the attached weight room. The third group consisted of three boys who were not trusted to work independently; they worked under the direct supervision of the teacher in the gym. Fifteen minutes into the lesson, the walking group arrived back, the boys emerged from the weight room, and the class quickly moved seamlessly into the next part of the lesson.

The preceding is an example of a class given choices to help develop their decision-making skills. The program worked for a number of weeks, and the students were very positive about it. The school was a rural secondary school in New Zealand.

Barrie Gordon, Victoria University of Wellington, New Zealand

CONFERENCE WORKSHOP OR SHORT COURSE

Don Hellison, and now his closest colleagues, often provides conference sessions, half-day workshops, and weekend short courses on TPSR. This has been an effective method of teaching the basics and inspiring large groups of teachers and other youth workers. In this method, a traditional keynote introduction sets the problem and the challenge to teachers to choose what's worth doing. The TPSR levels and strategies are presented as one way to teach, usually with a personal history of their development, and sometimes with inspirational images or video, and when possible, a hands-on workshop or master class with teachers participating as students. This direct approach has been hugely successful in familiarizing teachers and teacher educators with TPSR. It has also served to inspire untold numbers of teachers, coaches, youth workers, and administrators to "do" TPSR in their programs.

On some occasions, kids are brought in and Don or his associates present a more authentic master class working directly with kids to show kids responding to TPSR strategies, activities, and interactions. Modeling the strategies and answering questions that emerge from observing or participating in the experience via conference presentations, especially when kids are involved, has been particularly helpful to large numbers of teachers across this country and in Ireland, Australia, and New Zealand, in terms of imagining what teaching TPSR is really like.

The main disadvantage of the conference or short course approach is the lack of depth. Teachers are able to post the levels in their gymnasiums, and perhaps engage students in discussions, but most have difficulty sustaining or developing more than the superficial elements to effect real student empowerment or considering more powerful or fundamental changes in their PE and PA programs.

ONE-WEEK INTENSIVE ELECTIVE

Recognizing the need to provide TPSR beyond single-day workshops for teachers, Don designed and co-conducted with me weeklong three-credit intensive courses for graduate PETE students on-site at a high-needs middle school or high school summer enrichment program. Students met daily as a class before the children arrived, planned and taught two physical activity classes under our guidance, and then met again as a class to debrief and plan again. They also read TPSR and youth development materials and, following the on-site week, wrote a structured postexperience paper demonstrating their understanding of the model, assessing their personal strengths and weaknesses in implementing the TPSR approach, and commenting on any changes to their beliefs about teaching.

The advantages of the one-week intensive course are that PETE students are immersed in TPSR in a real setting with high-needs kids and an experienced instructor, are guided during their first attempts, and have a peer group with whom to share failures (often) and successes (eventually). The disadvantage is that a one-week intensive course happens fast, leaving novice teachers little time to think, read, discuss, and generally process some powerful and challenging experiences. Often students get stuck on barriers ("This can't work in my traditional physical education program!") and simply need more time to understand the issues and the implications of teaching differently. Furthermore, because it is an elective course, only a few PETE students who already have an interest in TPSR or high-needs students attend.

SEMESTER-LONG ELECTIVE

To remedy the restrictive time frame of the one-week intensive elective, Don and I cotaught a graduate PETE three-credit semester-long course on TPSR and youth development one day per week on-site at a community-based after-school program in a high-needs community. Students met each week as a class, taught TPSR basketball lessons to elementary-aged children, and then met again as a class to debrief and plan. Similar to the summer courses, students read selected TPSR and youth development materials and wrote a structured post-experience paper demonstrating their understanding of the approach and addressing their ability to implement the approach and changes, if any, to their beliefs about teaching.

The advantage was obvious: the course occurred over an entire semester allowing time for thoughtful engagement with ideas and informal conversation with the instructor. Graduate students could see and work through the problems they had implementing the approach and recognize the advantages of non-school-based programs over traditional physical education for teaching physical activity and personal and social skills.

Disadvantages included the frustrations of conducting a graduate course in an after-school setting in a community center that had limited physical activity space and no separate classroom space for planning and debriefing. Planning and debriefing were frequently interrupted because community center space is so limited. More important, some community center workers interfered in the weekly program because their priorities and values, especially disciplinary practices, conflicted with the plans, activities, and interactions PETE students had with their groups. The children were bewildered at times by two sets of teaching styles and rules. Again, an additional disadvantage was that the course served only the few graduate students who were already aware of and interested in TPSR.

WITHIN A REQUIRED ACTIVITY COURSE

Dave Walsh (2008) addressed this problem of "scaling up" TPSR to become a requirement in an undergraduate PETE program. His initiative involved a majors-only activity course—a course for content knowledge, not pedagogy, in which students were expected to polish their knowledge and skills of a variety of sports, learning common errors, corrections, progressions, and related conditioning essentials. To this traditional content course he added the TPSR structure, not as theory, but as part of the day-to-day class structure for all students. He reported that the PETE students initially rebelled—this TPSR approach wasn't what they believed they had to know. Over time, Walsh's students moved from believing they had to do the TPSR structure to beginning to buy in to the approach.

The main advantage of a required course structured in this way is that PETE students gain an in-depth lived experience of TPSR from an experienced instructor and participate in personal and social development strategies as students, and then as group leaders and teachers. They are required to spend time in a TPSR culture, which may contrast strongly with the so-called deep culture of PE. The main disadvantage of such a required course is that on-campus class experiences and peer teaching may not transfer well to younger students in school or youth development settings, perhaps particularly high-needs students.

WITHIN A REQUIRED ON-SITE UNDERGRADUATE METHODS COURSE

In an attempt to eliminate peer teaching and to provide more meaningful but guided practice teaching experiences, I moved my secondary methods course to a middle school PE program. I chose a high-needs middle school to provide a positive opportunity to meet our "high-needs field experience" requirement. The eight weeks we spend there provide enough time to get to know kids, enough opportunities to develop some confidence, and the possibility to try out and develop capacity for TPSR. We had previously required students to spend time individually in field placement at high-needs schools, which resulted in some nervous university students and parents objecting to the requirement. We also learned quickly that many students returned from these experiences with prejudices confirmed and with strong commitments to leave teaching altogether if the only job they could get was in a high-needs school. Our teacher education faculty knew we needed to expand experiences in high-needs placements in a way that confronted biases and provided positive instructional experiences beyond our existing electives. All of our preservice PETE students need positive high-needs field experiences.

The main advantage of the on-site secondary methods course was that undergraduate students received guided opportunities to teach in a high-needs school setting with effective and humane teachers, in contrast to placing them unguided in high-needs schools, especially those with dysfunctional programs and teachers. Our students also left feeling far more comfortable with low-income and minority students, and some with a commitment to teach in such schools.

The main disadvantage of the on-site methods class was a lack of control over the specific content and teaching approaches. Our university's five-day schedule contrasted with the school's six-day schedule, resulting in working with a class only once every other week. This lack of consistency limited our ability to get to know the students we were teaching each week, thereby rendering a TPSR approach (which is at its core relational) simply not possible. We could not establish the relationships necessary to develop the trust and consistency that underpin the approach. Instead, students taught a variety of lessons more consistent with a traditional, albeit primarily positive, physical education program.

REQUIRED METHODS COURSE IN AN AFTER-SCHOOL PROGRAM

For reasons similar to those driving the on-site methods class (to eliminate peer teaching, to practice basic teaching skills in a more meaningful way, and to provide guidance in a high-needs placement), our PETE students meet as a class on-site for eight 3-hour classes at an after-school community-based program. They teach two classes, followed by debriefing and planning. Because we have more control over content and teaching approaches in this after-school program, our students work in groups to conduct TPSR sessions in two different sports, while embedding traditional secondary methods lesson and unit planning, and teacher and student assessment. Additional assignments include reading TPSR and youth development materials, interviewing students, conducting service projects, and researching community programs and other physical activity opportunities.

In the after-school setting, PETE students can implement TPSR through two different sports with kids in the real world of small, crowded gyms and limited equipment. An additional advantage is the experience of teaching within a high-needs community-based program that does not begin with a negative culture of physical education. In this setting, teacher education students have control over what they teach and are far more expert in terms of physical activity than the youth workers employed by the agency. Other advantages are some flexibility in timing and the fact that kids seem to like talking and playing with young adults who clearly like to play sports and games. The teacher education students get the opportunity to understand the differences between traditional physical education culture and intermediary space physical activity programs in which student participation is voluntary. They also have to come to grips with the notion that effective teaching requires that kids be engaged in and successful at something that's meaningful to them. If the class sessions aren't fun, the kids won't be back next week.

There are disadvantages to methods courses in after-school programs. Because of relatively small numbers of participants and distinctly constrained facility space, teacher education students must work in groups—sharing planning and teaching responsibilities. Shared teaching is stressful and often seems disorganized; students can have difficulty relying on each other to plan and teach their lessons. When the more experienced teachers are asked to step back and let less experienced classmates take over, they can have difficulty refraining from intervening. Additionally, the drop-in nature of community-based after-school programs leads to inconsistent attendance by program participants. This affects middle and high school groups more than elementary groups, but the week-to-week uncertainty of attendance exacerbates the teacher education students' stress in planning class sessions and undermines progress in TPSR.

FRAMEWORK FOR A TEACHER EDUCATION PROGRAM

Initiated by Ray Petracek and currently led by Nick Forsberg, the HOPE (Health/ Outdoor/Physical Education) teacher education program at the University of Regina in Saskatchewan, Canada, moves beyond TPSR as an effective teaching option in physical education and youth development and toward TPSR as the functional philosophy for an entire health/outdoor/physical education teacher education program. Through the consensus of the program faculty, and over years of development, the TPSR goals have been adopted as the basis for their program, with the intent of weaving the TPSR terminology into their students' lives and identities as teachers and physical activity professionals. The University of Regina faculty asks students to be personally and socially responsible themselves as students first, then as professionals, and eventually as mentors to other professionals. The message throughout the program is that TPSR is something bigger than just the levels on a poster.

TPSR *in Action*

Taking personal and social responsibility (TPSR) is no less important in teacher education programs than it is with underserved youth in community outreach programs. The Health/Outdoor/Physical Education (HOPE) program in the Faculty of Education, University of Regina, Saskatchewan, recognizes and prepares future teachers through a four-year developmental program with a philosophical foundation built on TPSR.

I have been involved in the HOPE program for over 20 years. The program is based on the belief that aspiring teachers need to realize that they must become personally and socially responsible before they can ask their students to become personally and socially responsible. Every semester throughout the four-year program, HOPE student teachers are immersed in experiences related to course work or teaching practica that discreetly or overtly provide opportunities for them to engage with personal and social responsibility. Whether it is through the HOPE coaching program in the first year, service projects and school-based initiatives linked to outdoor education courses in the second year, or the HOPE mentoring program in the third and fourth years, student teachers begin to embody the principles associated with TPSR.

The hope is that as prospective teachers leave the program and enter the world of teaching, they recognize TPSR as not simply a model ready for implementation but as a way of being, who they are as teachers.

Nick Forsberg, PhD, Faculty of Education, University of Regina, Regina, Saskatchewan, Canada

First- and second-year undergraduate students read Don's TPSR book, and discussions revolve around taking responsibility and being self-directed and caring in their lives as university students (taking responsibility to be on time, turn in good work, be self-directed and caring as students in class), as practicing teachers and leaders in their field experiences (seeing the strengths of their students, taking the initiative to serve the schools), and as contributing members of their profession (serving as cooperating teachers to interns, volunteering in professional associations). Third-year students coach first-year students in their major and minor course selections and thus practice acting at Level IV on campus. Fourth-year students mentor third-year students in their internship assignments. TPSR is taught as a curricular model for physical education, together with other prominent models. It is a natural approach for professional preparation considering the heavy emphasis on personal and social goals articulated in the educational standards for health and physical education set by the province of Saskatchewan.

The advantages of this model of TPSR as a teacher education program philosophy are too numerous to mention. Nick Forsberg, in an interview for this chapter, could think of no disadvantages. In terms of replicating this model in other professional preparation programs, a number of barriers seem reasonable: achieving faculty consensus for a single philosophy is one; interpreting the Hellison text and applying these interpretations in a consistent programmatic way is another. The concept, however, of framing professional preparation around this unifying theme is inspirational.

SUMMARY THOUGHTS

This chapter has presented nine ways to educate preprofessionals about TPSR. These examples are drawn from my explorations as a PE teacher educator primarily concerned with curriculum and methods for physical activity specialists working with adolescents in schools. None of these explorations has resulted in a perfect solution for expanding professional preparation for TPSR. Each experimental configuration has distinct advantages and disadvantages, possibilities and constraints. The issues described in the following sections are lessons learned and issues to consider for those responsible for professional preparation.

Negotiating With Program Staff and Dealing With the Unexpected

Experiential learning is more powerful than theoretical learning. However, each on-site course requires detailed negotiations with the school-based or after-school program staff. Such negotiations must result in a formal "memo of understanding" that details shared arrangements, times, facilities and equipment, parking and safety procedures, program goals, and expectations. The negotiation of such a practical memo takes time and requires a careful understanding of the needs and interests of both parties, as well as clear goals and commitment to essential principles.

A major difficulty for the university instructor is learning to deal with unexpected events at on-site venues—changes in space allocations or cancellations without notice, for example—and designing instant alternative activities to avoid canceling the class. Teacher education students similarly are uncomfortable not knowing ahead of time exactly how many students they will be teaching, in which space, and with which partner. This unpredictability requires quick, imaginative thinking, keeping the essential priorities in mind, and adapting to the circumstances without taking time and energy away from the fundamental goals of the experience. In one sense, learning to anticipate and cope with this uncertainty is good training because such uncertainty is common in high-needs schools and youth development programs; but in another sense, it makes for a much more stressful course experience for all.

Addressing Course Requirements

Course instructors must negotiate with teacher education students and interns, especially in courses that are required within their degree programs. At the beginning of the experience, course instructors must explain and clarify course requirements, grading policies, and professional expectations for authentically attempting teaching behaviors that may be unfamiliar and uncomfortable. Teaching in such unpredictable settings is tricky and not for those who need predictable class activities, predesigned assignments, and rigid course calendars. In return for dealing with unpredictable events and anxious days, both instructors and students have an opportunity to engage in something authentic and worth doing in the search for a better solution to a problem that has persisted for too long.

Giving Up Familiar Teaching Behaviors

In many on-site settings, students are in unfamiliar territory and challenged to question or ignore a style of teaching that they may not consider problematic. The most difficult challenge in my experience has been helping students move out of the deep culture of physical education teaching or coaching and into alternative, less authoritarian demeanors in order to reach students accustomed to disengaging from physical education and physical activity instruction.

Abandoning comfortable teacher-controlled lesson plans because they are losing students' interest is very difficult, especially for undergraduates and those who model their teaching styles after strong competitive coaches. Helping these students move from direct instruction to student empowerment in appropriate ways is a slow and subtle process that involves failure and requires a deep understanding of new goals and strategies and a willingness to persist when doubtful of the results.

For some teacher education students, understanding why they might need TPSR or other indirect method may take weeks. Some never get it. Setting the problem of what's not working in traditional physical education, and explaining why this alternative is worth trying, remains an essential key to success for teacher education.

Learning From Students and On-Site Staff

Instructors have to recognize the strengths teacher education students have and learn to build on these, much as we expect our students to see the strengths, not deficiencies, of their students. We have racked our brains to find ways to resolve problems, only to see that teacher education students themselves have ideas and imagination that go far beyond our own. Teacher education students are not all the same, and drawing out their experiences as the basis of problem solving and positive teaching is often the only way to go.

Related to recognizing the contributions of teacher education students is acknowledging that we as instructors do not know much more than our students. With our own primarily white middle-class backgrounds and biases, and not much more experience than our students with low-income and oppressed minority cultures, we are often reminded of our lack of expertise. Our best allies in these times may be the on-site staff members who know their kids and communities far better than we do and often have insights from prior experiences that can help explain what has happened and help find a way forward.

Communicating With the Powers That Be

Focusing on TPSR to the exclusion of traditional teacher education content may raise hackles among our teacher education colleagues back on campus, because it implies criticism of existing programs. In addition, department chairs, deans, and tenure and promotion committees are likely to have more support for the concept of "the engaged university" than the practical realities of it, such as the time it takes to engineer course work and service projects. Despite these pressures, appealing to the university's espoused values of social justice and serving the underserved is a good way to quiet critics. We need to ensure that publications and presentations come to the attention of the appropriate people in power. Finally, writing successful grants can be very helpful.

Keeping Things in Perspective

Although we are vocal critics of traditional physical education and sport culture, and the schools or other institutions that support them, we should strive to see strengths, not deficiencies, not only in kids but also in the programs, schools, and community-based organizations where we work. We must keep in mind that if developing personal and social responsibility through physical education and physical activity programs were easy, it would have been done already. If improving programs and teaching in secondary schools were easy, we'd be out of a job, and if students were simple and easy to read, they'd ultimately be boring and not worth our attention.

⫸⫸⫸ TAKE-AWAYS ⫸⫸⫸

Here are some key points from this chapter that you might consider taking with you:

- To make TPSR come alive for teacher education students, it is essential to arrange for experience in practice teaching with children.
- Teaching on-site with any teaching approach requires much planning, negotiation, and accommodation of the unexpected.
- Teacher education students embody the deep culture of coaching and physical education and sometimes have trouble imagining themselves teaching in alternative ways. Instructors should build student awareness and confidence by convincingly setting the problem and the need for TPSR and drawing on the strengths students bring to the table.
- Teacher educators often do not have enough experience with underserved youth to understand and work though problems. Recognizing this and seeking help from on-site colleagues who do have such experience may provide a way forward.
- Those working with TPSR in PETE programs should be prepared for university administrators and colleagues who may not appreciate the value and time-intensive nature of learning TPSR. They often value tangible research articles over intangible changes in teaching perspectives. Instructors should decide what's most important for them and find a convincing rationale that works with their department's agenda and university's agenda.

C·H·A·P·T·E·R

9

Coaching Clubs and Other TPSR Program Structures

No more prizes for predicting rain. Prizes only for building arks.

—Louis V. Gerstner Jr.

■ ■ ■ ■ ■

Daryl Siedentop (1992) admonished us to think differently about PE and PA program development. Several PE program (or curriculum) models are available to PE and PA professionals, including TPSR and Siedentop's sport education. Schwab (1971) argued that program development needs to be based on a theory, either by drawing on the literature to find a suitable theory (which Schubert, 1986, thought was rarely applicable to practice), by modifying that theory to fit the situation, or, as both Siedentop and Schwab suggested, by creating one's own theory. It might be more accurate to call it one's own working theory-in-practice, signaling that a set of ideas is being tested and further refined in practice. To do this kind of work, a PE or PA imagination comes in handy.

This chapter and chapter 10 describe various issues and opportunities in different kinds of settings. In-school PE has one distinct advantage compared to most other settings: It is mandated in most school districts and therefore can exert some influence on a lot of kids (Shields and Bredemeier, 1995), although there has been some erosion of the requirement in a number of states. Unfortunately, this advantage is further diminished by funding restraints, which have increased class size and cost some teachers their jobs, as well as the deep culture of teaching PE (i.e., deeply rooted practices such as uniforms, whistles, showers for older kids, squads, and other trappings of traditional PE that discourage change). Although none of these practices are necessarily bad, they can hinder the cultivation of a PE imagination.

Myriad PA settings make generalizations difficult, but that same breadth offers countless opportunities to develop, try out, and practice innovative program models. Of course, deep culture is not limited to PE; it can be an issue in any well-established PA program or community-based organization. However, my experience in a number of PE and PA programs suggests that PA has fewer constraints, resulting in a range from very innovative programs to those that look a lot like free play.

Alternative schools offer both small classes and more curricular structure than after-school programs do. However, the structure does not often resemble

TPSR *in Action*

The Career Club Possible Futures program extends TPSR's notion of Level V—the transfer of life skills beyond the physical activity—by helping kids envision, explore, and contemplate meaningful possible future decisions. Career Club has two main goals: (1) empower youth to experience and reflect on coaching as an occupation by coaching a younger group of kids, and (2) link the skills (e.g., goal setting, communication, organizational) acquired from coaching to careers of their choosing. Career Club aims to balance kids' hopes and fears, which maximizes motivation, by consistently reinforcing the connection between the lessons learned during coaching and what is necessary for the realization of their futures. In addition, breaking down the tasks for coaching and the tasks for their own future aspirations into an exercise in "procedural knowledge" helps facilitate practical reflective discussions. They are shown as concretely as possible that any and all careers entail a similar set of procedural difficulties and opportunities.

Kids came to understand that coaching is much more difficult than they anticipated and that accomplishing their own goals would also be more difficult than they had initially thought. They learned that their own persistence, effort, and tenacity will be the primary factors in achieving their dreams.

David Walsh, Department of Kinesiology, San Francisco State University

that of traditional public school programs, because that traditional structure is one reason students wind up in alternative schools. But PE is not a priority in most alternative schools and is further hampered in some schools by students having to travel to suitable sport and exercise facilities. If PE is part of the curriculum, a volleyball or soccer game or an open gym sometimes comprises the entire program.

COACHING CLUBS

Nikos Georgiadis and I created the first coaching club almost two decades ago in a low-income, high-violence area of Chicago as an alternative structure for the implementation of TPSR. Nikos, a former professional basketball player, returned to Greece after receiving his doctorate, leaving me—a much less competent player (who fortunately had some basketball coaching experience)—at the helm. Basketball's popularity kept the kids coming to the voluntary before-school program, despite a policy of referring kids in trouble to the program. The principal and vice principal made this decision after observing the coaching club for three years, and I viewed this policy change as just another challenge. In truth, I didn't see much difference in the kids when the referral policy was instituted. By the third or fourth year, the coaching club had become part of the school's culture—that is, both kids and teachers recognized the coaching club as a legitimate part of the school. Moreover, I began receiving compliments from the teachers and administrators for reducing violence and developing leaders in the school. By the fifth year, I was invited to the eighth grade graduation ceremony and asked to tell the parents about the coaching club. That practice continued for the rest of the 17-year duration of the club.

Because the coaching club structure offers a specific PA model for TPSR, it has been adopted and adapted by, among others, Tom Martinek in Greensboro, North Carolina, schools; James Hollins of the Southwest Youth Collaborative in Chicago; Nick Cutforth in Denver schools; Dave Walsh in San Francisco schools and community youth organizations; Paul Wright in a Memphis YMCA; April Rogers in a school near Washington, DC; Frankie Giosa and Kermit Blakeley at alternative schools in the Chicago area; and Bryan McCullick in Athens, Georgia. It has also been adopted in Spain and perhaps in other states and countries. For this reason, it receives considerable attention in this chapter.

What's in a Name?

The term *coaching club* communicates to kids, parents, administrators, and other teachers that this is something different from a typical sport program. A coaching club emphasizes learning how to help others and become a leader. If it takes place in a Boys and Girls Club, it becomes a club within a club! To call attention to the specific physical activity for recruiting purposes, it is sometimes called a basketball or soccer (or whatever sport) *leadership* club. Coaching clubs have also included less competitive or noncompetitive physical fitness activities such as aerobics, weight training, and calisthenics; adventure education; martial arts; and tumbling. Any activity that voluntarily attracts kids will work. If the program leader wants to serve a specific group of kids, the activity needs to appeal to them. Basketball is a shoo-in in many urban neighborhoods, including the one being described here. One of my favorite comments came from an anonymous student who asked the vice principal, "How bad do I have to be to get in the coaching club?"

Advantages

Creating a coaching club offers the following advantages:

- Responsibility-challenged students can be given more attention and more practice at taking responsibility by keeping club membership small, in the range of 10 to 15. Sometimes assistance is available from cross-age student leaders, nearby university students, or aides, and the number can be adjusted.

- Kids have something meaningful to belong to—a club in which they have a voice, can make decisions, and can eventually become leaders.

- As long as the space is available and policies are not restrictive, the program leader can create the schedule, including how many days the club meets each week and for how long. A number of constraints have forced some coaching clubs to operate only one day a week over several years. However, end-of-year program evaluations suggest that clubs meeting once a week over time have a positive effect on the kids (Hellison and Wright, 2003).

- In an after-school setting, some of the usual in-school PE rules such as uniforms can be optional, and large-class management routines such as squads are not needed for smaller groups. Because attendance is voluntary, it's not essential to get it right, although attendance does indicate a small measure of responsibility. If attendance is kept, it can probably be done from memory as long as the group is small.

Issues

PE teachers may want to help some of their responsibility-challenged students but may not have the time or energy to take on another responsibility. Even if they do, getting strong administrative support is sometimes difficult for an alternative structure such as a coaching club, especially compared with the support normally afforded to interschool organized sports or even intramurals. A nearby university can sometimes provide volunteer interns to assist or even run a coaching club with minimal assistance either right away or after some experience with the kids. My colleagues and I have had quite a bit of success getting help from university students (Hellison et al., 2000).

Another issue is finding a location for the club if the gym is occupied by other activities. Often, improvising is necessary. I've conducted a martial arts coaching club on a stage with staggering temperatures from the stage lights and in classrooms by moving the chairs around. A key program leader criterion for exemplary extended-day programs is to "provide courageous and persistent leadership in the face of systemic obstacles" (Hellison and Cutforth, 1997; see figure 1.2 on p. 9).

An activity likely to attract responsibility-challenged students may be one in which the program leader possesses little skill at or knowledge of—for example, skateboarding. Of course, these skills can be learned with practice, but by being a bit vulnerable (see chapter 7), program leaders can be open to inviting the kids to teach them, providing an authentic Level IV experience.

Some university faculty and students desire to run club programs in schools or youth organizations. Many of the difficulties described earlier apply in these cases; moreover, they are outsiders working on others' turf. Dave Walsh (2002; 2006) found that two contact people at the site can be very helpful in offsetting these barriers. The first is the initial contact person, usually an administrator such as the school principal. The second should be someone who has direct contact with the kids such as a teacher or coach.

Sample Coaching Club Lesson

Because coaching clubs are so varied in content, it is impossible to offer a generic coaching club lesson plan. In this section, I describe a basketball lesson plan; but with a few adjustments, other team sports can become coaching clubs. For individual sports and other activities such as martial arts and adventure education, the program title changes to leadership club, but many of the same principles apply. For other detailed examples, see *Youth Development and Physical Activity* (Hellison et al., 2000).

Relational time at the beginning of the program can be augmented by offering the kids free time to pass and shoot on their own when they show up. The only rules are those of Level I—respect others, include everyone, and share the balls and space. With a small number of participants, ample time is available for touching base with most of them and even having one or two in-depth talks if warranted.

Either at this time or after the awareness talk, two kids who appear to be able to handle a limited leadership role can be invited to be coaches or assistant coaches (i.e., player-coaches or player-assistant coaches). They are given a simple specific practice plan written on a card and asked to make fair teams (in a private meeting without others hanging around) based on those who are participating that day. At first, to model good coaching, the program leader can be the coach of both teams (or an adult assistant can take one team). Assistant coaches can be added eventually. This is a role for younger kids or those who are unsure about coaching but want to try. At first, their job is just to run one drill. The coaches can sometimes invite kids to be assistant coaches.

The awareness talk, conducted with kids sitting in a circle, should be brief and focus on being a club member, which means showing up regularly, and on Level I as noted above. In my program, we called Level I self-control of your mouth and temper, which addressed most of the problems faced on a daily basis. (Remember the 10-word rule: keep every talk brief.) At the next meeting, ask if anyone remembers what this club is about. From then on, gradually introduce teamwork, which is substituted for effort in a coaching club, because in most cases effort is not an issue—but passing the ball is! Eventually self-coaching (a form of Level III, which involves goal-setting) and coaching (Level IV), and much later outside the gym (Level V), can be added, each followed over time by asking kids to include and explain these concepts in an expanded discussion about the purpose of the club. The program leader's talks should be very brief. Mostly, kids should do the talking.

After the awareness talk and the meeting with the player-coaches, the two teams conduct a practice based on the practice plans that the two coaches (or assistant coaches) have received, with assistance as necessary. Because new teams are created for each lesson, rivalries are less likely to form and shouldn't interfere with the purpose of the club. Players sometimes complain that they don't want to play with someone assigned to their team. They just need to be reminded that everyone, including famous professional athletes, have to play with people they don't like. It's just part of the game.

Before the game, player-coaches need to be reminded that they are in charge and therefore need to call timeouts to make offensive and defensive adjustments and solve problems that arise (with help as needed). If they cannot handle this

TPSR *in Action*

Project Effort, which focuses on fostering TPSR values among underserved youngsters, is in its 16th year of operation. Throughout its tenure it has served over 700 children and youth. Project Effort came about as part of a collaborative between the University of North Carolina at Greensboro's Department of Kinesiology and a principal of a local elementary school. She wanted students who were plagued with low grades, high office referrals, and school suspension to have a chance to be part of an after-school program that would help them channel negative energy in a positive way. Their school biographies indicated that they would be highly at risk for dropping out of school in their later years.

When the Project Effort Sport Club first started, all of the youngsters in the program lived in a low socioeconomic area of the city with one of the highest crime rates in Greensboro. With little adult supervision during after-school hours, a program was needed to occupy kids' discretionary time period.

Today, participating youngsters continue to come from Hampton, where they are recommended by teachers, counselors, and the principal. We have also expanded Project Effort to serve kids from other public housing communities, especially those with heavy immigrant families from Mexico, Viet Nam, and Africa.

Tom Martinek, University of North Carolina at Greensboro

responsibility at some point, the program leader needs to step in to help and sometimes to replace the leader with another club member or take over for the time being.

Club games have several rules that differ from those of traditional sport:

- Both teams must be taught to use a zone defense because guarding a zone rather than a specific player reduces one-on-one rivalries and trash talk. Eventually, if and when they are ready, player-to-player defense can be introduced, along with picks, two- and three-player games, posting up, and so on. The coaches' job at first is to teach the zone defense and have their teams practice it, which often means the coaches must first be taught the zone.

- On offense, team basketball is emphasized, using the all-touch rule, which requires that everyone on the team handle the ball in the front court before anyone can shoot. This is certain to generate protests and complaints, so the all-touch rule can be modified as soon as everyone understands and practices *team* basketball. For additional groans and protests, limit dribbling to three dribbles until players understand that this is a team game and that everyone deserves to be involved. Surprisingly, the kids get used to this rule (although often the program leader must first outlast them!), but they watch the other team carefully for violations. At times, however, the objections are strenuous, and it may take some bargaining (e.g., only three team members have to touch the ball) to resume the game. With the all-touch (or most-touch) rule, players learn not only teamwork but also how to move off the ball to get clear for a pass and how to pass more effectively.

- Because there are no referees, coaches and players must take responsibility for conducting a fair game. This can be a daunting task, but, as with most things, kids get better with persistence and practice.

- Players and especially coaches can call a timeout at any time to deal with problems or discuss strategy. At first, the program leader will need to call timeouts, because no one wants to stop the game. Once they experience conducting timeouts on their own, kids will begin to call them when a problem arises with their team or in the game or to make some improvement in their offense or defense. When a conflict breaks out and I start toward the group, what I want to hear is, "We don't need you; we can handle it." After some practice, they don't disappoint.

- The soft defense rule requires that the more highly skilled players not overplay the less skilled players on the opposing team. The kids understand why this rule has been created and are willing to relax their defense for kids who are clearly low skilled. But during an intense game, the higher-skilled players sometimes suffer from temporary amnesia.

- Using the term "winning" as in "we beat you" is discouraged by substituting "playing as well as you can" and "playing fair." This is an uphill battle because winning is so ingrained in the American culture (and in many PA and PE professionals!), despite none of us having control over who wins, only with improving ourselves and our team. With time the message sinks in, at least in the coaching club.

The program leader can participate in the game if another player is needed, which also serves as a way to role model passing and zone defense as well as defending without fouling and playing fair.

The group meeting follows the game. Again, students sit in a circle, but this time player-coaches (or in the beginning, assistant coaches) talk first, sharing their perceptions of how practice and the game went and who made positive contributions on their team. Then any player can talk about the practice or game as long as the comments are constructive. Finally, the program leader can share observations. It is crucial for the leader to talk last; otherwise, participants' voices will be muted.

Club members stay in the circle for reflection time. For each level or club goal that has been introduced, they can point their thumbs up, sideways, or down to indicate how they did with that level in the session (e.g., I respected others or showed self-control, I sometimes respected others, or I need to work on this). If they had time to work on individual goals, they can be asked to rate themselves on Level III according to whether they worked on their goal, went through the motions, or did not try at all. Journals can be used in place of thumbs, but the program leader must take the time to read their entries and respond to validate the process.

Coaching clubs can augment in-school PE if the teacher has the time and energy to start an after-school club for a popular sport. These clubs offer responsibility-challenged kids more attention and more leadership opportunities.

CROSS-AGE TEACHING AND LEADERSHIP

Cross-age teaching and leadership has already been described in chapter 5 as both a Level IV and Level V experience. Although the logistics of arranging for TPSR-trained older kids to teach and provide leadership for younger kids are challenging, it provides a unique experience for both groups and especially for the cross-age leaders who become leader, teacher, coach, and advisor of younger kids. Monitoring and feedback are important factors in the success of the program. (See Hellison et al., 2000, and Martinek and Hellison, 2009, for extended discussions of TPSR-based cross-age teaching.)

Older students can be fourth- and fifth-graders working with first-, second-, and third-graders. Or they can be eighth- or ninth-graders either working with sixth- or seventh-graders in their school or in a local youth organization, or working with younger kids in an elementary school. High school juniors and seniors can work with younger high school students or travel to the middle school or elementary school to assist there. In all these situations, cross-age leaders need to take on Level IV responsibilities (see chapters 3 and 5).

Some responsibility-challenged older students respond to being given leadership responsibilities. In a low-income minority community in Denver, Nick Cutforth's (2000) cross-age leaders were junior high students initially selected for his elementary program based on their poor disciplinary record. They came back weekly to their old elementary school as program teaching assistants. Terry Cooper had some of her most responsibility-challenged sixth-graders teach first-graders, and she reported that they were great teachers! I have had success with supposedly responsibility-challenged alternative high school students teaching younger kids in an elementary school as well as with inner-city students grade 7 through 12 teaching 10-year-olds from a different neighborhood.

Preparing students to become cross-age teachers creates yet another administrative headache: finding the time and energy to conduct mini-preservice teaching sessions. Here are some ways I have tried to prepare cross-age teachers:

- Peer teaching and coaching, being integral parts of TPSR, can help prepare students for working with younger kids, especially if accompanied by reflection on the experience.
- Students can be invited to take turns conducting the awareness talk and, with help, the group meeting and reflection time in a class or club setting. I've found that giving kids who are willing to coach and teach others a heads-up ahead of time allows them time to prepare mentally before taking on a leadership role.
- Reciprocal coaching (see chapter 5) can be extended so that kids demonstrate the skills to each other, point out important cues, observe, and give feedback as a lead-up to cross-age teaching.
- By developing a unit or mini-program on teaching, program leaders can give cross-age leadership candidates practice teaching lessons that they will use with younger kids. They enjoy watching videos of themselves in action, and feedback can help them focus on what is and is not working.

Tom Martinek (Martinek and Schilling, 2002) uses this progression for his students:

1. They still focus on personal needs.
2. They work on teaching skills, such as organizing and managing other kids and giving feedback.
3. They reflect on their teaching and how it has influenced their personal growth and knowledge about other kids.
4. They teach with compassion and teach others to be compassionate.

Tom's elaborate after-school youth leadership program is described in *Youth Leadership in Sport and Physical Education* (Martinek and Hellison, 2009).

TPSR IN ORGANIZED SPORT

Putting TPSR into practice in organized sport (or interscholastic athletics) is in some ways a formidable undertaking. As I noted in chapter 1, character development rhetoric is an integral part of organized sport, although whether sport truly builds character is a matter of debate. These traditional programs, however, do provide structure in kids' lives as well as supervised places during their free time, and they require kids to make commitments. Organized sport has great appeal in our culture; it is a magnet for kids, who tend to develop strong ties to the sport, their teams, and their coaches.

Then why is putting TPSR into practice in organized sport so difficult? The primary problem is the influence of the professional sport model that has trickled all the way down to youth sport programs. Most organized sport programs, sometimes even at the T-ball level, try to replicate the winning-is-everything, elitist, spectator-driven, commercialized orientation of the big-time sport model. Despite attempts to humanize sport for kids, including a number of rule modifications, too many coaches and parents value winning over participation, fair play, and personal and social development (hence the alternative goals of the coaching club). And too many coaches believe in their own authority rather than in sharing power with their players. In the inner city, the myth of playing in the NBA too often goes unanalyzed. Occasionally, coaches even intentionally use it as a motivator. I am always amazed when I see professionals trained as school psychologists, social workers, or special education teachers leave their training on the sidelines when they become coaches, sometimes even with special education kids! In short, the cultural appeal of organized sport has its dark side.

Nevertheless, TPSR has been implemented here and there in organized sport. Moreover, former professional basketball player Nikos Georgiadis argued that the motor elite sorely need this perspective, because they are victims of the professional sport model and its values. Sport psychologist Gloria Balague told me that she agreed, saying that the levels of responsibility should apply to elite athletes as well.

Walt Kelly, a veteran football coach, and Cynthia Luebbe began to use TPSR in their high school classes in Bozeman, Montana. Kelly then decided to try out these ideas in football. He reconceptualized the levels, as shown in table 9.1,

Table 9.1 Walt Kelly's Football Team Levels of Responsibility

Level	Name	Description
I	Preplayer	The first and foremost goal is to respect the rights and feelings of teammates, opponents, coaches, officials, and spectators by using self-control (rather than coach control). This includes controlling one's abusive behavior, such as put-downs and arrogance, and disruptive behavior, such as interfering with practice. It also includes negotiating differences. This is a prerequisite to participating on the team and requires the highest need for direct supervision.
II	Player	The second level involves becoming involved in the activities of the team, learning from failure, redefining success so that success can be experienced (e.g., improvement as success), losing oneself in the game, and having fun. Again, the goal is to shift this responsibility to the players.
III	Self-coach	The goal of the third level is to help the players manage their own development, to be their own coach. Players face a number of conflicts at this stage—between peer pressure and their own goals, between "looking good" and self-acceptance, etc. The coach's role is to help players to see these conflicts and to experiment with solutions.
IV	Coach	The goal of the fourth level is to learn how to support and help others, to extend oneself beyond one's own needs and interests, and to become an assistant coach.

so that being a player meant being at Level II. Level I meant that the player was working on the qualities needed to become a player. At Levels III and IV, the concepts of self-direction and coaching were added. He taught these levels to his players in awareness talks and required that they do self-evaluations during scheduled reflection times at the end of practice. This self-evaluation consisted of written comments for each level, followed by written feedback from Kelly. He also conducted group meetings in which players could share their ideas about practice, game plans, and decisions.

Kelly, a former U.S. marine, reported that TPSR forced him to rethink his coaching style and to shift from issuing commands to collaborating and negotiating with his players. Walt began his TPSR journey over 20 years ago and recently telephoned while I was writing this third edition to update me on the TPSR work he is still doing.

Bill White put TPSR into practice with his interscholastic wrestling and gymnastics teams in Portland, Oregon. All his senior athletes were Level IV assistant coaches; they helped run practice and coach the younger athletes. In addition, certain athletes had specific Level IV roles, such as the nutrition coach who taught everyone about healthy weight-reducing practices in wrestling. His athletes were responsible for making decisions about whether to come to practice (Level II) and, with assistance at first, what kind of workout to do (Level III). During group meetings, players decided who would start. That way, the decision of whether to come to practice became a team decision. Many of White's athletes were considered at-risk students in school. In gymnastics competitions, officials would regularly deduct points for their dress and "non-gymnastics attitude." Despite this, his team took several city titles in gymnastics and placed in the top three in the state every year he coached. He coached wrestling for a shorter time, and his ideas turned around a struggling wrestling team almost immediately. The point here is not that winning is important but that a coach who employs TPSR can win, too.

Kostas Keramidas (1991) used TPSR with his junior basketball team, which plays in a highly competitive league in Greece. He reported that the TPSR approach has reduced the influence of the star system imported from the United States ("Be like Mike" or more recently, like LeBron), that most of his players have reached Level IV, that their reflection time journals show they are thinking, and that their basketball skills have improved. Referees and coaches praised his team for their unselfish play and their performance. Because his team has performed so well, other coaches in the league started using reflection time journals, not to help their players become more responsibly reflective but, assuming this idea was imported from the American sport model, in the hope of improving the win–loss records of their teams! And so it goes.

RESPONSIBILITY-BASED FITNESS CENTERS

Compared with some other activities, fitness lends itself more to having kids take responsibility. The activities—stretching, weight training, push-ups and sit-ups, running, stationary bicycle—are easy to learn and don't require much motor skill feedback to improve. The mechanics are simple for most kids, and once they learn the basic mechanics of a push-up, a bench press, or jogging, improvement will come with regular training. Moreover, fitness is easily individualized. Students start by performing the exercise correctly, record their performance, and work from there at their own pace.

The one obstacle to running a self-directed fitness center is developing students' conceptual knowledge so that they can be self-directed. They may need to learn about warm-up, overload, intervals, aerobic and anaerobic training, heart rate measurement, and body fat reduction. Concepts posters and a brief multiple-choice (or other) test to screen students for the threshold knowledge necessary to work on their own is one simple way to deal with this issue (and something I have found to be effective). This process has the additional benefit of being self-directed, so that students must learn the concepts on their own and schedule their test taking. If necessary, they can be issued cards authorizing those who have passed the test to be on their own in the fitness center. Students who can manage only Level I would require active supervision if they are to be allowed in the center.

Despite these advantages, a program leader must monitor students who go to the center, unless a university student interested in fitness is available. Kids who are willing and able to take on leadership responsibilities can, with some training or past experience, assist at the center.

At Rock Springs High School in Wyoming, Leslie Lambert and Paul Grube (1988) created such a center. Because they wanted to nurture students toward more decision making and self-management, they integrated TPSR into the activities of the center. As a result, "participation has increased, most notably in the students' feelings of responsibility for their learning and class involvement" (p. 72).

TPSR ON THE PLAYGROUND AND AT RECESS

Curt Hinson (2001) adapted TPSR for the playground and recess. Hinson wrote that his interest began this way:

> When I tried to place too much control over them I ended up in a power struggle with kids who didn't know how to act appropriately. That's when I went in search of a method that could help me to teach students to be self-responsible. (p. 63)

Hinson adapted the levels of responsibility by reducing the five levels to three "levels of behavior":

- Unacceptable (e.g., not following directions, arguing, hitting, or pushing)
- Acceptable (e.g., following directions, taking care of equipment, respecting others)
- Outstanding (e.g., cooperating with others, helping others, being a role model)

Posters of these levels were placed where kids could see them regularly, such as the cafeteria and classrooms, and, when possible, they were reminded of the levels before they went to the playground—such as by asking them for examples of the levels.

Once kids understood the levels, they could make choices about how they wanted to be on the playground. The key to Hinson's approach was for students to choose their behaviors rather than for adults to tell them what to do. Ideally, unacceptable behaviors would not make them popular playmates, but they sometimes needed some assistance to figure that out. The playground supervisor's job was to help students who were behaving unacceptably to identify their level of behavior and, if it was unacceptable, to change it on their own. Some children, however, needed help to solve a particular problem, such as an argument, or to understand how they could change to acceptable and outstanding behaviors. The supervisor could make suggestions, but the child needed to make the final decision.

Kids who blame others for what is happening don't understand self-responsibility. They may need some help to shift their thinking to what they need to do rather than what others are doing. As a last resort, the supervisor can step in and solve the problem. If a child's behavior is still unacceptable after other options have been attempted, removing the child from recess may be necessary.

TPSR IN THE CLASSROOM

TPSR has been implemented here and there in elementary and secondary classrooms. Most of these initiatives have relied heavily on the levels, ignoring the rest of the framework. In almost all cases, results of the PE teacher's implementation of TPSR prompted other teachers to inquire about it and request help in trying some of the ideas in their classrooms.

Classroom Applications

Most often, the levels are posted, sometimes with students doing the artwork, sometimes with considerable creativity. For example, Vicki Jorgensen, an elementary music teacher in Ashland, Oregon (who learned of the levels from the school's physical education teacher, Keith Kimball), created a four-color rainbow, with one color for each level. She called it "Put a rainbow in your life!" and the idea spread to most of the classrooms in the school. Teachers Tom Martinek worked with in an elementary school used selected Calvin and Hobbes cartoons to illustrate each of the levels.

Teachers have also modified TPSR strategies for use in the classroom. Steve Hoy, teaching a sixth-grade class in Billings, Montana, used the cumulative levels along with the talking bench (out in the hall) and a Level Zero table where students could separate themselves from their classmates to cool off and make a plan to improve. He reported that TPSR has helped his kids learn how to manage themselves.

One high school math teacher reported some success in giving his students the choice of learning content cooperatively, competitively, or individually. Traditionally, students have been in competitive contexts—who has the best test score, who has the right answer in class—but recently, both specific cooperative learning and individualized instruction strategies have been made available to teachers. From a TPSR perspective, students should probably be exposed to all three learning processes but eventually be allowed to choose the one or two that work best for them.

Ray Petracek (1998), teaching all subjects to his class of grade 7 students in Regina, Saskatchewan, had his kids make journal entries at the end of the day to rate themselves on the percentage of time during the day that they functioned at each of his adapted levels of responsibility.

- No control ___%
- Self-control ___%
- Involvement with effort ___%
- Self-direction ___%
- Caring for others ___%
- Responsible leadership ___%

Every Monday morning Ray assisted his students in setting class goals for the week. He also kept track of incidences of not being prepared for class, disrespecting his right to teach, disrespecting others' right to learn, and issuing a put-down or threat. He used these data to give feedback to his students, to discuss the problems, and to make plans to solve them. Finally, he gave them a written assignment from time to time, asking them to describe a situation in which all of the levels are used.

Health Education Applications

Because some physical education teachers also teach health education, those who use TPSR sometimes experiment with it in that area. In addition, TPSR addresses a key issue in health education: taking responsibility for one's physical, emotional, and social health. Because of these factors, many of the classroom applications have been in health education.

Bill White may have been the first to implement TPSR in health education. His Portland, Oregon, high school health education program was a semester course that included a number of short units, such as nutrition, drug education, sex education, and so on. Bill began the course with a mental health unit that featured the levels. Through awareness talks, discussions (similar to group meetings), and reflection time, he encouraged students to see the relevance of the levels in their lives both in and out of school. He focused on the necessity of respect in social relations, the importance of participation and effort in learning or improving anything, the relevance of self-direction for the many choices students face on a daily basis, the need to be cared for and helped, and the benefit of offering these things to others. After this initial unit, the levels were applied to subsequent units so that students were confronted with issues of self-control, effort, self-direction (making personal decisions), and caring about others in drug and sex education, in nutrition decisions, and even in driver education.

Chris Hare (1998), a high school health education teacher in a Chicago suburb, was aware that he was just "spitting out information," but he also knew that his students needed to learn to make health-related decisions for themselves, based on their needs and interests, as long as no one was adversely affected. As a result, he created his own levels of responsibility for his classes (see figure 9.1). His levels focused on the climate he was trying to establish to teach health education in an empowering way.

I: Self-Responsibility

- Effort on homework
- Coming to class prepared with the materials they need

II: Self-Control

- Right to be included in class discussions, to make a positive contribution to class
- Right to peaceful conflict resolution in class discussions

III: Self-Direction

- Participation in class, sharing one's thoughts
- Becoming independent thinkers, not subject to peer pressure

IV: Out of the Classroom

- Health education applications in life
- Caring about and helping others (e.g., helping one's family develop a fire escape plan)

V: Self-Actualization

- Setting long-term goals
- Reaching self-fulfillment and one's potential

FIGURE 9.1 Chris Hare's levels of responsibility for his health education classes.

In her wellness course, Mary Sinclair uses the levels to help students reflect on their personal and social wellness. Students score themselves on a 1 to 10 scale on each level, and Sinclair asks them to make open-ended written comments. Figure 9.2 shows how Sinclair redefined the levels to represent wellness attitudes, values, and behaviors.

Wellness Responsibility Levels

How would you grade yourself on self-responsibility for your wellness? Using the responsibility levels, rate yourself by circling the number you believe best represents your effort at each of the levels (10 being the highest rating). For Levels Zero and I, 10 represents the absence of negative attitudes and behaviors. Discuss your self-evaluation below by elaborating and using examples to support your self-perceptions.

Self-Control and Respect

Low --- High

1   2   3   4   5   6   7   8   9   10

Level Zero: Abusive, destructive health behavior. No ownership of own health.

Level I: Minimal investment in personal wellness. Lack of awareness about personal needs and skills. Health behaviors not unhealthy but not necessarily constructive.

Level II: Participation and Effort

Low --- High

1   2   3   4   5   6   7   8   9   10

Willing to put effort into own wellness. Disciplined. Open to ideas and experiences. Ready to risk change. Ready to develop self-awareness. Self-knowledge (first connection between class and personal wellness).

Level III: Self-Direction

Low --- High

1   2   3   4   5   6   7   8   9   10

Accepting responsibility for all aspects of own health. Owning goals and problems. Using skills of "response-ability" to internalize and work problems out. Self-initiated goal setting and self-evaluation. High level of personal awareness.

Level IV: Helping Others

Low --- High

1   2   3   4   5   6   7   8   9   10

Role model for wellness. Help others with their wellness.

FIGURE 9.2   Mary Sinclair's levels of responsibility for wellness.

Leslie McBride and I taught health education and physical education as one course to high school students using TPSR as the framework (Hellison and McBride, 1986). We introduced physical, emotional, and social health concepts in a format similar to awareness talks in the classroom. The students then went to the gym to experience these concepts. Classroom group meetings and reflection time for evaluating the effect of the experience on their health followed. The class discussed student participation in community action projects as outgrowths of these experiences.

SCHOOLWIDE ADOPTIONS OF TPSR

I have heard of a few schools that adopted some version of TPSR schoolwide. Closer to home, several schools and even one school district have invited me to conduct TPSR workshops and presentations. The impetus for these invitations came from the success of one or more PE teachers using TPSR in the school or district. I approach these invitations wary of across-the-board adoptions of TPSR or any other singular approach. Although students would benefit from having consistency across the curriculum—in some ways similar to a wraparound approach, especially if fully implemented in the halls, on the playground, and in extracurricular activities—such adoption may force teachers to abandon some of the things that work well for them and substitute a value-based approach that some teachers don't believe in. The test score mania, which has shrunk the margins that creative teachers work in, is a perfect example. After all, developing one's own values and beliefs is not an objective, scientific exercise. Science can't prove that TPSR, or any other approach for that matter, is good for kids. It can only show whether it works. My message in this book, as well as in any TPSR professional preparation work I do, is best expressed by Hugh Prather (1972):

> And so I am left with this belief: that there are no answers, that there are only alternatives. . . . If my words affirm you, [take them in], but if they cause you to distrust your own experience, spit them out.

I also relied on this quote in introducing my book *Beyond Balls and Bats* (Hellison, 1978), perhaps reflecting a lack of progress in my thinking. But I'd like to think it shows consistency in my belief that teachers can be self-directed.

Having shared my thoughts and feelings about mandatory adoptions, it may surprise you that I still accept invitations to discuss schoolwide adoption of TPSR. For starters, I share with teachers my skepticism about one size fitting all, just as I am doing now. I also teach that buy-in of foundational TPSR values—empowering kids to take personal and social responsibility and see whether it works in their lives plus developing the kind of teacher–student relationship that supports the transfer of these values to life—is essential. But if some do buy in, they need to adapt TPSR to their own setting, kids, and style and progress by self-paced successive approximations.

One middle school librarian volunteered to direct the schoolwide operation of TPSR. She created ID cards that stated whether the student was at cumulative Level III or IV. Students at Level III could use their IDs as hall passes, go to the library on their own, and enjoy other perks. Students at Level IV were eligible to do these things as well as engage in peer mediation, peer and cross-age teaching, and similar activities. Some teachers did not buy in, but most did, and students were receptive to receiving perks (no surprise). I struggled with the behavior modification involved in such a system and with definitions of being responsible that were entirely behavioral, thereby promoting doing the right thing without necessarily valuing or believing in it. I was involved in this implementation process, but given the importance of empowering the teachers as well as students who were using my value system, I kept my mouth shut. As suggested earlier, teachers tend to interpret the levels as behaviors rather than as intentions, attitudes, and behaviors. In my experience, this conflict comes with the territory.

TAKE-AWAYS

Here are some key points from this chapter that you might consider taking with you:

- Alternative structures that are voluntary, such as coaching clubs, cross-age teaching programs, and fitness centers, can offer small groups more relational experiences, provide more opportunities for leadership, and permit kids to specialize in activities they enjoy or want to improve in.

- Current structures such as classroom courses, health education courses, and playground activities can integrate TPSR values and sometimes supplement TPSR already present in the school.

- Integrating TPSR into interscholastic sport can modify the "winning is everything" perspective and promote teamwork, goal setting, human decency, and leadership.

10

Getting Started

The only person you get to change is yourself.

—*Carolyn Boyes-Watson*

▪ ▪ ▪ ▪ ▪

It may seem strange to name one of the last chapters in the book Getting Started, but readers who haven't tried TPSR and want to do so are faced with doing just that. As Kallusky advised (in Hellison et al., 2000, p. 207), "Start small, start smart, start and don't stop."

Getting started in implementing TPSR depends on many factors. Before suggesting some specific strategies for getting started, let's review some of these factors and their implications for TPSR.

CONTEXT

Although the TPSR core values, program leader's responsibilities (i.e., program themes), and the entire framework have been implemented in a wide range of settings, the specific context still influences the implementation process. For example, in-school PE differs from after-school PA, and public schools differ from alternative schools for high-needs kids. Settings also vary within a category, such as school (e.g., urban, rural, and the many different kinds of small schools now dotting the educational landscape). There are also "schools within schools," magnet schools, block scheduling, and other structural changes within schools—the list goes on.

It is risky to generalize, but a few observations may help to clarify the variety of ways TPSR can be employed. Public school PE is generally organized around large classes of 25 to 50 students. (If 50 students in a PE class sounds like an exaggeration, check the class sizes in southern California and New York City, among others.) Management and direct instruction typically dominate the teaching styles in these programs. TPSR is often used as a management tool to deal with discipline in class, but authentic implementation of TPSR conflicts with teacher-directed classroom management strategies (see McCaslin and Good, 1992). Because discipline is high on the management agenda, it's not surprising that TPSR is often adopted for that reason, as one data-based study found (Mrugala, 2002), and not for its core values. Fortunately, the same study also revealed that some teachers, after adopting the cumulative levels for management purposes, gradually shifted their priorities toward both a more holistic view of their students and being more relational with them. This result is supported by a review of a number of TPSR programs in urban and high-needs settings, which showed kids learning to be more respectful in TPSR programs (Hellison and Walsh, 2002).

The cumulative levels (chapter 3) address the class size issue by offering a simplified way to have kids evaluate their level of responsibility that day. However, problems described in chapter 4 arise when adopting cumulative levels. The intention is to give kids an opportunity to evaluate their own level of responsibility, not for the program leader to be the judge and jury or to bully students into "behaving." Used in a top-down way, it becomes just one more way to manage students without honoring the TPSR framework.

In addition, if Level V is omitted because outside-the-gym behavior cannot be evaluated in class, then TPSR becomes a less effective vehicle for life skills and values. For some—perhaps many—PE teachers, that was never their goal anyway. Their primary concern might be to reduce discipline problems in the gym (see chapter 8). TPSR can reduce the adversarial relationship between students and program leaders (in this case, PE teachers), but not without leaders respecting kids, listening to them, giving them a say in what goes on, and very gradually shifting responsibility to them. None of this is a problem as long as program leaders who don't adhere to the basic tenants of TPSR refrain from claiming to be doing TPSR (or worse, "Hellison's stuff"). Actually, all program leaders need to modify TPSR to fit their needs, so they always own it. But when key concepts and values are ignored, it is truly and fully their stuff!

Public school PE has experienced a major shift toward a standards-based curriculum nationally and in many states. This effort has been led by the National Association for Sport and Physical Education, which in 2004 promulgated six content standards (Lund and Tannehill, 2010). My concern, expressed in chapter 1, is that standards can become rigid mandates for all PE teachers. Lund and Tannehill were aware of this issue and suggested that a variety of options could be provided for teachers and that perhaps districts could adopt some specific curriculum models for guidance.

PA programs come in many shapes and sizes, making generalizations difficult. Some are part of after-school community schools with a director and staff who may or may not be associated with the school. Some are under the supervision of an in-school PA director who is responsible for physical activities outside of PE. Community-based organizations such as Boys and Girls Clubs and YMCAs have their own guidelines and initiatives. Micro-programs (e.g., the TPSR-based programs in Greensboro, Memphis, and San Francisco) are often housed in schools or community-based organizations but maintain a high degree of autonomy. In fact, a major feature of PA programs is flexibility.

Although the No Child Left Behind policy contained specific curricular requirements for after-school programs receiving federal funds, the federal landscape is changing. Many PA programs enjoy wide latitude in such areas as meeting time (how long, how often); choice of activities, either by the program leader, the kids, or some combination (if kids want a specific activity, that can usually be arranged); policies on uniforms, showers, squads, and other typical PE traditions; attendance, which may or may not be required, depending on the specific program; and discipline procedures (unruly kids can be sent home or suspended from a program for a specific period of time without administrative red tape; leaders just need to tell them to leave and when they can return). These PA programs occupy intermediate space (Noam, Biancarosa, and Dechausay, 2003);

they should not resemble being in school nor should they look like free play on the playground or in the street. Despite the apparent looseness of after-school PA programs, specific criteria for exemplary after-school programs in urban settings have been identified in the literature (see figure 1.2 on p. 9).

SELF-ASSESSMENT

Adopting a new program or curriculum model is a headache for most PE and PA professionals because it disrupts their current practice. And because it is new, stress escalates as problems pile up. Trying something different is often difficult for both kids and staff. That's why, before embarking on this journey, it is important to decide whether TPSR is worth doing (chapter 1). The TPSR questionnaire in figure 10.1 is designed to assist this decision-making process by asking specific questions that reflect TPSR's core values and the program leader's responsibilities (i.e., program themes). The primary issue is whether these principles are compatible with the setting and the program leader's beliefs and style (or style-to-be).

TPSR Teacher Questionnaire

1. Do you like kids, and can you relate to them?
2. Do you try to treat all kids as individuals?
3. Do you spend some time consciously focusing on students' strengths?
4. Do you listen to students and believe that they know things?
5. Do you share your power as a teacher with students?
6. Do you help your students solve their own conflicts so that they can do so on their own?
7. Do you help your students learn to control their negative statements and temper, or do they rely on you to control them?
8. Do you help students include everybody in the activities so that they can do so on their own?
9. Do you give students opportunities to work independently and on their own goals?
10. Do your students have a voice in evaluating each lesson and solving problems that arise?
11. Do your students have opportunities to individually reflect on how well they respect others, put effort and cooperation into their activities, are self-directed, perform helping and leadership roles, and try these things in their lives?
12. Do your students have opportunities to assume meaningful leadership roles such as teaching and coaching?
13. Do you place some emphasis on transferring the levels from your class to students' lives outside your program?
14. Do your students leave your program understanding what taking responsibility means and how it applies to them?

FIGURE 10.1 Answering these questions will help you decide whether TPSR is worth doing.

This is not a beginner's version. The questions represent an ideal TPSR program, but they also provide a vision to shoot for. Although sitting on a one-legged chair doesn't work very well, the chair needs to be built a leg at a time. It is helpful to envision the TPSR implementation process as a series of quasi-sequential stages toward the complete model as described in earlier chapters. Take a step, evaluate it (ah, self-reflection again), tinker with it if needed, and move on to the next step in the process. During this process, the focus is primarily on the task at hand, doing the current step in the progression as effectively as possible while attending to backsliding and similar interruptions. Keep in mind that this is only one stage in a developmental process and that more development lies ahead.

The TPSR questionnaire can be a compatibility check with both the levels of responsibility and the five themes. Here are the themes and the questionnaire items that ask about them:

- Empowerment: questions 4, 5, 6, 7, 8, 9, 10, 11, 12
- Self-reflection: questions 10, 11
- Integration of responsibility with the physical activity lesson: questions 6, 7, 8, 9, 11
- Teacher–student relationship: questions 1, 2, 3, 4, 5
- Transfer outside the gym: questions 12, 13

FIRST STEPS

One of the key criteria in figure 1.2 is to "provide courageous and persistent leadership in the face of systemic obstacles" (Hellison and Cutforth, 1997). In my experience, that is much easier said than done. Obstacles depend to a large extent on the setting and the leadership of the principal or site director. Kids are not obstacles; kids are kids! They are the reason for doing this work. Of course, as has already been stated, when introducing anything new, especially if the process differs considerably from the familiar, a good rule of thumb is to outlast the kids. That just means hanging in there while hanging on to what's worth doing. Eventually, TPSR implementation will get easier, especially as relationships with kids become less adversarial and as at least some kids begin to work independently, to help each other, and to take on small and then larger leadership roles. These changes in turn free the program leader to work with the kids who are "responsibility challenged" and help those who need a little push to become more self-directed or caring.

So what are these first steps? Some suggestions are coming up, but they are just that—suggestions. Program leaders need to create their own steps (ah, empowerment). Sometimes early in the step-by-step process, the program leader gets bogged down. Getting stuck in an early step may just mean that, right now, no more changes can be made. The kids may be on the verge of rebelling, or the program leader may be fully occupied with whatever changes have already been made. Maybe his or her "chaos level" or comfort zone has been reached or exceeded. Or the setting contains barriers that are too difficult to negotiate. Slowing down or stopping sometimes makes good sense, but eventually, digging deeper will help to make the TPSR program more authentic.

KID QUOTES

"If you want to go around musty [without a shower], it's your choice."—High school freshman

"It helped me believe in myself."—Seventh-grader

"What I disliked about this program is that we should have had it a long time ago."—Sixth-grader

The general rule—to start small, start smart, but start and don't stop—was introduced in the opening paragraph of this chapter. The safest way to begin is to add or adjust something that will only minimally disrupt the program. If this small change works, it opens the door to taking more steps. If the change doesn't work, the program leader should take a step back. PE teachers who have a number of classes can reduce the risk further by experimenting with one class for a trial period. If it works better than the current program, expansion can proceed. If the trial fails, the teacher can step back. For PE teachers who choose to work with one class at first, some select their most disruptive class, figuring they have little to lose. Others start with one of their best-behaved classes, reasoning that if it doesn't work there, it won't work anywhere.

As a cautionary note, give the change enough time to succeed or fail on its own merits. Remember, everyone in the program will be new at this. My advice on outlasting the kids' initial attitudes as well as those of the critics applies here: Outlast the initial struggle and the inevitable mistakes.

It makes sense to start at the beginning, by introducing Levels I and II in a brief awareness talk. Respect for others and active participation are familiar territory to PE and PA professionals, and although the TPSR framework differs considerably from traditional practice, empowerment is less pronounced at first and therefore less challenging for program leaders with little experience in letting go of authority. If nothing else, the levels offer a vocabulary and a progression for talking with kids about *self*-control and the importance of effort in developing skills and fitness (or, if it makes more sense for a particular group, talking about their responsibilities without using the levels structure). Teaching practices that don't encourage students to take responsibility obviously will hinder the development of personal and social responsibility, but awareness is a beginning. Keep the awareness talks brief. Long-windedness is typical of beginners and sometimes veterans as well.

Also, check students' body language (are eyes rolling?) to better recognize whether they are understanding or buying in to the message. Use language kids understand and can relate to. The word *respect* might work for Level I, but *self-control* might be better. Maybe another word is better yet. Or ask the kids what words they would use. One of Missy Parker's students suggested "Just do it" for Level II when that Nike slogan was popular.

Fran Zavacky (1997), an elementary school PE teacher in Virginia, together with her students, her teaching partner, and his students wrote descriptions stating what each level would look like in the physical education setting. Students accepted the descriptions because they resulted from collaboration between students and teachers. The discussions involved in developing the descriptions helped create an environment where students had the courage to try new things without worrying about their peers' reactions. The students began to see how they could fit in and still succeed at their individual developmental levels. During the school year, we watched the students grow into cooperative, caring young people who challenged themselves more than we as teachers could have done, and who supported each other in ways we did not anticipate. (p. 30)

As a variation of Fran's process, consider having students suggest some respect rules for the class. Ask them to share things they don't want done to themselves, and perhaps include them in a revised definition of Level I. In a creative twist, elementary school teacher Aleita Hass-Holcombe has used a tape recorder in the corner of the gym so that her children could go over and listen to the latest awareness talk message from the secret agent!

After awareness talks are under way, adding a brief reflection time at the end of every session is a natural follow-up because it gives students a chance to apply the levels to themselves. It's one thing to hear the program leader saying something like "I want you to take more responsibility for controlling your criticism of others." It's quite another to have to demonstrate self-control in the program or else face evaluating yourself for not being under control. A simple show of hands (yes or no) for Levels I and II or pointing thumbs up (yes), sideways, or down (no) is quick and easy to teach and learn. This also provides an opportunity to get some sense of how kids evaluate themselves, how honest they are.

Occasional—and then more frequent—group meetings can be inserted into the program. Kids can gather after the physical activities and share one thing they liked or disliked about the program that day. Even if only two students are called on, student voices are being acknowledged. If time permits, the rest of the group can be asked by a show of hands who agrees with those who spoke. That way, everyone has a small opportunity to contribute their views. Running an effective group meeting takes more skill than conducting an awareness talk or reflection time, although all of these strategies require some skills. The program leader has to pay close attention to kids' comments on the program and each other in order to respond appropriately, including making some change that has been suggested if it could improve the program. If no adjustments are ever made, the group meeting process becomes meaningless to the kids.

ADVANCED STEPS

Somewhere in this process, Levels III and IV need to be integrated into the program. These advanced levels require that kids be empowered to practice them. Strategies that introduce a moderate version of empowerment, such as station choice for Level III and reciprocal coaching for Level IV, provide limited oppor-

TPSR *in Action*

I have discovered that TPSR crosses over into new cultures and societies through my experiences in South Africa, specifically in the Kayamandi Township. During my time in Kayamandi, the leaders of a local nonprofit asked me to run two sport programs for the community children, and we were also asked to train the facilitators from the community on how to deliver a sport program based on positive youth development. My thoughts immediately jumped to the TPSR model. Although this environment was completely different from anything that I had ever experienced, we shared the fundamental belief in teaching youth how to take personal and social responsibility. I worked with the facilitators to fine-tune the TPSR model so that it could be effective in the Xhosa culture, and our approach continued to evolve as we ran the two sport programs for over 30 underserved youth. We focused on *imbeko* (respect) with the children, and we watched this transfer into the soccer games, with trash cans serving as goalposts and bare feet running everywhere. Through this experience, I discovered that the TPSR model has the potential to effect change in the lives of youth in countries and cultures outside of the United States.

Meredith Whitley, Michigan State University

tunities for kids to demonstrate responsible self-direction and leadership. This process will need to be individualized and peppered with brief one-on-one guidance meetings, because students differ, sometimes widely, in their ability to be self-directed and take on leadership roles, even in the early stages. Some need more direct instruction; some soar without much assistance. The smaller the class size, the more individualizing and nurturing can be done (obviously). In all cases, individual progressions will be needed (see the Level III and IV strategies in chapters 3 and 5).

Level V can wait until at least some students show that they can handle the first four levels reasonably well. Exploring transfer outside the gym is difficult because the climate is usually much less supportive. Kids therefore need successful experiences with Level V in class first (see Level V strategies in chapters 3 and 5).

For most program leaders, changing how physical activities are taught is the most difficult part of implementing TPSR, for the following reasons:

- Unlike the physical activity lesson, the awareness talk, group meeting, and reflection time are new add-ons rather than a common aspect of daily teaching and coaching.

- Embedding responsibility in the activity lesson requires changing standard practices that most program leaders have been doing for some time and probably with considerable confidence.

- Integration also requires the knowledge and pedagogical skills to teach the physical activity; the knowledge, pedagogical skills, and qualities to teach responsibility described earlier; and the ability to integrate the two.

Except for courageous souls, it is best to tiptoe into embedding responsibility strategies in the planned activities. Some strategies can be integrated without disrupting the curriculum or program plan, such as the following:

- Introduce inclusion activities and rules (e.g., in floor hockey, everyone must touch the puck before the team shoots).
- Set up stations with different tasks, and progress to students choosing stations they want to work at.
- Introduce self-paced challenges, such as an individualized progression of soccer kicking and trapping activities.
- Reciprocal coaching is easy to work into most motor skill drills by partnering students. Teach three or so skill cues to help the coach guide his or her partner at a specific task, such as taking five shots at the basket.

Physical activity lesson strategies for discipline and motivation problems can meet an immediate need. Consider the following:

- If needed, install a talking bench for arguments between two students, although they may need guidance in how to talk to each other about the problem.
- DeLine's (1991) "no plan, no play" strategy, or sit-out progressions, could be effective for abusive game players; both are described in chapter 6.
- Task modification (e.g., "Do as many sit-ups as you can," "Get close enough to the goal [or target] so you can be successful; then back up") might improve students' motivation in drills.

Advanced integration strategies require that the program leader have confidence in dealing with uncertainty and possible chaos. They also require kids who are at least somewhat competent at the first steps in taking responsibility. The following are examples of ways to integrate TPSR into physical activity, further empowering students:

- The accordion principle can be used occasionally for the entire group, but it is more useful for individuals and small groups when they can be entrusted to choose from some options, officiate their own games, take on leadership roles, or assume other responsibilities described in past chapters. Many such strategies can be employed in small steps or in advanced applications of TPSR.
- Instead of one game, a choice of games can be offered—for example, competitive and recreational, or competitive and cooperative, or game play versus practice, perhaps using task cards for the practice. This approach requires a brief talk beforehand about how to choose and a brief reflection time afterward to ask students whether their choices worked for them.

Some program leaders have deviated markedly from this progression. In New Zealand, Barrie Gordon reported that a local middle school PE teacher, with Barrie's help, implemented TPSR and within three months had her students choosing their own fitness activities in the first 15 minutes of class. In a surprise move, one of the two classes in which she implemented TPSR voted to come in for physical education on a day that school was not in session!

Jeff Walsh (Hellison, 1983) took a two-hour workshop and then called me about three months later to say that he thought he had everything that I talked about in place with his kids, and he did! Mike DeBusk took a TPSR class and then implemented his whole program plan at once in a PA program for kids in trouble. He followed that experience with installing the whole TPSR model in his elementary school PE class. His program was so "by the book" that when he visited one of my programs, he said to me, "You aren't doing the model!" Matt Smith (1990) started his junior high school students with awareness talks and then jumped to the development of personal plans for Level III time. He then added reflection time and group meetings. Chicago-area elementary PE teacher Kathy Woyner introduced awareness talks, reflection time, and self-grading at the same time in her upper-elementary PE classes.

As I've argued, TPSR program leaders can continue to advance their understanding and practice of TPSR indefinitely. The suggestions throughout this book represent a buffet of choices. They need to be carefully selected, taking stock along the way to be certain that TPSR practices already in place don't drop off the agenda (unless they are being replaced by more promising ideas and strategies).

It is helpful to be imaginative—"What's possible?"—at this stage. For example, in response to criticism of the traditional two- or three-week unit that emphasizes exposure over improvement (Siedentop, 1991), Liz Nixon and I added a Level III day near the end of every third unit in a Portland, Oregon, high school PE program. During Level III time, students chose to work on selected skills in the current unit, skills from previous units, or fitness activities offered in all units. We placed students not willing or able to handle such independence in a teacher-directed group and gave them a one-week unit focused on a specific activity. For this to work, the teacher-directed group needs to be offered to everyone (some may want to do it to be with their friends or for other reasons). Those who haven't proven themselves able to do Level III work should be "invited" to join the teacher-directed group (e.g., "So far you haven't been able to be responsible on your own, so you'll have to be with me until you're ready"). Level IV student leaders can help monitor the Level III activities while the program leader takes charge of the teacher-directed group. Sometimes an advanced student leader can assume this responsibility.

Such scheduling depends on the teaching station and available equipment, but creativity also helps. I've conducted volleyball drills in the wrestling room and volleyball and martial arts stations in the weight room (beware of flying missiles!).

A related approach is to select one physical activity as the theme for the year or semester. Each week, students develop further in the theme activity. Fitness is a common theme, but a sport would work by creating a modified version of sport education (Siedentop, 1994). I have had some success in an alternative high school concentrating on volleyball for about half of each PE class for the entire year, to the point that students began to see themselves as a volleyball team rather than a class.

Before the program formally begins, Level III time—where kids work on their goals or personal plans, or just hang out—can be offered, along with relational time and, if necessary, role taking. If things are going well, Level III time can be extended into the lesson.

TEACHING AS A SUBVERSIVE ACTIVITY

When trying to make program changes, the setting matters. Conducting in-school PE is not a walk in the park in some—perhaps many—schools. Often, there is little support for change unless it comes top down from the administration. Many times, colleagues (who often complain about the current state of affairs) oppose change, and any effort to change the status quo, even in just one class, has to take place amid a hundred other pressing duties and responsibilities. Therefore, motivation has to be high just to get started.

In some schools, innovative teaching is treated as a subversive activity. For this reason, new program leaders need to be careful about sharing a new approach such as TPSR with other staff. They may not be very enthusiastic and may say things like, "We've tried that before" or "You'll learn better eventually." The motivation for these rebuffs can take many forms, including jealousy or the fear that they may be asked to do something new. Typically, staff and administrators won't spend much time checking on what one program leader is doing unless they have reason to suspect that something weird is going on. If the kids like TPSR (and they often do because they are given choices and opportunities to share their ideas and to lead), they can certainly tell their parents about it, but if they talk to other students, who in turn complain to other staff members about not being given choices and so on, look out!

Telling parents can sometimes work wonders. Walt Kelly, a high school physical education teacher in Bozeman, Montana, was called into the principal's office to discuss what he was doing in PE. Walt prepared himself for a reprimand, but the principal just wanted to know what he was teaching about responsibility. Parents had been calling the principal to share their excitement about what their kids were learning from Walt! Jeff Walsh's principal, a former coach and physical education teacher, pressured him to go back to traditional PE. When Jeff told his kids about the principal's request, they groaned and asked what they could do about it. Jeff replied, "Nothing, unless you want to tell your parents." The next day the principal came to see Jeff and said, "Jeff, we could have worked it out!" He left Jeff alone after that.

Class size is an obstacle to doing TPSR effectively, but Jeff Walsh knew better than to argue with his school district about how his large classes interfered with his curriculum goals. Instead, he went to his principal (the same guy) and argued that he needed class size reductions for safety reasons. After a month had passed with no action, he wrote the school district. They came out, observed, and told the principal to cut the class size! (Good thing Jeff was tenured!)

The vice principal of a large high school told Bill White and me that he had no money to pay for videos of skills being correctly performed, which we needed to individualize our classes. So we wrote a proposal for a small state grant for classroom improvements. We didn't get the grant, but when the vice principal read a copy of the letter, he called us in and said he had no idea that we were teaching responsibility and honoring individuality, something he, as a fat kid, never got. He gave us the money.

Those who stay in the mainstream won't need to confront most of these problems. But those who try to implement TPSR or some other departure from business as usual need to be prepared to weather the storm. Fortunately, education has become more enlightened and open to change in recent years, especially from truly student-centered administrators and teachers, but it doesn't hurt to anticipate problems that usually accompany the implementation of innovative practices.

Even if the staff is supportive, kids may not be very receptive. The longer they have been doing traditional PE, especially if they were successful or having fun, the more difficult it will be for them to adapt to change. (Remember my story from chapter 7 about the kid in my class who wrote an essay in English called "PE Makes You Hate"!) Taking small steps enables students to adjust to change. One of the program leader's qualities discussed in chapter 7, persistence, sometimes calls for outlasting students. Of course, persistence needs to be accompanied by listening and observing, sizing up the situation, and making adjustments. The goal, however, remains the same: to help kids become more responsible.

◀◀◀ TAKE-AWAYS ▶▶▶

Here are some key points from this chapter that you might consider taking with you:

- Because TPSR is, at its heart, a way of teaching, the first decision is whether TPSR is worth the resistance that might be encountered. The TPSR teacher questionnaire (figure 10.1) can help, as long as it is understood that the statements describe an ideal version of TPSR, a distant vision for most of us. That's okay, because implementation is a gradual progression toward the ideal version of TPSR.

- The first steps usually involve the introduction of Levels I and II in a brief awareness talk, followed soon after by a brief reflection time at the end of the lesson.

- Subsequent steps involve gradually implementing the other levels and a group meeting, and eventually introducing responsibility strategies during the physical activity lesson.

- Sometimes TPSR needs to be treated as a subversive activity because the various stakeholders—other teachers, administrators, parents, and even students—may find these ideas too radical. In these instances, it helps to rely more on actions and less on arguments as much as possible, but, as an old military saying goes, be prepared to "keep your head down and out of sight!" On the other hand, parents can be effective advocates of the program if they notice positive changes in their children (which means they have observed some examples of Level V, transfer outside the gym).

11

Assessment and Evaluation Strategies

with Paul M. Wright

Those personal qualities that we hold dear are exceedingly difficult to assess, [so] we are apt to measure what we can, and eventually come to value what is measured.

—Arthur Wise

■ ■ ■ ■ ■

Assessment of in-school PE typically includes the evaluation of students' performances, teachers' performances, and sometimes the program itself. Of these, student assessment receives the highest priority, although the standards/accountability movement has influenced both teacher assessment and program evaluation. Assessment of after-school programs varies considerably from site to site. However, the need for external (and sometimes internal) funding, accompanied by an increasing demand for assessment plans and results, has ratcheted up the need for valid assessment procedures.

Much has been written about program evaluation in general (e.g., Greene, 2000) as well as specific applications in PE (e.g., Lund and Tannehill, 2010) and after-school programs (e.g., Eccles and Gootman, 2002). O'Sullivan and Henninger (2000) have even written on the assessment of "student responsibility and cooperation" in PE. Despite the growth of designs and procedures for program evaluation and learner assessment, McLaughlin (2000) raised important concerns about the overemphasis on measuring program impact. The reality, she argued, is that "process is product in a quality youth organization" (p. 24). Rather than focus on fixing specific (e.g., quantitative) deficits such as dropout rates and drug abuse, youth programs "might be more accurately judged on interim measures such as the development of leadership skills, emotional competencies, and attitudes of responsibility" (p. 24). In other words, as Karen Pittman memorably stated, "Problem free does not mean fully prepared" (Benson, 1997, p. 18).

For TPSR to work effectively, feedback must be gathered in the form of assessment from a number of sources, and the assessment strategies used need to reflect the core values and themes of TPSR thereby prioritizing human decency, positive relationships, and the whole person as well as self-reflection, empowerment, and transfer. Therefore, in this chapter we share a number of field-tested strategies and instruments that align with and support assessment in TPSR programs. A number of the instruments described here can also be located on the TPSR Toolbox Group Web site (www.tpsr-alliance.org/toolbox).

STUDENT ASSESSMENT

Student assessment ought to reflect the presence of TPSR in two ways: first, by giving students feedback on the program leader's perceptions of the extent to which they are taking personal and social responsibility in class, and second, by empowering students to share in the assessment process. Both of these approaches are built into the TPSR daily program format as multiple chances for reflection and discussion regarding individual and group responsibility. Informal strategies such as program leader observations, verbal checks for understanding, and debriefing sessions are very important in helping the program leader and students stay focused on what is important in the program and how they are doing.

Some program leaders may want (or need) to complement ongoing informal student assessment with more formal and systematic approaches. Although these strategies require additional time and planning, many of us find they are worth it because they help us document student performance, establish goals for improvement, assess change over time, and share student work. The next two sections provide specific examples of informal and formal assessment strategies we have found particularly useful and easy to align with TPSR.

Informal Student Assessments

Informal assessment and feedback on student responsibility should be continual and integrated with TPSR instruction. In this section we highlight how this can be accomplished in the group meeting and reflection time. These parts of the TPSR daily program format involve students in the assessment process.

The group meeting enables students to evaluate the class as a whole and comment on how specific individuals acted in class that day. Sometimes in the group meeting, students criticize other students—for example, for not cooperating or losing their temper. These incidents must be handled carefully, but as long as the student or students being criticized have an opportunity to respond and the process is carried out respectfully, everyone involved receives feedback. Program leaders also have an opportunity to share their feedback with students, not only about the process but also about whether the criticism was justified. In addition, student leaders and coaches need to be encouraged to tell everyone how their assignment—their mini-lesson or their team coaching performance—went and what positive contributions the students they worked with made to the group or team.

Again, this approach provides feedback for everyone involved (along with the benefit of pointing out student role models of Level IV), and it gives program leaders an opportunity to share their feedback. They must, however, share their feedback last! The program leader is only one voice in this process, and students' authority to share their views may be usurped if the program leader talks first. Of course, he or she can take over—this isn't a full-fledged democracy, although it should be heading in that direction. But taking control is only necessary if kids need guidance—for example, on how to talk to each other or how to focus or listen more. Too much "guidance" can set back the empowerment process. A balance needs to be achieved so that kids' voices are respected.

Reflection time more directly addresses student assessment, because the point is to have kids assess themselves on how well they put the levels into practice that day. If they point their thumbs, raise their hands, hold up a number of fingers, or tap in and out, the program leader receives feedback about their perceptions and can make occasional comments—"Yes, I saw that," "You're being hard on yourself," "I thought that needed some work," "Should that be a goal for you?"

Formal Student Assessments

Sometimes very little is required to make the shift from informal to formal assessments. The type of reflection and processing that occurs during the group meeting and reflection time, as described in the previous section, can be made formal simply by having students write it down in a daily log or assessment (see figures 11.1 and 11.2 for examples).

Another option would be to periodically ask students to write reflections in a program journal. Diane Coleman, an elementary PE teacher in Memphis, Tennessee, made use of the journaling strategy to work around the time constraints placed on her (i.e., seeing the kids twice a week for only 25 minutes in which she had to address personal and social responsibility as well as all of the other content mandated in the national standards; NASPE, 2004). Ideally, strategies such as daily logs, assessments, and journals would be used in addition to, rather than instead of, group processing. With that said, an added benefit of these strategies is that they provide documentation of student performance and give the program leader another mode of providing feedback (i.e., written responses to the students' work).

Creating and Using Rubrics

Documenting the reflective process is valuable, but some program leaders also want assessment strategies and procedures that allow them to categorize or rate student performance. The rubric Don developed that is shown in figure 11.3, although "excessively general" for a rubric according to one assessment expert, illustrates the concept of rubric use with the levels. Another example, developed by Paul, is shown in figure 11.4. Either of these rubrics can be used, appropriately tightened and worded to be age appropriate, by the program leader to give students feedback or to grade their levels of personal and social responsibility.

Student Daily Log

Name: _____ Date: _____

Please rate aspects of today's program below by putting a check in the box after each item that best represents your opinion. Be honest in your responses. Some items are about the program leader, some are about the class in general, and some are about you personally.

Program aspect	Strongly agree	Agree	Not sure	Disagree	Strongly disagree
Today, the program leader talked about the importance of respect and self-control.					
The program leader encouraged everyone to participate and try hard.					
The program leader let students ask questions and make suggestions today.					
In today's lesson, students had a chance to lead or demonstrate.					
Today, the program leader talked about being responsible outside of school.					
Overall, everyone in class showed respect and good self-control today.					
We, as a class, participated and tried hard today.					
Today, several students asked questions and made suggestions.					
Today, several students had an opportunity to lead or demonstrate.					
Today, I showed respect and had good self-control.					
I participated and tried hard today.					
I made suggestions and asked questions in today's discussion.					
I was able to lead or demonstrate in today's lesson.					

Please add any additional comments you have about today's lesson: _____

_____

_____

_____

_____

FIGURE 11.1 A sample daily log for students is a simple method of formal assessment.

From D. Hellison, 2011, *Teaching personal and social responsibility through physical activity, 3rd edition* (Champaign, IL: Human Kinetics).

Kung Fu Club Assessment

Name: _____ Date: _____

Please rate the program so far (1 = Needs work; 2 = Okay; 3 = Great):

Good experience _____   Learned something _____
Good workout _____   Instructor _____

Rate your level of responsibility so far (1 = Needs work; 2 = Okay; 3 = Great):

Self-control _____   Leadership _____
Effort _____   True martial artist _____
Self-direction _____

Rate your fitness level so far (1 = Needs work; 2 = Okay; 3 = Great):

Strength _____   Flexibility _____
Cardio _____   Body composition _____

Rate your martial arts skills so far (0 = Not yet; 1 = Working on it; 2 = Good at it; 3 = Can teach it):

Attention stance _____   Block up/down _____
Bow _____   Jab _____
Fighting stance _____   Cross _____
Switch _____   Footwork with partner _____
Double switch _____   Polish the mirror _____
Slide _____   Toe fighting _____
Step _____

Describe a goal that you will work on for next week: _____

_____

_____

_____

_____

Write in any other comments you wish to add: _____

_____

_____

_____

_____

Thanks!

FIGURE 11.2 This sample student assessment for a kung fu club allows students to easily assess themselves and the program.

Responsibility Rubric

Name: _____ Date: _____

	Consistently	Sporadically	Seldom	Never
Contributes to own well-being	☐	☐	☐	☐
Demonstrates effort and self-motivation	☐	☐	☐	☐
Is independent	☐	☐	☐	☐
Sets goals	☐	☐	☐	☐
Contributes to others' well-being	☐	☐	☐	☐
Respects others	☐	☐	☐	☐
Helps others	☐	☐	☐	☐
Exhibits leadership	☐	☐	☐	☐

FIGURE 11.3 A simple rubric illustrating rubric use with the levels.

From D. Hellison, 2011, *Teaching personal and social responsibility through physical activity, 3rd edition* (Champaign, IL: Human Kinetics).

Rubric for Assessing Responsible Behavior

Name: _____ Date: _____

Responsible behavior	Description	All of the time	Most of the time	Some of the time	None of the time
Respect	Student does no harm to others verbally or physically; includes/works well with others; resolves conflicts peacefully if they emerge.	3	2	1	0
Participation	Student tries every activity and takes on various roles when asked.	3	2	1	0
Effort	Student tries hard to master every task and focuses on improvement.	3	2	1	0
Self-direction	Student stays on task without direct instruction or supervision whether working alone or with others; does not seem to follow bad examples or succumb to peer pressure.	3	2	1	0
Caring	Student helps, encourages others, and offers positive feedback.	3	2	1	0

FIGURE 11.4 A sample rubric for assessing students' levels of personal and social responsibility.

From D. Hellison, 2011, *Teaching personal and social responsibility through physical activity, 3rd edition* (Champaign, IL: Human Kinetics).

Although rubrics provide valuable information, they do not involve students in the assessment process. To achieve this, student leaders could be directed to use such rubrics to evaluate students they have worked with. Students could also evaluate themselves using the rubric. These different uses of the rubric can comprise a progression from program leader directed to student directed. Yet another way to share power with students and involve them in the assessment process is to ask for their input in the development of a responsibility rubric. Who knows? They might come up with one that is not excessively general!

Having the program leader and students fill out rubrics separately and compare notes can also be interesting. Hichwa (1998) had his middle school PE students grade themselves with a modified rubric: *Done consistently, Done most of the time,* or *Done inconsistently.* They wrote their self-grades for the following on 5-by-7-inch cards:

- Works to personal best
- Follows rules and is cooperative
- Takes care of equipment
- Is thoughtful and helpful to others
- Improves fitness and skill scores

Hichwa also graded each student in the same way and met individually with students whose ratings did not match his to discuss the differences. Another useful strategy he developed was using an attendance form to record his daily observations, as follows:

- 1 = Works and tries hard
- 2 = Follows rules
- 3 = Respects equipment
- 4 = Respects others
- 5 = Cares for and helps others

If the behavior was negative, he placed a minus next to the number. This system gave him specific data to discuss with his kids.

Don created a self-evaluation approach for skill development based on rubrics. From time to time, he hands students a list of the skills they have been learning and practicing and asks them to rate themselves. The evaluation categories range from a low score of 1 to a high score of 5:

- 1 = I haven't tried it yet.
- 2 = I'm working on it.
- 3 = I can demonstrate it correctly.
- 4 = I can perform it correctly in a game or situation.
- 5 = I can teach it to someone so that they learn it correctly.

For rubrics such as these to work as self-assessments, program leaders must take some time to teach kids what each category means. It is also important to make sure they are comfortable being honest (i.e., they won't be singled out or given a consequence if they admit to a shortcoming). We have used this approach with both middle and high school students, and most of them needed help to get started. However, they often express interest in evaluating their skills this way after they understand what to do.

The rubric examples give students the opportunity to measure themselves against set categories. Other assessments, such as the sample in figure 11.2, provide opportunities for students to assess themselves on the TPSR levels as well as their development in fitness, motor skills, and conceptual knowledge. It is worth noting for PE teachers under pressure to address all of the NASPE (2004) standards that assessing personal and social responsibility is not in conflict with assessing the other content you teach; it can be integrated with and even shape the assessment of performance in other learning domains. Many of our students who are not particularly fond of writing show interest in charting their progress in assessment workbooks. Jerry Guthrie's workbook *Be Your Own Coach* (1982) used soccer to illustrate some creative ways for students to measure their own progress. They are shown in figures 11.5 and 11.6.

Measuring Your Skills

Name: _____ Date: _____

You can measure soccer skills and body fitness in several ways:

Counting: How many juggles? _____

Timing: How fast through cones? _____

Accuracy: How many accurate shots? _____

Sometimes you may combine two or more of these measurements:

How many hops over the ball in 30 seconds? _____

FIGURE 11.5 A sample from Jerry Guthrie's assessment workbook.
Adapted from Guthrie 1982.

Record-Keeping Tips

Keeping regular and accurate records of your self-coached practice is easy when you follow a couple of simple tips:

1. *Keep your recording simple and convenient.* Carrying a three-by-five index card or notebook will allow you to make regular recording of your skill measurements.

2. *Transfer your measurements from the small record to a permanent chart.* A wall chart posted in a conspicuous place will allow you to see how your measurements look over a long period.

FIGURE 11.6 Tips for helping students to improve their record-keeping skills.

Giving Students a Say in Grading

Although the issue of grading applies more directly to PE teachers, TPSR program leaders in other settings may also want or need to periodically evaluate their students' overall performances. We suggest thinking of ways to give students a voice in that process, too. In many of the preceding examples, rubrics were used to rate performance on specific tasks or behaviors that should be demonstrated along the way in a program (i.e., formative assessments). As noted, these formative assessments can be administered by the program leader or the student. The same option exists at the end of a program or unit when it is time to make a final determination regarding the students' overall performance (i.e., summative assessment). In most schools and programs that serve youth, adults make these decisions on their own without involving their students. In a TPSR program, this practice has serious limitations:

> As long as grading is not part of the assessment process, the feedback from assessment can facilitate the development of responsibility. However . . . if a teacher links assessment to grading, students must share in this process in order to be true to [TPSR]. . . . Truly authentic assessment [of responsibility] must . . . include a gradual shift in responsibility from the teacher to the students. (Parker and Hellison 2001, p. 27)

Giving students a say in grading, or self-grading, can be done in other ways as well. Lambert and Grube (1988) had their high school students in Rock Springs, Wyoming, grade themselves using the responsibility levels. The teachers scheduled conferences to resolve conflicts between their grades and those of their students. The result became part of the grade. Junior high school teacher Jeff Walsh and high school teachers Gayle McDonald and Tom Hinton created the self-grading scorecard shown in figure 11.7 to offer students input on their grades. They developed one-sentence descriptors for various aspects of each level. Both the student and the teacher grade the student on each component, and the teacher then assigns a grade after considering the student's input.

Redefining Success in Self-Grading

Chapter 5 includes a set of Level II strategies to help students redefine success so that, with sufficient effort, they can reach it. As it applies to PE, one approach that makes TPSR sense is to build redefining success into the grading system. Doing this pretty much eliminates students' comparing grades, at least in relation to "who's best." At the same time, students must learn to respect definitions of success other than their own (i.e., not making fun of less skilled students who have defined success as improvement or even participation). Students may prefer to be graded by their improvement, especially if their performance in the skill or fitness component being assessed can be improved or, from a standards perspective, should be improved. Another approach is to give students the choice of being graded on improvement or achievement, or some combination of the two. This approach could be taken even further by giving students options that assess various skills, talents, or intelligences. For example, at the end of a volleyball unit, students could choose to be graded on

Self-Grading Scorecard

Name: _____ Date: _____

Level	Behavior	Self-grade	Teacher grade
I	Does not call others names	_____	_____
I	Controls temper	_____	_____
I	Does not disrupt class	_____	_____
II	Is on time to class	_____	_____
II	Tries new activities	_____	_____
II	Listens to instructions	_____	_____
III	Makes and follows contract	_____	_____
III	Writes in journal every day	_____	_____
IV	Shares equipment	_____	_____
IV	Treats others kindly	_____	_____
IV	Shows good sporting behavior	_____	_____

FIGURE 11.7 A self-grading scorecard like this one can give students a voice in the grading process.

From D. Hellison, 2011, *Teaching personal and social responsibility through physical activity, 3rd edition* (Champaign, IL: Human Kinetics). Adapted from Jeff Walsh, Gayle McDonald and Tom Hinton.

improvement or achievement in either a skill test *or* a cognitive test on rules, tactics, and skill analysis.

Self-evaluation forms such as the self-report in figure 5.2 in chapter 5 (see pp. 75-76) help students become aware of their own needs, thereby setting the stage for goal setting. Gary Kuney combined several of these options in a contract he offered to his K-8 students as shown in figure 11.8. In this self-grading contract for fitness, he first asked students to rate their present fitness and their goal. Note that they could choose *I don't care*. We've found that students treat all the choices more seriously when the full range is included. Moreover, if they truly don't care, we'd like to know. We want them to have the opportunity to express their low motivation to us (rather than behind our backs); then we can negotiate. They also have a choice of whether to participate in some competitive events. Finally, they get to choose how they will be evaluated. Gary's contract is complicated: lots of choices for kids, and lots of work for him. We include it here only to broaden the ways we think about redefining success in self-grading, and it doesn't hurt anyone to see a program leader willing and able to pull off something like Gary's plan.

What About Level V (Outside the Gym)?

Jeff Walsh, Gayle McDonald, and Tom Hinton created the scorecard shown in figure 11.7 before Don had conceived of Level V, which explains why they did

Self-Grading Contract

Name: _____ Grade: _____

Rate Your Present Fitness Level

____ Pro   ____ Excellent   ____ Good   ____ Okay   ____ So-so

____ Could be better   ____ I don't care

Where Would You Like to Be?

____ Pro   ____ Excellent   ____ Good   ____ Okay   ____ So-so

____ Could be better   ____ I don't care

Grouping I Want to Be In

____ Noncompetitive   ____ Competitive

Select Four Goals or One Lab and Two Goals

____ Goal A: Book report on fitness

____ Goal B: Pass test on fitness concepts

____ Goal C: Improve fitness

____ Goal D: Give written report on history

____ Goal E: Work with others in positive manner

____ Goal F: Give it your best shot

____ Goal G: Adhere to safety rules

____ Lab A: Aerobics development lab

____ Lab B: Strength development lab

I agree to fill this learning plan.

Student:_____

Witness (teacher): _____

FIGURE 11.8   Gary Kuney's self-grading fitness contract for K-8 students.
Adapted from Gary Kuney.

not include it. Even now, exclusion of Level V is a common practice of in-school PE teachers, as pointed out in an earlier chapter. Although we usually view such omissions as a flaw in the practice of TPSR, grading is about student performance in class, so it may not be possible or necessary to assess Level V in terms of performance. However, we suggest that the least program leaders can do is assess students' understanding of Level V. Written reflections, informal assessment during reflection time, and student self-reports can all be used to demonstrate how well students understand the various TPSR responsibilities and life skills as well as their applications in other settings.

Figure 11.9 is an open response "quiz" Paul gave a group of inner-city high school students in Memphis to assess what they had learned about life skills in his program. Of course, student responses may not correspond with their actual behavior in other settings, but assessments such as these at least document how well the students understand Level V. Information from such assessments

Life Skills

Name: _____ Date: _____

In this program we have discussed a number of life skills and responsibilities you can develop here and apply in other places such as home and the classroom. In the space below, write down at least three life skills or responsibilities we have discussed, and give an example (using complete sentences) of how you could use each skill in another setting—that is, outside the gym.

Skill 1: _____

Example: _____

_____

_____

_____

Skill 2: _____

Example: _____

_____

_____

_____

Skill 3: _____

Example: _____

_____

_____

_____

FIGURE 11.9　A sample quiz used to assess student learning.

can also stimulate program leaders' reflection, increase their understanding of their students' perspective, guide instructional decisions, and provide student-generated examples to integrate into discussions of Level V.

TEACHER EVALUATION

Few job descriptions include the phrase *effectively implement TPSR in physical activity programming.* In fact, most TPSR program leaders are using this particular approach by choice. Whether they work in youth agencies or schools, they no doubt have a long list of responsibilities and things they are accountable for in their professional roles. As with other professionals, they probably undergo some form of periodic review or evaluation based on these. Our objective in this section is to provide a set of strategies that program leaders may use to evaluate themselves with regard to their use of TPSR. We place heavy emphasis on self-reflection and the idea of fidelity in this section and share some tools that may provide helpful guidelines for self-assessment.

Reflective Practice

Affective and social–moral development are not high on typical school district priorities, so TPSR program leaders may not be evaluated on those qualities that facilitate TPSR. Despite the fact that the current national standards for PE (NASPE, 2004) suggest that personal and social responsibility are part of the "content" PE teachers are supposed to deliver, we have encountered very few programs in which this expectation is taken as seriously as developing sport skills, improving fitness, achieving high levels of moderate to vigorous physical activity, or simply keeping kids busy. PA programs based on youth development principles are more likely to support staff evaluations that reflect affective and especially social development qualities. Program leaders may have to assess their own effectiveness in making TPSR work.

One option for program leaders is to keep a reflective journal in which they self-grade their implementation of TPSR goals and teacher skills and qualities (see chapter 7) on a daily basis. The first time Don tried this in a high school class that met daily, he realized that on many of the days that the lesson was relatively smooth, his implementation of TPSR was weak. His interpretation was that the "good" days were good primarily because the kids didn't give him much trouble, not because he implemented TPSR effectively. Keeping a critical eye on implementation and not being satisfied with random success has been part of Don's personal growth as a program leader and the continual refinement of TPSR.

Another way to self-assess is to provide honest answers to the TPSR teacher questionnaire shown in chapter 10, figure 10.1. If most of the answers are positive (i.e., *Yes* or *I'm working on it* or *I want to do that*), the program leader is exhibiting the basic TPSR qualities. To self-assess more specifically, program leaders should check one of these categories for each statement:

- I am doing this now.
- I want to implement this soon.

- This is a long-range goal for me.
- I need to think about it some more.
- This isn't relevant for my situation.

Assessing Fidelity

Many TPSR program leaders are naturally great with kids, share the values we have been discussing, and create very positive learning environments. Yet they still wonder, regarding TPSR, "Am I doing it right?" We know this because they ask us. This question brings up the idea of fidelity, or the extent to which TPSR is really being implemented. TPSR cannot have much effect on students if it is not being implemented, and this really comes down to the program leader. Buchanan's (1996) study is a good example of that. She spent 120 pages describing her study, including her data and the analysis of her results. Her conclusion could have been expressed in one sentence: The program leaders had not bought in to TPSR and therefore did not implement much of it very successfully. Assessing the fidelity of TPSR implementation on an ongoing basis and using this information for reflection and continual improvement may prevent situations like this.

As noted earlier, one simple way to monitor implementation is to keep a daily journal that reflects on the extent to which TPSR was put into practice that day and how well it worked. Five minutes can be set aside for this task, or the daily lesson or program plan can be used for this purpose (write all over it in a different colored ink to differentiate reflections from the original lesson plan notes). A shortcut is for program leaders to assign themselves a letter grade for the extent of program implementation that day (e.g., A = full implementation).

As an example of a more comprehensive approach, consider a postteaching reflection tool that Paul uses to assess his own teaching in a community-based TPSR program he runs for at-risk youth in Memphis. This tool was created to match an observation tool he created called the TARE (Tool for Assessing Responsibility-Based Education; Wright and Craig, 2009). The TARE Postteaching Reflection Form can be found in the appendix (pp. 187-193) as well as on the TPSR Toolbox Web site (www.tpsr-alliance.org/toolbox). The TARE observation tool and the postteaching reflection tool focus on specific responsibility-based teaching strategies that are often used by TPSR program leaders.

Of course, the strategies discussed here leave lots of things out, but they can serve as reasonable indicators of TPSR implementation. Some of these are fundamental, such as modeling respectful behavior and setting clear expectations. Others are more empowerment based and go beyond what PE teachers and youth workers typically do (i.e., give students choices, provide leadership opportunities, discuss transfer, and even give students a role in assessment!). After rating themselves on implementation of these strategies (from *Never* to *Extensively*), program leaders can add comments to explain the rating or provide examples.

The next section of the TARE Postteaching Reflection Form directs program leaders to assess their implementation more holistically relative to TPSR themes such as integration, transfer, and empowerment. These are also rated from *Never* to *Extensively,* and space is provided for comments.

The final section of the instrument allows for an overall rating of student performance related to the TPSR levels. This helps add some context to the program leader's implementation ratings. Remember Don's example about days the kids were pretty good but he realized his implementation was weak. It can happen the other way, too; we've both had days when we did everything we set out to do and implemented TPSR strategies to the hilt, but it was just a tough day in terms of the kids' behavior.

As noted, Paul uses this postteaching reflection in his own work, but his program meets only once a week. Filling one of these out after every lesson might not be feasible for program leaders who teach multiple lessons per day. Those with less time in their schedules for this type of reflection and analysis could complete it just one time each week. This would still document the strategies being used and could help establish goals to improve TPSR implementation.

An observation tool such as Paul's original TARE tool could be useful for TPSR research and program evaluations. However, most program leaders don't have the luxury of a colleague or supervisor who is familiar enough with TPSR to observe them and provide useful feedback. For those who do have such an opportunity, consider using the TARE or perhaps the simpler TPSR Feedback Form that Don developed (see the appendix on pp. 194-195).

PROGRAM EVALUATION

Evaluating the effectiveness of a TPSR program is no simple task. After-school and community-based programs often serve small numbers of students and have high turnover rates. In fact, the more committed program leaders are to working with underserved youth, the less likely they are to have a program that lends itself to a "clean" evaluation. Although teachers in the schools often have greater numbers of students and more stability (depending on the school), they encounter other obstacles related to the marginalized status of PE in many schools. For these reasons, process-oriented evaluations conducted by TPSR program leaders themselves are common and often quite valuable.

Multiple Sources of Evidence

Depending on a program leader's context and reason for evaluating the program (e.g., for research, funding, oversight, program improvement, or assessing impact), it is usually wise to draw on multiple sources of evidence. In many cases, our program evaluations make use of the kind of information described in the earlier sections of this chapter. Compiling multiple sources of evidence, such as student assessments, program leader reflections, and program records on attendance and retention (depending on the setting), can provide a well-rounded picture of a program and make a case for its effectiveness or areas for possible improvement (or both).

Some version of the following evaluation procedures have been used in many TPSR programs and usually in combination (Hellison and Martinek, 2006; Hellison and Walsh, 2002):

- Include in a journal or on your daily plan observations and feelings about this approach—whether it continues to make sense, whether this is something worth standing for as a PE or PA professional. Try to separate these comments from whether the approach is working.

- Remember that no one can say much about the impact of TPSR if they can't first demonstrate that it was implemented. So consider some form of periodic fidelity check whether it involves a self-assessment or observation and feedback from a colleague.

- Use reflection time and group meeting comments as a source of student perceptions (write them down when possible).

- Keep track of relevant student behaviors, such as the amount of name calling, on-task participation, independent work, and helping others.

- Describe level-related activities and incidents as completely as possible for one lesson early in the program and then again later in the program to help determine the extent of change (either positive, negative, or no change).

- Ask kids how respectful or self-directed they are near the beginning of the year and then again near the end of the year to evaluate change.

- Keep track of behaviors on a regular, or even daily, basis—for example, by marking the appropriate level number next to each student's name.

- Administer anonymous student evaluations of the program. Ask them what they learned about themselves and about relating to others, as well as whether they've improved. See figures 11.10 and 11.11 for examples of anonymous student evaluations that we have given out to our students.

- Consider giving out pre-and post-questionnaires. You may consider constructing your own, or check out two that have been published in academic journals and are available on the TPSR Toolbox Web site (www.tpsr-alliance.org/toolbox). These are the Contextual Self Responsibility Questionnaire (Watson, Newton, and Kim, 2003) and the Personal and Social Responsibility Questionnaire (Li et al., 2008).

- Use written reflections or knowledge tests related to the levels to show the extent to which the students understand them.

- Talk with the students' classroom teachers, administrators, and playground or bus duty supervisors to see whether they believe TPSR is having any effect.

- Find out whether your students' classroom teachers assign conduct ratings. If so, you can get a glimpse into their level of responsibility outside the gym. For example, Don's fourth- through eighth-grade students are rated on self-control in their classroom, so he can look for improvements on their report cards and by talking with their classroom teachers.

When looking at the preceding list, it is important to remember that no one we know of has tackled all of these procedures, and certainly not in a single program evaluation. We recommend choosing just a few data sources or assessment strategies that really address key issues, problems, or program goals.

Culminating Projects

Because of the contexts many TPSR program leaders work in, few are able to conduct the type of program evaluations many academics are interested in (e.g., demonstrating statistically significant decreases in violence or substance

Coaching Club Evaluation

Date: _____

1. Why do you come to the Coaching Club? _____

_____

_____

2. What, if anything, did you learn about basketball in the Coaching Club? _____

_____

_____

3. What, if anything, did you learn about yourself in the Coaching Club? _____

_____

_____

4. How could the Coaching Club be improved next year? _____

_____

_____

5. What should Don do differently? _____

_____

_____

_____

FIGURE 11.10   An example of an anonymous student evaluation of a coaching club.

abuse). However, many of us have found that culminating activities and group projects can yield compelling products that illustrate some of the unique and meaningful things that can be accomplished in TPSR programs, even if they are hard to measure.

In 1999, Amy Rome (a first-grade teacher at the time) collaborated on a project with Paul in which the two taught yoga and tai chi movements to Amy's first-graders using TPSR. This program involved weekly physical activity lessons and the integration of these lessons (including the TPSR levels) into classroom activities throughout the week. This program was conducted in one of Chicago's public K-8 schools in the Chinatown neighborhood. The student body was made up of poor Chinese immigrants and poor African American students whose families lived in the nearby housing projects. Amy had invited Paul to initiate this program in part because of racial tensions that were an ongoing problem at this school.

Student Program Evaluation

Date: _____

Please circle the response that best matches your thoughts about this program.

1. Have you worked on the short-term goals you set in this program?

   Yes   No   Not sure

2. Do you think your behavior in this program has improved?

   Yes   No   Not sure

3. Do you think this program helped you do better in school?

   Yes   No   Not sure

4. Would you take another class like this if you had the chance?

   Yes   No   Not sure

5. Do you think this program is a good thing for students in your school?

   Yes   No   Not sure

Briefly answer each of the following questions.

1. What did you like the most about this program? _____

_____

_____

_____

_____

2. What did you dislike about this program? _____

_____

_____

_____

_____

3. Do you have any suggestions to improve this program? _____

_____

_____

_____

_____

FIGURE 11.11 An example of an anonymous student evaluation of the program.

From D. Hellison, 2011, *Teaching personal and social responsibility through physical activity, 3rd edition* (Champaign, IL: Human Kinetics).

At the end of the year, Amy's first-graders had the opportunity to demonstrate what they had learned at a schoolwide brotherhood assembly. In the weeks leading up to the demonstration, the lessons were devoted to planning and rehearsal. When the day of the assembly came, the first-graders (about half Chinese and half African American) worked together seamlessly to demonstrate not only a series of complex and elegant movements but also an extremely high level of composure, self-confidence, focus, and effort. This student performance was an ideal culminating experience to highlight how much the students had learned in this program. It also gave the students the opportunity to serve as role models in their school community for brotherhood as well as personal and social responsibility. Video documentation of the event served as an effective piece of evidence to support the overall evaluation of the program.

In 2001, Stein Garcia (at the time a master's degree student working with Don) and several other program leaders made a short martial arts movie with students from a TPSR Martial Arts Club operated in the after-school hours at another of Chicago's public K-8 schools. This school is on Chicago's West Side and served African American students who were all living at or below the poverty level. Stein, who had the necessary technical expertise and equipment, led this film project, which spanned several weeks. He and the other program leaders worked with the students to write a script, sketch out scenes, and choreograph fight sequences using the skills they had been working on in the club. Of course, the film, titled *Defending the Way*, had a story line that reinforced TPSR values. The final product was a DVD that included the slick "movie" complete with outtakes and special features such as interviews with the school's principal, the students' classroom teachers, and several of the stars (students) themselves. Although we may not be able to attribute a decrease in dropout rates or improvements in standardized test scores to a program that served only 10 or 12 students per semester, this group project and the product it generated provides compelling evidence of the creativity, hard work, commitment, and responsibility that can be part of a well-implemented TPSR program.

The final example offered in this section is a book project Paul did in collaboration with Diane Coleman (the Memphis PE teacher mentioned previously) in 2004. This project was also carried out with first-graders and extended on the work Paul had begun with Amy Rome in Chicago. By this point, Paul had found that the traditional TPSR daily program format was better suited for students who were at least in the upper elementary grades. To introduce students in the primary grades to TPSR, he created a story that incorporated yoga poses, animal walks, and tai chi–like movements. The story is about a young tiger cub that wanted to be a leader. The tiger cub goes on a journey that involves meeting a number of animals that help the cub learn what true leadership is (i.e., the TPSR levels).

Paul worked with one of Diane's first-grade PE classes for several lessons until they not only knew the various movements in the story but also knew the story itself well enough that they could tell it on their own. At this point, each student was able to choose one character from the story to highlight. In each case, that student was asked to pose for a digital photo demonstrating the pose or movement representing that character (e.g., jumping like a frog). To go along with their photos, students were asked to color pictures of their characters to use as illustrations for the book. Finally, some of Paul's undergraduate students helped to interview the first-graders about what they learned from the story, what they liked most about it, and what they liked the least.

Eventually, all the student photographs and illustrations were integrated with the text of the story into a self-published book. Kid quotes were included as an appendix. The students were thrilled to see themselves in print when Paul read the book to them. A copy of the book was also given to the school's library so the students could show their parents and friends what they had created. The students' classroom teacher was willing to extend the project by having them take one of the themes from the story, caring, as the focal point of acrostic poems they wrote the following month. By the time it was finished, this project had integrated TPSR instruction with authentic assessment strategies and crossed curricular lines while doing it, from the gym to the library and into the classroom. The book along with each student's individual photo, illustration, poem, and interview quotes provided rich and varied data to assess what individual students and the group as a whole had learned along the way.

These examples highlight the potential of creative group projects to provide culminating experiences and generate meaningful artifacts for evaluating TPSR programs. Such projects can result in concrete products such as a performance, a movie, or a book that convey some of the hard-to-measure but extremely important aspects of a TPSR program. These products can augment a program evaluation and provide a unique way of communicating the program's value to stakeholders such as principals, center directors, parents, and funders. Projects such as these provide true authentic assessments of student responsibility because they cannot be successful if students are not willing to engage, try hard, cooperate, and be responsible. The end products often demonstrate the integration of affective development with cognitive and psychomotor development. In fact, all of the examples offered here show the integration of these learning domains as well as the use of higher-order thinking skills in TPSR programs.

To make one final point regarding culminating projects, we remind you of McLaughlin's (2000) comment that "process is product" in programs such as this. Although the performance, the DVD, and the book are wonderful products, the educational value was in the process that led to their creation and the extent to which it challenged and allowed students to be responsible.

≪≪ TAKE-AWAYS ≫≫

Here are some key points from this chapter that you might consider taking with you:

- Whether assessing students, the program, or oneself, self-assessment and reflection are important parts of the process in TPSR.
- Students' personal and social responsibility can be assessed with a rubric, by grading specific responsibility qualities, and in other ways. But obtaining input from the kids in group meetings and reflection time as well as having them fill out the rubric or responsibility grades themselves will not only empower them (if attention is paid to their views) but also provide more information. Student self-assessment, like all empowerment strategies, requires a gradual progression.
- If students are helped to build their own definitions of success into individual criteria for their personal goals as well as their grades, they will be

more likely to explore their unique strengths and weaknesses and expand their understanding of self-assessment (beyond evaluating themselves on set criteria).

- Program evaluation should begin with an investigation of how much and how well TPSR has been implemented (i.e., fidelity). After that, other strategies can be used to assess its effectiveness.

- Good ways to assess program effectiveness include writing journal entries, keeping track of student behaviors and comments, asking students to evaluate the program anonymously, and requesting evaluations of students from outside observers such as administrators, teachers, and parents.

- PE and PA professionals who want their teaching and leadership to be evaluated may have to do it themselves. This is especially true if they want their TPSR qualities to be evaluated. One way to do this is to self-grade on a daily basis, especially in relation to the implementation of TPSR goals and strategies as well as the skills and qualities listed in chapter 7. Another way is to take the TPSR teacher questionnaire (see chapter 10, figure 10.1).

- Program leaders should consider group projects that will be developmentally appropriate and engaging for their students. If well planned, these teach students about responsibility while also providing an assessment of their levels of responsibility. Moreover, the artifacts that come from these projects can add an important dimension to TPSR program evaluations.

Epilogue

A life is not important, except in the impact it has on other lives.

—*Jackie Robinson*

■ ■ ■ ■ ■

What's worth doing is, in my view, the most important question that PE and PA professionals need to ask themselves, and it's a question that needs to be asked periodically throughout their careers. That goes for me, and perhaps you as well.

The TPSR core values are a way of being that provides a moral compass for the TPSR framework, a path to implementation for those who decide that it might be worth doing. If that is you, and you do get involved, feel free to join the TPSR Alliance (www.tpsr-alliance.org) at no cost and perhaps even attend our yearly TPSR conference.

As I continue to ask myself, Is this stuff still worth doing? I'm forced back to the drawing board again and again to reflect, rethink, and reimagine. So far, TPSR has survived this process, but there are no guarantees. As many of you know, if you take this journey, you will need to return to your own drawing board again and again. As I said in the first chapter, there is no silver bullet. If something comes along that in your view would work better for your kids and more accurately represents the kind of contribution you want to make, by all means use that.

The scope of this third edition of this book has been widened to include both PE and PA in order to recognize the growing contributions of youth development and alternative programs and schools. The world is changing. PE has had a distinguished past (Siedentop, 1990) but faces an uncertain future. PA programs have had an uneven but at times impressive history as well (Addams, 1972; Halpern, 2003) and seem to offer a promising future.

In case I have failed to convey the messiness of this process, I will close the same way I closed the previous editions of this book and *Beyond Balls and Bats* (1978), with a saying by Hugh Prather (1970):

> Ideas are clean.
>
> I can take them out and look at them.
>
> They fit nicely into books.
>
> They lead me down the narrow way
>
> And in the morning they are there.
>
> Ideas are straight.
>
> But the world is round
>
> And a messy mortal is my friend.
>
> Come walk with me in the mud.

Appendix

ASSESSMENT TOOLS

The TARE Postteaching Reflection and TPSR Feedback forms contained in this appendix are provided to support high-quality TPSR implementation. The items contained in each of these tools focus on specific aspects of the model and serve as good indicators of quality implementation. These tools include basic directions and could be modified to serve different purposes. For example, the TARE Postteaching Reflection Form was originally designed to guide practitioners' self-assessment, but it could be slightly adapted for use by an observer. The same principle is true for the TPSR Feedback Form—it was originally developed to support program observation or supervision but could be readily converted to a self-assessment form.

The TARE Postteaching Reflection Form (pp. 187-193) was adapted from the Tool for Assessing Responsibility-Based Education (TARE) observation instrument. The original tool was validated and tested favorably for reliability. This postteaching reflection variation is designed to serve as a self-report complement to the direct observation tool. The structure and content are completely aligned to facilitate triangulation. Dr. Paul Wright, who led the development of the observation tool, later developed and field-tested this instrument. He has used it in his own TPSR programs to guide reflection and assess fidelity of TPSR implementation. He has also used it as a tool to train others.

The TPSR Feedback Form (pp. 194-195) was developed by Don Hellison at the University of Illinois at Chicago and last revised in 2007. The clear case for the tool's validity stems from the fact that it was created by the TPSR model developer. It aligns with specific elements included in this book such as lesson format, student goals, and program leader goals. The tool was field-tested and refined by Hellison as he evaluated and supported health and physical education teachers at three alternative schools in the Chicago area. It may be useful for members of the TPSR community who are training others to implement the model. It might also be useful for university faculty to use as an evaluation and feedback tool for preservice physical education teachers who are learning about TPSR or NASPE's (2004) national standard 5. The basic content of the form could also be reframed and used to guide postteaching reflection or self-reporting regarding TPSR implementation.

Program leaders could use either one or both of these tools to document their implementation of the model over time. Setting aside time to self-assess implementation by rating the various items after each lesson (or once a week if that's too much) could help practitioners document what they are currently doing and identify areas for improvement. These same tools could be used to structure periodic observations by a supervisor, mentor, or colleague. Provided they understand the model and know what to look for, such individuals could lend an outsider's perspective on implementation. Having someone observe a lesson, rate the various items, and then discuss with the program leader afterward can be a useful form of feedback that stimulates reflection and program improvement. Individuals who are conducting research or a comprehensive evaluation of a TPSR program may want to combine these strategies (program leader self-assessment and periodic observation by an outsider) to get a more complete picture of TPSR implementation. Beyond record keeping and data collection, we hope these tools will be used to promote reflection, support planning, and enhance implementation fidelity in TPSR programs.

Tool for Assessing Responsibility-Based Education (TARE) Postteaching Reflection Form

Instructor and Program Information

Instructor name: _____

Date of report: _____ Day of week: _____

School/program name: _____

_____

Setting: _____

Locale (urban, rural, suburban): _____Youth grade level/age: _____

Activity content: _____

_____

_____

_____

_____

_____

_____

Instructor gender: _____Instructor race/ethnicity: _____

Reporting period: ☐ Single lesson   ☐ Several recent lessons

                    ☐ Other _____

Student Information

Approximate number in class: _____ Participant gender(s): _____

Race/ethnicity background(s): _____

_____

_____

_____

_____

_____

Special education included (circle one):   Yes   No   Not sure

From D. Hellison, 2011, *Teaching personal and social responsibility through physical activity,* 3rd edition (Champaign, IL: Human Kinetics).

Part 1: Brief Overview of Lesson(s)

Provide some information on the context, content, and goals of the lesson(s) being reported.

_____

_____

_____

_____

_____

_____

_____

_____

_____

_____

_____

_____

_____

_____

_____

_____

_____

_____

_____

_____

_____

_____

_____

From D. Hellison, 2011, *Teaching personal and social responsibility through physical activity, 3rd edition* (Champaign, IL: Human Kinetics).

Part 2: Responsibility-Based Teaching Strategies

For the time period being reported, use the scale provided to rate your use of each of the nine responsibility-based teaching strategies below. More explicit definitions for these strategies can be found in part 6 of this form. After selecting your rating, provide some comments to justify that rating (i.e., give concrete examples of things you did and said that would serve as evidence). In cases where you realize you did not make full use of the strategy, you may want to identify ways that you could have or that you might in future lessons.

Teaching strategies	4 (Extensively)	3 (Frequently)	2 (Occasionally)	1 (Rarely)	0 (Never)	Comments to justify rating
Modeling respect	4	3	2	1	0	
Setting expectations	4	3	2	1	0	
Providing opportunities for success	4	3	2	1	0	
Fostering social interaction	4	3	2	1	0	
Assigning management tasks	4	3	2	1	0	
Promoting leadership	4	3	2	1	0	
Giving choices and voices	4	3	2	1	0	
Involving students in assessment	4	3	2	1	0	
Promoting transfer	4	3	2	1	0	

Extensively: This strategy was seamlessly addressed directly and evidenced in multiple ways throughout the lesson through your words and actions.

Frequently: This strategy was addressed directly and evidenced at several points in the lesson through your words and actions.

Occasionally: Some of your words and actions connected to this strategy either directly or indirectly during the lesson.

Rarely: This strategy was not generally integrated into your teaching but may have been reflected in some isolated words or actions.

Never: Throughout the entire lesson, none of your words or actions clearly conveyed or aligned with this strategy.

From D. Hellison, 2011, *Teaching personal and social responsibility through physical activity, 3rd edition* (Champaign, IL: Human Kinetics).

Part 3: Personal–Social Responsibility Themes

For the time period being reported, use the scale provided to assess your overall application of these general themes. After selecting your rating, provide some comments to justify that rating (i.e., give concrete examples of things you did and said that would serve as evidence). In cases where you realize you did not address a theme very strongly, you may want to identify ways that you could have or that you might in future lessons.

Themes	4 (Extensively)	3 (Frequently)	2 (Occasionally)	1 (Rarely)	0 (Never)	Comments to justify rating
Integration: The extent to which responsibility roles and concepts are integrated into the physical activity	4	3	2	1	0	
Transfer: The extent to which connections are made to the application of life skills in other settings	4	3	2	1	0	
Empowerment: The extent to which you share responsibility with students	4	3	2	1	0	
Teacher–student relationship: The extent to which you treat students as individuals deserving of respect, choice, and a voice	4	3	2	1	0	

Extensively: This theme was seamlessly addressed directly and evidenced in multiple ways throughout the lesson through your words and actions.

Frequently: This theme was addressed directly and evidenced at several points in the lesson through your words and actions.

Occasionally: Some of your words and actions connected to this theme either directly or indirectly during the lesson.

Rarely: This theme was not generally integrated into your teaching but may have been reflected in some isolated words or actions.

Never: Throughout the entire lesson, none of your words or actions clearly conveyed or aligned with this theme.

From D. Hellison, 2011, *Teaching personal and social responsibility through physical activity, 3rd edition* (Champaign, IL: Human Kinetics).

Part 4: Student Responsibility

For the time period being reported, provide a holistic rating for these general areas of student responsibility. Consider observed student behavior and interactions throughout the lesson. Keep in mind that this rubric assesses the group overall and not individual students.

Areas	4 (Very strong)	3 (Strong)	2 (Moderate)	1 (Weak)	0 (Very weak)	Comments
Self-control: Student does no harm to others verbally or physically; includes and works well with others; resolves conflicts peacefully if they emerge.	4	3	2	1	0	
Participation: Student tries every activity and takes on various roles if asked.	4	3	2	1	0	
Effort: Student tries hard to master every task and focuses on improvement.	4	3	2	1	0	
Self-direction: Student stays on task without direct instruction or supervision, whether working alone or with others; does not seem to follow bad examples or succumb to peer pressure.	4	3	2	1	0	
Caring: Student helps, encourages others, and offers positive feedback.	4	3	2	1	0	

Very strong: All students displayed this responsibility throughout the lesson with no observed exceptions.

Strong: Most students displayed this responsibility throughout the lesson with only minor or isolated exceptions.

Moderate: Many students displayed this responsibility, but many did not; several exceptions were observed.

Weak: Some students displayed this responsibility, but many did not; exceptions were frequent or serious enough to impede learning.

Very weak: Few, if any, students displayed this responsibility, and the majority struggled to do so; exceptions were frequent or serious enough that at least some portions of the lesson were rendered ineffective.

From D. Hellison, 2011, *Teaching personal and social responsibility through physical activity,* 3rd edition (Champaign, IL: Human Kinetics).

Part 5: Additional Comments or Plans

From D. Hellison, 2011, *Teaching personal and social responsibility through physical activity, 3rd edition* (Champaign, IL: Human Kinetics).

Part 6: Extended Descriptions of Responsibility-Based Teaching Strategies

Modeling respect (M): The teacher models respectful communication. This would involve communication with the whole group and individual students. Examples include using students' names; engaging in active listening; making eye contact; recognizing individuality; maintaining composure; providing developmentally appropriate instruction; talking "with" rather than "at" students; showing an interest in students; and exhibiting unconditional positive regard. Counter examples include exhibiting indifference; being disengaged; losing one's temper; and deliberately embarrassing a student.

Setting expectations (E): The teacher explains or refers to explicit behavioral expectations. Examples include making sure all students know where they should be and what they should be doing at any given time; giving explicit expectations for the activity or performance; and explaining and reinforcing safe practices, rules and procedures, or etiquette.

Providing opportunities for success (S): The teacher structures lessons so that all students have the opportunity to successfully participate and be included regardless of individual differences. Examples in physical activity include making appropriate adaptations for inclusion; and providing opportunities for practice, skill refinement, and game play. Examples in less active modes include allowing students to volunteer answers in a discussion or succeed in a nonphysical task.

Fostering social interaction (SI): The teacher structures activities that foster positive social interactions. Examples include fostering student-to-student interactions through cooperation, teamwork, problem solving, peer coaching, and partner drills in which communication is encouraged. Counter examples include not engaging in random student interactions and facilitating pseudo group discussions that involve only teacher–student exchanges.

Assigning management tasks (T): The teacher assigns specific responsibilities or management-related tasks that facilitate the organization of the program or a specific activity. Examples include asking students to take attendance, serve as timekeepers, set up equipment, keep score or records, or officiate a game.

Promoting leadership (L): The teacher allows students to lead or be in charge of a group. Examples include allowing students to demonstrate for the class, lead stations, teach or lead exercises for the whole class, or coach teams.

Giving choices and voices (V): The teacher gives students a voice in the program. Examples include letting students engage in group discussions, vote as a group, and make individual choices; inviting student questions or suggestions; eliciting student opinions; and letting students evaluate the teacher or the program.

Involving students in assessment (A): The teacher allows students to have a role in their own assessment. Examples include self-assessment or peer-assessment related to skill development, behavior, attitude, etc.; student-centered goal setting; negotiation between teacher and student on the student's grade or progress in the class.

Promoting transfer (Tr): The teacher directly addresses the transfer of life skills or responsibilities beyond the program. Examples of topics include working hard and persevering in school; being a leader in the community; keeping self-control to avoid a fight after school; setting goals to achieve goals in sports or life in general; being a good team player when in other contexts such as the workplace; and thinking independently to avoid peer pressure and make good life choices.

From D. Hellison, 2011, *Teaching personal and social responsibility through physical activity*, 3rd edition (Champaign, IL: Human Kinetics).

TPSR Feedback Form

Date: _____

Program leader: _____

Supervisor: _____

What's worth doing?	Is it working? *(Yes, No, Somewhat)*	Feedback
Daily program format		
1. Relational time: The teacher shows effort to relate positively to students.		
2. Awareness talk: The teacher reminds students of their goals (with student participation).		
3. Physical activity lesson: The teacher integrates student goals into the lesson and solves problems as needed.		
4. Group meeting: The teacher listens to students' positive and negative comments about the lesson, as well as suggestions to improve the lesson.		
5. Self-reflection time: Students self-evaluate how well they carried out their goals, including outside the gym.		
What's worth doing?	Is it working? *(Yes, No, Somewhat)*	Feedback
Student goals and levels		
1. Respect others' rights and feelings, and exhibit self-control		
2. Show effort and teamwork		
3. Exhibit self-direction and goal setting		
4. Help others, exhibit leadership		
5. Outside the gym		
Program leader goals		
1. Relate well with students		
2. Integrate content and TPSR		
3. Share power with students gradually		
4. Emphasize self-reflection		

(continued)

From D. Hellison, 2011, *Teaching personal and social responsibility through physical activity, 3rd edition* (Champaign, IL: Human Kinetics).

TPSR Feedback Form   *(continued)*

Additional Comments

_____

_____

_____

_____

_____

_____

_____

_____

_____

_____

_____

_____

_____

_____

_____

_____

_____

_____

_____

_____

_____

_____

_____

_____

_____

_____

_____

References and Resources

Addams, J. 1972. *The spirit of youth and the city streets.* Urbana, IL: University of Illinois Press. (Originally published in 1909 by Macmillan.)

Arnold, P.J. 1988. *Education, movement and the curriculum.* London: Falmer.

Ayers, W. 1989. *The good preschool teacher: Six teachers reflect on their lives.* New York: Teachers College Press.

Banks, W.H., and C. Smith-Fee. 1989. Middle school PE: Assertiveness training. *Journal of Physical Education, Recreation and Dance* 60: 90–93.

Beedy, J.P., and T. Zierk. 2000. Lessons from the field: Taking a proactive approach to developing character through sports. *CYD Journal: Community Youth Development* 3: 6–13.

Benson, P.L. 1997. *All kids are our kids: What communities must do to raise caring and responsible children and adolescents.* San Francisco: Jossey-Bass.

Berlin, R.A., N. Dworkin, N. Eames, A. Menconi, and D.F. Perkins. 2007. Examples of sport-based youth development programs. In *New directions for youth development: Sport-based youth development* (Special monograph), ed. D.F. Perkins and S.L. Menestrel, 85–108. San Francisco: Jossey-Bass.

Berman, S. 1990. Educating for social responsibility. *Educational Leadership* 48: 75–80.

Boyes-Watson, C. 2001. Healing the wounds of street violence. *CYD Journal: Community Youth Development* 4: 16–21.

Bredemeier, M.E. 1988. *Urban classroom portraits: Teachers who make a difference.* New York: Lang.

Bressan, E.S. 1987. Physical education and social change in South Africa. In *Proceedings of the fifth curriculum theory conference in physical education,* ed. M. Carnes and P. Stueck, 128–138. Athens, GA: University of Georgia.

Buchanan, A.M. 1996. *Learner's and instructors' interpretations of personal and social responsibility in a sports camp.* Doctoral dissertation, Texas A&M University.

Camino, L.A. 2002. CO-SAMM: A tool to assess youth leadership. *CYD Journal: Community Youth Development* 3: 39–43.

Carnegie Council on Adolescent Development. 1992. *A matter of time: Risk and opportunity in the nonschool hours.* Report of the Task Force on Youth Development and Community Programs. New York: Carnegie Corporation of New York.

Compagnone, N. 1995. Teaching responsibility to rural elementary youth: Going beyond the at-risk boundaries. *Journal of Physical Education, Recreation and Dance* 66: 58–63.

Csikszentmihalyi, M., and J. McCormack. 1986. The influence of teachers. *Phi Delta Kappan* 67: 415–419.

Cuban, L. 1993. The lure of curricular reform and its pitiful history. *Phi Delta Kappan* 75: 182–185.

Cutforth, N. 2000. Connecting school physical education to the community through service learning. *Journal of Physical Education, Recreation and Dance* 71: 39–45.

Cutforth, N., and M. Parker. 1996. Promoting affective development in physical education: The value of journal writing. *Journal of Physical Education, Recreation and Dance* 67: 19–23.

DeBusk, M., and D. Hellison. 1989. Implementing a physical education self-responsibility model for delinquency-prone youth. *Journal of Teaching in Physical Education* 8: 104–112.

deCharms, R. 1976. *Enhancing motivation: Change in the classroom.* New York: Irvington.

DeLine, J. 1991. Why . . . can't they get along? *Journal of Physical Education, Recreation and Dance* 62: 21–26.

Delpit, L.D. 1988. The silenced dialogue: Power and pedagogy in educating other people's children. *Harvard Educational Review* 58: 379–385.

DeWitt-Wallace Reader's Digest Fund. 1995. *Strengthening the youth work profession.* New York: Author.

Denton, D.E. 1972. *Existential reflections on teaching.* North Quincy, MA: Christopher.

Dill, V.S. 1998. *A peaceable school: Cultivating a culture of non-violence.* Bloomington, IN: Phi Delta Kappan Educational Foundation.

Divoky, D. 1975. Affective education: Are we going too far? *Learning,* 25.

Dreikurs, R., and V. Soltz. 1964. *Children: The challenge.* New York: Hawthorn.

Dryfoos, J.G. 1991. Adolescents at risk: A summation of work in the field—programs and policies. *Journal of Adolescent Health* 12: 631–637.

Eccles, J., and J.A. Gootman. 2002. *Community programs to promote youth development.* Washington, DC: National Academy Press.

Ennis, C.D., M.A. Solmon, B. Satina, S.J. Loftus, J. Mensch, and M.T. McCauley. 1999. Creating a sense of family in urban school using the "Sport for Peace" curriculum. *Research Quarterly for Exercise and Sport* 70: 273–285.

Foster, H.L. 1974. *Ribbin', jivin', and playin' the dozens: The unrecognized dilemma of inner city schools.* Cambridge, MA: Ballinger.

Fraser-Thomas, J., J. Cote, and J. Deakin. 2005. Youth sport programs: An avenue to foster positive youth development. *Physical Education and Sport Pedagogy* 10: 19–40.

Georgiadis, N. 1990. Does basketball have to be all W's and L's? An alternative program at a residential boys' home. *Journal of Physical Education, Recreation and Dance* 61: 42–43.

Gibbons, S.L., V. Ebbeck, and M.R. Weiss. 1995. Fair play for kids: Effects on the moral development of children in physical education. *Research Quarterly for Exercise and Sport* 66: 247–255.

Giebink, M.P., and T.L. McKenzie. 1985. Teaching sportsmanship in physical education and recreation: An analysis of interventions and generalization effects. *Journal of Teaching in Physical Education* 4: 167–177.

Glasser, W. 1965. *Reality therapy.* New York: Harper & Row.

Glasser, W. 1977. Ten steps to good discipline. *Today's Education* 66: 61–63.

Goodlad, J. 1988. Studying the education of educators: Values driven inquiry. *Phi Delta Kappan* 69: 105–111.

Gordon, B. 2009. Merging teaching personal and social responsibility with sport education: A marriage made in heaven or hell? *Healthy Lifestyles Journal* 56: 13–16.

Gordon, G.L. 1999. Teacher talent and urban schools. *Phi Delta Kappan* 80: 304–306.

Greene, J.C. 2000. Understanding social programs through evaluation. In *Handbook of qualitative research,* ed. N.K. Denzin and Y.S. Lincoln, 981–999. Thousand Oaks, CA: Sage.

Greene, M. 1986. Philosophy and teaching. In *The handbook of research on teaching,* 3rd ed., ed. M.C. Wittrock, 479–504. New York: Macmillan.

Guthrie, J. 1982. *Be your own coach.* Portland, OR: ASIEP.

Halpern, R. 2003. *Making play work*. New York: Teachers College Press.

Hare, C. 1998. *Incorporation of the responsibility levels into the health curriculum*. Unpublished paper.

Hattie, J., H.W. Marsh, J.T. Neill, and G.E. Richards. 1997. Adventure education and outward bound: Out-of-class experiences that make a lasting difference. *Review of Educational Research* 67: 43–87.

Hellison, D. 1973. *Humanistic physical education*. Englewood Cliffs, NJ: Prentice Hall.

Hellison, D. 1978. *Beyond balls and bats: Alienated (and other) youth in the gym*. Washington, DC: AAHPER.

Hellison, D. 1983. Teaching self-responsibility (and more). *Journal of Physical Education, Recreation and Dance* 54: 23, 28.

Hellison, D. 1985. *Goals and strategies for teaching physical education*. Champaign, IL: Human Kinetics.

Hellison, D., and N. Cutforth. 1997. Extended day programs for children and youth: From theory to practice. In *Children and youth: Interdisciplinary perspectives,* ed. H. Walberg, O. Reyes, and R. Weissberg, 223–249. San Francisco: Jossey-Bass.

Hellison, D., N. Cutforth, J. Kallusky, T. Martinek, M. Parker, and J. Stiehl. 2000. *Youth development and physical activity: Linking universities and communities*. Champaign, IL: Human Kinetics.

Hellison, D., and N. Georgiadis. 1992. Teaching values through basketball. *Strategies* 5: 5–8.

Hellison, D., and T. Martinek. 2006. Social and individual responsibility programs. In *The handbook of physical education,* ed. D. Kirk, D. Macdonald, and M. O'Sullivan, 610–626. Thousand Oaks, CA: Sage.

Hellison, D., and L. McBride. 1986. A responsibility curriculum for teaching health and physical education. *Oregon Journal of Health, Physical Education, Recreation, and Dance* 20: 16–17.

Hellison, D., and T.J. Templin. 1991. *A reflective approach to teaching physical education*. Champaign, IL: Human Kinetics.

Hellison, D., and D. Walsh. 2002. Responsibility-based youth program evaluation: Investigating the investigations. *Quest* 54: 292–307.

Hellison, D., and P. Wright. 2003. Retention in an extended day program: A process-based assessment. *Journal of Teaching Physical Education* 22: 369–381.

Hichwa, J. 1998. *Right fielders are people too*. Champaign, IL: Human Kinetics.

Hinson, C. 1997. *Games kids should play at recess*. 2nd ed. Wilmington, DE: PE Publishing.

Hinson, C. 2001. *Six steps to a trouble-free playground*. Wilmington, DE: PE Publishing.

Hirsch, B.J. 2005. *A place to call home*. New York: Teachers College Press.

Hoffman, D.M. 2009. Reflecting on social emotional learning: A critical perspective on trends in the United States. *Review of Educational Research* 79: 533–556.

Horrocks, R.N. 1977. Sportsmanship. *Journal of Physical Education, Recreation and Dance* 48: 20–21.

Horrocks, R.N. 1978. Resolving conflict in the gymnasium. *Journal of Physical Education, Recreation and Dance* 49: 61.

Howe, Q., Jr. 1991. *Under running laughter: Notes from a renegade classroom*. New York: Free Press.

Intrator, S.M., and S. Siegel. 2008. Project Coach: Youth development through sport. *Journal of Physical Education, Recreation and Dance* 79: 17–23.

Jones, R.S., and L.N. Tanner. 1981. Classroom discipline: The unclaimed legacy. *Phi Delta Kappan* 63: 494–497.

Keramidas, K. 1991. *Strategies to increase the individual motivation and cohesiveness of a junior male basketball team.* Master's thesis, University of Illinois at Chicago.

Kohn, A. 1993. Choices for children: Why and how to let students decide. *Phi Delta Kappan* 75: 8–20.

Kunjufu, J. 1989. *Critical issues in educating African American youth.* Chicago: African American Images.

Lambert, L., and P. Grube. 1988. The physical/motor fitness learning center: A university-school collaborative effort. *Journal of Physical Education, Recreation and Dance* 59: 70–73.

Lampert, M. 1987. Mathematics teaching in schools: Imagining an ideal that is also possible. In *Mathematical Sciences Education Board, The teacher of mathematics: Issues for today and tomorrow* (pp. 37–42). Washington, DC: National Research Council.

Lawson, H.A. 1984. Problem-setting for physical education and sport. *Quest* 36: 48–60.

Lawson, H.A. 2005. Empowering people, facilitating community development, and contributing to sustainable development: The social work of sport, exercise, and physical education. *Sport, Education and Society* 10: 135–160.

Li, W., P.M. Wright, P. Rukavina, and M. Pickering. 2008. Measuring students' perceptions of personal and social responsibility and its relationship to intrinsic motivation in urban physical education. *Journal of Teaching in Physical Education* 27: 167–178.

Lickona, T. n.d. *Eighteen strategies for helping kids take responsibility for building their own character.* Unpublished manuscript.

Lickona, T. 1991. *Educating for character: How our schools can teach respect and responsibility.* New York: Bantam.

Lund, J., and D. Tannehill. 2010. *Standards-based physical education and curriculum development.* Sudbury, MA: Jones & Bartlett.

Lyon, H.C., Jr. 1971. *Learning to feel: Feeling to learn.* Columbus, OH: Merrill.

Maddi, S.R., S.C. Kobasa, and M. Hoover. 1979. An alienation test. *Journal of Humanistic Psychology* 19: 73–76.

Martinek, T., and J.B. Griffith. 1993. Working with the learned helpless child. *Journal of Physical Education, Recreation and Dance* 64: 17–20.

Martinek, T., and D. Hellison. 2009. *Youth leadership in sport and physical education.* New York: Palgrave Macmillan.

Martinek, T., and T. Schilling. 2002. *Developing compassionate leadership in underserved youth.* Unpublished paper.

Masser, L. 1990. Teaching for affective learning in elementary physical education. *Journal of Physical Education, Recreation and Dance* 61: 18–19.

McCaslin, M., and T.L. Good. 1992. Compliant cognition: The misalignment of management and instruction goals in current school reform. *Educational Researcher* 21: 4–17.

McDonald, J.P. 1992. *Teaching: Making sense of an uncertain craft.* New York: Teachers College Press.

McLaughlin, M. 2000. *Community counts.* Washington, DC: Public Education Network.

McLaughlin, M.W., and S.J. Heath. 1993. Casting the self: Frames for identity and dilemmas for policy. In *Identity and inner city youth: Beyond ethnicity and gender,* ed. S.J. Heath and M.W. McLaughlin, 210–239. New York: Teachers College Press.

Meadows, B.J. 1992. Nurturing cooperation and responsibility in a school community. *Phi Delta Kappan* 73: 480–481.

Mesa, P. 1992, November. *Keynote address.* First Annual At-Risk Youth Conference, Lake Tahoe, NV.

Mosley, W. 1992. *White butterfly.* New York: Washington Square Press.

Mosston, M., and S. Ashworth. 1994. *Teaching physical education.* 4th ed. New York: Macmillan.

Mrugala, J. 2002. *Exploratory study of responsibility model practitioners.* Doctoral dissertation, University of Illinois at Chicago.

Murray, C.H., S.N. Smith, and E.H. West. 1989. Comparative personality development in adolescents: A critique. In *Black adolescents,* ed. R.L. Jones, 49–77. Berkeley, CA: Cobb & Henry.

National Association for Sport and Physical Education (NASPE). 2004. *Moving into the future: National standards for physical education.* 2nd ed. Reston, VA: Author.

Nicholls, J.G. 1989. *The competitive ethos and democratic education.* Cambridge, MA: Harvard University Press.

Nicholls, J.G., and S.P. Hazzard. 1993. *Education as adventure: Lessons from the second grade.* New York: Teachers College Press.

Noam, G.G., G. Biancarosa, and N. Dechausay. 2003. *After-school education: Approaches to an emerging field.* Cambridge, MA: Harvard University Press.

Noddings, N. 1992. *The challenge to care in schools.* New York: Teachers College Press.

Norton, D.L. 1976. *Personal destinies: A philosophy of ethical individualism.* Princeton, NJ: Princeton University Press.

Orlick, T. 1978. *The cooperation book of games and sports.* New York: Pantheon.

Orlick, T. 1980. *In pursuit of excellence.* Champaign, IL: Human Kinetics.

O'Sullivan, M., and M. Henninger. 2000. *Assessing student responsibility and teamwork.* Reston, VA: National Association of Sport and Physical Education.

Parker, M., and D. Hellison. 2001. Teaching responsibility in physical education: Standards, outcomes, and beyond. *Journal of Physical Education, Recreation and Dance* 72: 26–36.

Pastor, P. 2002. School discipline and the character of our schools. *Phi Delta Kappan* 83: 658–661.

Petitpas, A.J., A. Cornelius, and J. Van Raalte. 2008. It's all about relationships. In *Positive youth development through sport,* ed. N. Holt, 61–70. London: Routledge.

Petracek, R. 1998. *Strength building log.* Unpublished paper.

Power, F.C. 2002. Building democratic community: A radical approach to moral education. In *Bringing in a new era in character education,* ed. W. Damon, 129–148. Palo Alto, CA: Hoover Institution Press.

Prather, H. 1970. *Notes to myself. My struggle to become a person.* Moab, UT: Real Person Press.

Prather, H. 1972. *I touch the earth, the earth touches me.* New York: Doubleday.

Puka, B. 1987. Moral development without the philosophical captivation. *Moral Education Forum* 12: 4–20.

Quinn, J., and J. Dryfoos. 2009. Freeing teachers to teach. *American Educator* 33: 16–21.

Raffini, J.P. 1980. *Discipline: Negotiating conflicts with today's kids.* Englewood Cliffs, NJ: Prentice Hall.

Raths, L.E., M. Harmin, and S.B. Simon. 1966. *Values and teaching.* Columbus, OH: Merrill.

Raywid, M.A. 2006. Themes that serve schools well. *Phi Delta Kappan* 88: 654–656.

Richards, A. 1982. Seeking roots from Hahn. *Journal for Experiential Education* 5: 22–25.

Romance, T.J., M.R. Weiss, and J. Bokoven. 1986. A program to promote moral development through elementary physical education. *Journal of Teaching in Physical Education* 5: 126–136.

Rothstein, R. 2004. *Class and schools: Social, economic, and social reform to close the black-white achievement gap.* New York: Economic Policy Institute.

Rubin, L. 1985. *Artistry in teaching.* New York: Random House.

Schafer, W. 1992. *Stress management for wellness.* 2nd ed. Fort Worth, TX: Harcourt Brace Jovanovich.

Schilling, T., T. Martinek, and C. Tan. 2001. Fostering youth development through empowerment. In *Sport in the twenty-first century: Alternatives for the new millennium,* ed. B.J. Lombardo, T.J. Caravella-Nadeau, H.S. Castagno, and V.H. Mancini, 169–179. Boston: Pearson.

Schlosser, L.K. 1992. Teacher distance and student disengagement: School lives on the margin. *Journal of Teacher Education* 43: 128–140.

Schon, D.A. 1987. *Educating the reflective practitioner.* San Francisco: Jossey-Bass.

Schubert, W. 1986. *Curriculum: Perspective, paradigm, and possibility.* New York: Macmillan.

Schwab, J.J. 1971. The practical: Arts of eclectic. *School Review* 79: 493–542.

Shields, D.L.L., and B.J.L. Bredemeier. 1995. *Character development and physical activity.* Champaign, IL: Human Kinetics.

Siedentop, D. 1980. *Physical education: Introductory analysis.* 2nd ed. Dubuque, IA: Brown.

Siedentop, D. 1990. *Introduction to physical education, fitness, and sport.* Mountain View, CA: Mayfield.

Siedentop, D. 1991. *Developing teaching skills in physical education.* 3rd ed. Mountain View, CA: Mayfield.

Siedentop, D. 1992. Thinking differently about secondary physical education. *Journal of Physical Education, Recreation and Dance* 63: 69–72, 77.

Siedentop, D. 1994. *Sport education: Quality PE through positive sport experiences.* Champaign, IL: Human Kinetics.

Siedentop, D. 2001. *Introduction to physical education, fitness, and sport.* 4th ed. Mountain View, CA: Mayfield.

Sizer, T.R. 1992. *Horace's school: Redesigning the American high school.* Boston: Houghton Mifflin.

Smith, M. 1990. Enhancing self-responsibility through a humanistic school program. *Journal of Physical Education, Recreation and Dance* 63: 14–18.

Stiehl, J., G.S.D. Morris, and C. Sinclair. 2008. *Teaching physical activity: Change, challenge, and choice.* Champaign, IL: Human Kinetics.

Tappan, M.B. 1992. Educating for character: How our schools can teach respect and responsibility [Book review]. *Journal of Teacher Education* 43: 386–389.

Thomas, C.E. 1983. *Sport in a philosophic context.* Philadelphia: Lea & Febiger.

Tom, A.R. 1984. *Teaching as a moral craft.* New York: Longman.

Trulson, M.E. 1986. Martial arts training as a "cure" for juvenile delinquency. *Human Relations* 39: 1131–1140.

Veal, M.L., C.D. Ennis, D. Hellison, T. Martinek, and M. O'Sullivan. 2002. *Physical activity in high schools: Building models of caring.* Presentation at the American Alliance of Health, Physical Education, Recreation and Dance National Convention, San Diego.

Walsh, D.S. 2002. Emerging strategies in the search for effective university-community collaborations. *Journal of Physical Education, Recreation and Dance* 73: 50–53.

Walsh, D.S. 2006. Best practices in university-community partnerships: Lessons learned from a physical activity program. *Journal of Physical Education, Recreation and Dance* 77: 45–56.

Walsh, D.S. 2008. Helping youth in underserved communities envision possible futures: An extension of the personal and social responsibility model. *Research Quarterly for Exercise and Sport* 79: 209–221.

Watson, D.L., M. Newton, and M. Kim. 2003. Recognition of values-based constructs in a summer physical activity program. *The Urban Review* 3: 217–232.

Weinberg, R.S., and D. Gould. 1999. *Foundations of sport and exercise psychology.* 2nd ed. Champaign, IL: Human Kinetics.

Weiner, L. 1993. *Preparing teachers for urban schools: Lessons from thirty years of school reform.* New York: Teachers College Press.

Williamson, K.M., and N. Georgiadis. 1992. Teaching an inner-city after-school program. *Journal of Physical Education, Recreation and Dance* 63: 14–18.

Willis, J.D., and L.F. Campbell. 1992. *Exercise psychology.* Champaign, IL: Human Kinetics.

Wright, P.M., and M.W. Craig. 2009. *Tool for Assessing Responsibility-Based Education (TARE): A reliability study.* Paper presented at the American Alliance for Health, Physical Education, Recreation and Dance National Convention, Tampa, FL.

Zavacky, F. 1997. Motivating the I. *Teaching Elementary Physical Education* 8: 30–31.

Index

Note: The letters *f* and *t* after page numbers indicate figures and tables, respectively.

A

accordion principle 90*t*, 91-92, 100
Adams, H. 105
all-touch rule 136-137
Andersen, D. 97
apprenticeship 120-121
assertiveness 40
assessment and evaluation strategies
  program evaluation 175-180
  student assessment 162-173
  take-aways on 180-181
  teacher evaluation 173-175
assumptions 18*f*, 19-20
awareness levels 7*f*
awareness talk
  in daily program format 27*f*, 49
  description of 28
  guidelines for 53-55
Ayers, B. 106, 107

B

Balague, G. 139
Barkley, C. 42, 43
Beale, A. 104, 121
being relational with kids
  courage to confront 105
  different cultural backgrounds and 112-114
  four relational qualities 103-105
  kid quotes 107
  program leader qualities and skills for 106-112
  relational time 27*f*, 49, 50-53, 106
  as responsibility of program leader 25-27
  take-aways on 114
Benson, P.L. 10
Benton, R. 97
Beyond Balls and Bats (Hellison) 146, 183
Beyond the Ball 19
Bing, D. 43
Blakeley, K. 133
Boyes-Watson, C. 149
Bredemeier, B.J.L. 33, 113
Brees, D. 41
Brookfield, S.D. 31
Buber, M. 110
Buchanan, A.M. 174
Buckle, M. 4

C

Camino, L.A. 88
Career Club Possible Futures program 132
caring, Level IV
  description of 21*t*, 32*t*, 34*f*, 40-42, 43*f*
  strategies 78, 80-85
Castenada, A. 19
Castenada, R. 19
causes of social problems 14
checklist of personal goals 77*f*
classroom, TPSR in
  classroom applications 143
  emphasis on levels 142
  health education applications 143-146
coaching club evaluation 177*f*
coaching clubs
  advantages of 133-134
  background on 132-133
  issues in 134
  kid quotes on 135
  sample coaching club lesson 134-137
  typical sports program versus 133
Cody, K. 61
Coleman, D. 163, 179
Compagnone, N. 55
conference workshop or short course 122-123
conflict resolution, peaceful 37
conflict resolution strategies
  emergency plan 90*t*, 97
  making new rules 90*t*, 97-98
  self-officiating 90*t*, 96-97
  sport court 90*t*, 96
  talking bench 90*t*, 97
contract, self-grading 170, 171*f*
contracts, written 78, 79*f*, 80*f*
Cooper, T. 138
core values 18*f*-19
Cote, J. 18
courage to confront 105
courage to resist peer pressure 21*t*, 90*t*, 99-100
cross-age teaching and leadership 138-139
Cuban, L. 107
cues, student leader 82*f*-83*f*
cultural backgrounds of students 112-114
cumulative levels 32*t*, 33-35, 61-62
Cutforth, N. 59, 85, 133, 138

D

daily program format
 awareness talk 27*f*, 28, 49, 53-55
 basic description of 18*f*, 27*f*-28
 empowerment and 49, 50
 group meeting 27*f*, 28, 49, 56-58
 kid quotes on 52
 physical activity plan 27*f*, 28, 49, 55-56
 relational time 27*f*, 49, 50-53
 self-reflection time 27*f*, 28, 49, 58-62
 take-aways on 62
Deakin, J. 18
DeBusk, M. 97, 157
decency, promoting 18
DeCharms, R. 13
decision-making ability of students 26, 53, 104
DeLine, J. 156
Delpit, L.D. 113
Denton, D. 106, 107
Dewey, J. 6, 63
Doolittle, S. 112, 117
Dravecky, D. 103
Dreikurs, R. 91
drill and exercise leadership 81, 82*f*
Dryfoos, J.G. 14
dysfunctional families 10

E

effort and cooperation (participation or involvement), Level II
 description of 21*t*, 32*t*, 34*f*, 37-38, 43*f*
 strategies 69-73
embedding, defined 18*f*, 24-25
embedding responsibility in physical activity content
 kid quotes on 65
 Level I strategies 67-68
 Level II strategies 69-73
 Level III strategies 73-78
 Level IV strategies 78, 80-85
 Level V strategies 85-86
 physical activity content 63-66
 strategy progression 66-67
 take-aways on 86
Emerson, R.W. 49
empowerment
 daily program format and 49, 50
 gradual 22-23
 levels of responsibility and 45
 struggles with 98-100
Ennis, C.D. 108
evaluation and assessment strategies
 program evaluation 175-180
 student assessment 162-173
 take-aways on 180-181
 teacher evaluation 173-175

F

fattening one's bag of tricks 87, 90*t*
Feedback Form, TPSR 175, 185, 194-195
fidelity, assessing 174-175
fitness centers, responsibility-based 141
five clean days 90*t*, 95
five levels of responsibility. *See also* embedding responsibility in physical activity content
 cumulative levels 33-35
 empowerment and 45
 in framework for TPSR 18*f*, 20-22
 Level 0, irresponsibility 33, 34*f*, 43*f*
 Level I, respect and self-control 21*t*, 34*f*, 35-37, 43*f*
 Level II, participation or effort and cooperation 21*t*, 34*f*, 37-38, 43*f*
 Level III, self-direction 21*t*, 34*f*, 38-40, 43*f*
 Level IV, caring 21*t*, 34*f*, 40-42, 43*f*
 Level V, role models outside the gym 21*t*, 42-43, 170-173
 level modifications 44
 progression of levels 32*t*-33
 take-aways on 45
football, TPSR in 139-140*t*
Forsberg, N. 19, 107, 126, 127
Foster, H.L. 113
framework for TPSR
 assessment 18*f*, 28
 assumptions 18*f*, 19-20
 basic description of 17, 18*f*
 core values 18*f*-19
 daily program format 18*f*, 27*f*-28, 49-62
 embedding strategies 18*f*, 24-25, 63-86
 levels of responsibility 18*f*, 20-22, 31-45
 program leader responsibilities 18*f*, 22*f*-27
 take-aways on 29
Fraser-Thomas, J. 18

G

Garcia, S. 86, 179
genuineness and vulnerability 109-110
Georgiadis, N. 32, 57, 66, 72, 84, 111, 132
Gerstner, L.V. 131
Giosa, F. 133
Giraffe Club 85
Glasser, W. 93
goal-setting progression 74-77
Goodlad, J. 63
Gordon, B. 122, 156
Gordon, G.L. 108
Gould, D. 77
grading 169-170, 171*f*
Grandma's law 90*t*, 94
group meeting
 in daily program format 27*f*, 49
 description of 28, 49, 56-57

guidelines 57-58
options 58
purpose of 57
Grube, P. 141, 169
Guilford Interfaith Hospitality Network
(GIHN) 24
Guthrie, J. 168

H

Hahn, K. 40, 42
Hansen, K. 39
Hare, C. 144
Harlem RBI 9, 12
Harmin, M. 51
Hartinger, K. 59
health education applications 143-146
Hellison, D. 77, 119, 120, 122, 127, 167, 175,
176, 185
helping and leadership problems 100-101
helping others and leadership. *See* Level IV
Henninger, M. 161
Hichwa, J. 19, 20, 44, 167
Hinson, C. 44, 142
Hinton, T. 169, 170
Hirsch, B.J. 112
Hockett, P. 61
holistic self-development 18-19
Hollins, J. 133
HOPE (Health/Outdoor/Physical Education)
program 127
Howard, K. 87
Howe, Q. 11, 53, 88, 108, 111, 112, 113
Hoy, S. 143
humor, sense of 111-112
Hurley, T.J. 105

I

ID cards 146-147
independence, on-task 21*t*, 73-74
individuality of each student 26, 52, 103
intensity scale 72-73
intuition and self-reflection 110-111
irresponsibility, Level Zero 33, 34*f*, 43*f*

J

James, W. 41
Jones, J. 19
Jordan, M. 99
Jorgensen, V. 143
journal writing
for class evaluations 58
in physical education 59
for program leaders 173

K

Kallusky, J. 149
Kelly, W. 78, 139, 140, 158

Kennedy, D. 44
Keramidas, K. 141
kid quotes 11, 26, 33, 52, 65, 93, 107, 135,
153, 163
Kimball, K. 143
Kohn, A. 13, 78
Kramer, T. 62
Kuney, G. 170, 171*f*
Kunjufu, J. 10

L

Lambert, L. 141, 169
Lawson, H.A. 14, 87
Level 0, irresponsibility 33, 34*f*, 43*f*
Level I, respect and self-control
defined 21*t*, 34*f*, 35-37, 43*f*
strategies 85-86
Level II, participation or effort and cooperation
defined 21*t*, 34*f*, 37-38, 43*f*
strategies 69-73
Level III, self-direction
defined 21*t*, 34*f*, 38-40, 43*f*
strategies 73-78
Level IV, caring
defined 21*t*, 34*f*, 40-42, 43*f*
strategies 78, 80-85
Level V, role models outside the gym
assessment and 170-173
Career Club and 132
defined 21*t*, 42-43
group meetings and 58
strategies 85-86
transfer 22*f*, 25
levels of responsibility. *See also* five levels of
responsibility
basic description of 18*f*, 20-22
cumulative levels 33-35
empowerment and 45
five levels 35-43*f*
kid quotes on 33
level modifications 44
progression of levels 32*t*-33
take-aways on 45
Lickona, T. 22, 55, 107
life skills
emphasis on 11-12
quiz 172*f*
Lifka, B. 84
listening and caring 108-109
log, student daily 164*f*
Luebbe, C. 139
Lund, J. 4

M

Manning, W. 27
Martinek, T. 23, 24, 38, 41, 66, 77, 78, 84, 85,
94, 121, 133, 136, 139

Masser, L. 42
McBride, L. 146
McCarthy, J. 51
McCullick, B. 133
McDonald, G. 169
McDonald, J. 23, 170
McLaughlin, M. 4, 5, 10, 109, 161, 180
Mead, M. 3
meeting, group
  in daily program format 27f, 49
  description of 28, 49, 56-57
  guidelines 57-58
  options 58
  purpose of 57
Mesa, P. 14
Morris, G.S.D. 68
Mosley, W. 37
Mosston, M. 23

N

Nacu, J. 81
negotiation 90t, 92-93
Nicholls, J. 38, 108
Nixon, L. 157
No Child Left Behind policy 150
Noddings, N. 11, 18, 53, 63, 105, 107
no plan, no play 90t, 93

O

one-liners, awareness talk 54-55
on-task independence 21t, 73-74
organized sport, TPSR in 139-141
O'Sullivan, M. 161
Outward Bound 40

P

Parker, M. 39, 44, 59, 121, 153
participation or involvement (effort and
    cooperation), Level II
  description of 21t, 32t, 34f, 37-38, 43f
  strategies 69-73
Pastor, P. 91, 92
peer pressure, courage to resist 21t, 90t, 99-100
peer teaching and coaching 81
personal physical activity plan
  as checklist 77f
  goal setting for 77-78
  as written contract 79f, 80f
Petitpas, A. 9
Petracek, R. 126, 143
physical activity plan in daily program format
    27f, 28, 49, 55-56
physical education teacher education (PETE),
    TPSR for
  advantages of 117-120
  apprenticeship 120-121
  conference workshop or short course 122-
    123

framework for teacher education program
    126-128
nine ways to teach TPSR for 120f
one-week intensive elective 123
required methods course in after-school
    program 125-126
semester-long elective 124
site-based practicum or internship 121
summary thoughts on 128-130
take-aways on 130
within required activity course 124
within required on-site undergraduate
    methods course 125
Pittman, K. 161
player-coaches 83
playful spirit 111-112
playground, TPSR on 142
Play It Smart 9
Power, C. 56
Prather, H. 146, 183
program evaluation
  culminating projects 176-177, 179-180
  multiple sources of evidence 175-176, 177f,
    178f
program leader, qualities of
  genuineness and vulnerability 109-110
  intuition and self-reflection 110-111
  listening and caring 108-109
  sense of humor and playful spirit 111-112
  sense of purpose 107
  strong leader 106-107
program leader responsibilities
  being relational with kids 25-27
  embedding 24-25
  framework of TPSR and 18f
  gradual empowerment 22-23
  self-reflection 22f, 23-24
  transfer 22f, 25
Project Coach 9
Project Effort 136
Project Rebound 9
Puckett, K. 41

Q

qualities and skills of program leader
  genuineness and vulnerability 109-110
  importance of strong leader 106-107
  intuition and self-reflection 110-111
  listening and caring 108-109
  sense of humor and playful spirit 111-112
  sense of purpose 107
questionnaire, TPSR teacher 151f-152
quotes, kid 11, 26, 33, 52, 65, 93, 107, 135,
    153, 163
quotes, teacher education student 123

R

Raths, L.E. 51

Raywid, M.A. 8, 9, 10
recess, TPSR at 142
reciprocal coaching 80-81, 138
Reeder, M. 38, 69
referral 90*t*, 95-96
reflection, importance of 17, 23-24
reflection-in-action 87, 88-90, 101
reflection time in daily program format 27*f*, 28, 49, 58-62
reflective practice for program leaders 173-174
relational time 27*f*, 49, 50-53, 106. *See also* being relational with kids
respect, Level I 21*t*, 32*t*, 33, 34*f*, 35-37
respect for cultural differences 114
responsibility-based fitness centers 141
Right Fielders Are People Too (Hichwa) 19
Rink, J. 9
Robinson, D. 43
Robinson, E. 17
Robinson, J. 183
Rogers, A. 133
Rogers, C. 110
Rome, A. 177, 179
Rose, B. 109
Rothstein, R. 8, 9, 10
Rubin, L. 110
rubrics for assessment 163, 166*f*, 167-168

S

Schafer, W. 105
Schilling, T. 23
Schon, D.A. 89
schoolwide adoptions of TPSR 146-147
scorecard, self-grading 170*f*
self-control and respect, Level I
    defined 21*t*, 34*f*, 35-37, 43*f*
    strategies 67-68
self-direction, Level III
    defined 21*t*, 32*t*, 33-34*f*, 38-40, 43*f*
    strategies 73-78
self-evaluation form 60*f*
self-evaluation methods 59
self-grading contract 170, 171*f*
self-grading scorecard 170*f*
self-modification of tasks 69-70
self-officiating 90*t*, 96-97
self-paced challenges 70-71
self-reflection
    daily program format and 27*f*, 28, 49, 58-62
    intuition and 110-111
    problem setting and 87-88
    program leader responsibilities and 22, 23-24
self-report for goal setting 75*f*-76*f*
sense of purpose 107
SEPE (sport, exercise, and physical education) 14

Shields, D.L.L. 33
Siedentop, D. 4, 131
Silberman, C. 63
silver bullets, no 14, 15
Simon, S.B. 51
Sinclair, C. 68
Sinclair, M. 145
site-based practicum or internship 121
sit-out progression 90*t*, 92-93
Sizer, T. 4, 7, 19
Smith, M. 157
social and educational issues 10-11
social-emotional learning (SEL) 11-12
social problems, causes of 14
Socrates 23
Soltz, V. 91
solutions bank 87, 89-90
sport, organized 139-141
sport court 90*t*, 96
starting a TPSR program
    advanced steps 154-157
    context 149-151
    first steps 152-154
    innovation as subversive activity 158-159
    kid quotes on 153
    self-assessment 151*f*-152
    take-aways on 159
Stiehl, J. 68
student
    decision-making ability of 26, 53, 104
    individuality of 26, 52, 103
    strengths of 26, 52, 103
    voice of 26, 52-53, 104
student assessment
    formal student assessments 163, 164*f*, 165*f*
    informal student assessments 162-163
    rubrics for 163, 166*f*, 167-168
student daily log 164*f*
Student Health and Fitness Act 9
success, redefining 71-72

T

table, Level Zero 143
talking bench 90*t*, 97
Tan, C. 23
Tannehill, D. 4
Tappan, M.B. 13
TARE (Tool for Assessing Responsibility-Based Education) 174, 175, 185, 187-193
task cards 70, 71*f*
teacher-directed group 90*t*, 94-95
teacher education program. *See* TPSR in PE teacher education
teacher education student quotes 123
teacher evaluation
    assessing fidelity 174-175
    reflective practice 173-174
teaching and leadership, cross-age 138-139

teaching by invitation 90*t*, 98
teaching personal and social responsibility
(TPSR). *See also* TPSR framework
birth of 5-6
as working theory-in-practice 6-8
Teaching Physical Activity: Change, Challenge, and Choice (Stiehl, Morris, and Sinclair) 68
Templin, T. 3
10-word rule 54, 135
three Rs for teaching prosocial behavior 44
Tom, A. 53
TPSR Alliance 183
TPSR Feedback Form 175, 185, 194-195
TPSR framework
assessment 18*f*, 28
assumptions 18*f*, 19-20
basic description of 17, 18*f*
core values 18*f*-19
daily program format 18*f*, 27*f*-28, 49-62
embedding strategies 18*f*, 24-25, 63-86
levels of responsibility 18*f*, 20-22, 31-45
program leader responsibilities 18*f*, 22*f*-27
take-aways on 29
TPSR in action
in aquatic medium 104
Career Club Possible Futures 132
Climbing Club 39
fitness program 122
Grandma's law 94
Guilford Interfaith Hospitality Network 24
leadership class 69
Leadership Mentor program 108
Police Activities League 4
Project Effort 136
school for kids with behavioral problems 89
in South Africa 155
teacher education program 127
Team Support advisory program 51
Youth Leader Corps 66
Youth Sport Club for refugee boys 36
TPSR in classrooms
classroom applications 143
emphasis on levels for 142
health education applications 143-146
TPSR in PE teacher education
apprenticeship 120-121
conference workshop or short course 122-123
framework for teacher education program 126-128
nine ways to teach TPSR for 120*f*
one-week intensive elective 123
required methods course in after-school program 125-126
semester-long elective 124

site-based practicum or internship 121
summary thoughts on 128-130
take-aways on 130
TPSR for 117-120
within required activity course 124
within required on-site undergraduate methods course 125
TPSR teacher questionnaire 151*f*-152
TPSR Toolbox Web site 162, 176
transfer outside the gym, Level V
assessment and 170-173
Career Club and 132
defined 21*t*, 42-43
empowerment and 45
group meetings and 58
level modifications and 44
strategies 85-86
teach for transfer 22*f*, 25
Trujillo, J. 108

V

values 7, 12-13
values of TPSR, core 18*f*-19
voice of each student 26, 52-53, 104
vulnerability and genuineness 109-110

W

Walsh, D. 83, 121, 124, 132, 133, 134
Walsh, J. 59, 95, 157, 158, 169, 170
Washington, G. 42
Weinberg, R.S. 77
Weiner, L. 14
wellness responsibility levels 145*f*
what's worth doing 3-5, 15
White, B. 55, 56, 140, 158
White, G. 89
Whitley, M. 36, 155
Williams, R. 111
Williamson, K.M. 32
Wise, A. 161
Woyner, K. 157
Wright, P.M. 12, 121, 133, 161, 163, 174, 175, 179, 180
written contracts for personal plan 78, 79*f*, 80*f*

Y

Youth Development and Physical Activity (Hellison et al.) 134
youth development programs 8-10
Youth Leader Corps 24
Youth Leadership in Sport and Physical Education (Martinek and Hellison) 139

Z

Zavacky, F. 153, 154
Zero, Level 33, 34*f*, 43*f*

About the Author

Don Hellison, PhD, is a professor in the college of education at the University of Illinois at Chicago and codirector of the Teaching Personal and Social Responsibility (TPSR) Alliance. He has extensive experience working with high-risk youth, was a distinguished research fellow at Adelphi University, and has been a visiting professor at numerous universities in the United States and in Canada.

Much of Hellison's work focuses on the development, implementation, and evaluation of alternative physical activity program models that teach life skills and values, especially for underserved youth.

He has published six books and numerous articles and book chapters. Hellison has received many awards, including the Gulick Medal (AAHPERD's highest honor) and the International Olympic Committee's President's Prize. He has received grant support for 25 projects, served on three editorial boards, and was editor of *Quest* for two years. He has given keynote addresses, made presentations at professional meetings, and conducted workshops for teachers and youth workers in most of the 50 states, several Canadian provinces, and Israel, Korea, Ireland, New Zealand, Australia, England, and Spain. He has also served on numerous committees for several professional associations.